Praise for

INFONOMICS

and DOUGLAS B. LANEY

Becoming data-driven is not just a game, it's a serious business contest that Laney shows you how to win. The insights, frameworks, and real-world examples throughout this book provide a complete picture of why and how to become an information-savvy organization.

—Judd Williams, Chief Information Officer, NCAA

Laney's work redefines information as a true strategic asset, and shows how we CDOs can be instrumental in unlocking new ways for companies to grow and be relevant in the new connected modern economy.

—Rajeev Kapur, Chief Data Officer, Kimberly-Clark

We will one day look back at Doug's work and say, it is the groundbreaking work that firmly put data and data leadership in the middle of the business arena not as the white elephant, but as the phoenix: a formal player at the boardroom table.

—Althea Davis, Chief Data Officer, ABN AMRO

Doug Laney has put together a smart, practical book that applies traditional rules of business economics to the emerging information marketplace. *Infonomics* is an excellent field guide to knowing what actions can be taken to better measure, manage, and monetize your company's data assets now and in the future.

—Dr. Jim Short, Lead Scientist and co-founder
of the Center for Large Scale Data Systems (CLDS)
at the San Diego Supercomputer Center

Infonomics provides a broad, deep, and practical framework that information professionals can build on; it's full of real world illustrations and I think it is a seminal work. If you are serious about "treating information as an asset" then *Infonomics* is a must read.

—Phillip Radley, Chief Data Architect,
BT Group, plc.

Infonomics is a must read for business leaders who intend to succeed in data monetization, a requisite organizational capability for firms competing in the Digital Economy. Doug offers rich examples and detailed foundations that leaders can draw upon as they formulate their data strategies.

—Dr. Barbara Wixom, Principal Research Scientist,
MIT Sloan Center for Information Systems Research

Doug Laney brings decades of practical experience to *Infonomics*, providing a stepwise framework for C-level executives to answer the "Why" to monetize data question, as well as how to operationalize the monetization of data throughout the enterprise and position themselves to innovate, compete, and lead in their markets. I recommend this book as a must read to enable full potential of all the idle data in your enterprise.

—Gokula Mishra, Senior Director, Global Data & Analytics,
Supply Chain, McDonald's Corporation

Through a myriad of relevant examples, Doug successfully brings together data management, analytics, and economics in a book that offers practical guidelines to manage, improve, and monetize an organization's data assets. The book is not only a must read for Chief Data Officers, but for any other executive interested in succeeding in the Information Age.

—Leandro Dallemule, Chief Data Officer, AIG

Thank you, Doug, for an engaging read and for giving Data a well-deserved "seat at the table." This is a must have book, not only for CDOs, CIOs, and Data Strategists but, for any executive interested in creating a data driven, info-saavy company. Laney serves up a treasure trove of insights and observations, while also asking some embarrassingly basic questions that beg to be answered by most companies.

—Dianna Serio, SVP, Enterprise Data Strategy,
First American Financial Corp

The secret is out now. *Infonomics* encapsulates the characteristics comprising the kinds of companies we favor: they treat and deploy their information as an asset, and fully appreciate its economic value. Since Laney's pioneering work in data warehousing, he has had a sense of information as something other than a business byproduct or occasionally-interesting resource, and has now graciously passed this on to the rest of us.

—Warren Weiss, General Partner,
Foundation Capital

Since the dawn of data warehousing, information's real and potential value to organizations in every industry and geography has skyrocketed to the point of underpinning the global economy today. But little has been explored about how to fathom and harvest this value. *Infonomics* provides the foundation to master what has been intuitively known for years, but not well understood at all. It is essential reading for all corporate management, not just "data folks."

—Bill Inmon, renowned "Father of the
Data Warehouse Concept," author and entrepreneur

Infonomics is a pragmatic handbook for C-level executives that will enable them to speak, collaborate, and take action on their newest and most valuable asset: information. Laney is spot on by elevating the "asset status" of information…one to be curated, enriched, protected, and monetized judiciously.
—Steve Bakalar, VP, Digital Transformation, Georgia-Pacific

As it dawns to us what it means to be in the Information Age, our society find itself poorly equipped with the tools, language, and levers needed to manage this resource effectively. While qualifying and quantifying information value may not be obvious, Doug Laney shows it can be done. Filled with real-world examples, simple frameworks, and straightforward practical advice, *Infonomics* will benefit business leaders, information professionals, and policy-makers alike.
—David Vaz, Data Governance and Stewardship,
National Australia Bank

Reading *Infonomics* will be engaging and will constantly trigger thoughts of value creation opportunities awaiting organizations, including ones that are immediate. I highly recommended reading this book regardless of your industry or organizational role.

—Evon Jones, Diversified former CIO Bausch & Lomb, Liz Claiborne and Hallmark Cards

Infonomics is everything you always wanted to know about how to treat and benefit from information as an actual corporate asset, but didn't even know how or what to ask. It is a must read by CEOs, CMOs, CFOs, CIOs, business leaders, enterprise architects, and everyone involved with data.

—Maurice Levy, Retired CEO and chairman, Publicis Groupe

Doug Laney's *Infonomics* is an engaging read with interesting twists and turns for valuing data assets. I found myself looking forward to every "next chapter." As a current CDO, this book will become one of my most valuable "go to" resources. Thank you, Doug, for this thought provoking read.

—Sherri Zink, SVP and Chief Data Officer, BlueCross BlueShield of Tennessee

Infonomics is a must-read for anyone interested in profiting from or managing the rapidly growing information assets held by businesses. It also provides important insights for accountants, who should be thinking about information assets and how they might be reported to business stakeholders. Laney's engaging style and careful thinking make for a compelling read.

—Jon Davis, University of Illinois School of Business, Accountancy Department Head

Doug Laney's well-researched and compelling text is a much-needed breath of fresh air. Laney formalizes the case for finally treating information as the truly valuable asset that it is. *Infonomics* challenges longheld—and, quite frankly, largely dated—beliefs about data, governance, and IT roles. It may well make you and your organization uncomfortable in the short term—and that's a good thing.

—Phil Simon, award-winning author of *Analytics:*
The Agile Way and faculty member at the
Arizona State University W. P. Carey School of Business

Infonomics easily provides the clearest thought leadership for companies on the true economic value of information. In time, textbooks will be rewritten and balance sheets recalculated to account for the monetary value of information. Doug is pioneering the establishment of this new asset class with inspiring examples, useful metrics, and sound logic.

—Brandon Thomas, Chief Data Officer, Zions Bank

Doug Laney makes a compelling case for accounting for information as a corporate asset. *Infonomics* expertly guides organizations to uncover their hidden treasures and realize economic benefits from information assets. A must read for all CIOs.

—Cherif Amirat, Ph.D., Chief Information Officer, IEEE

This is a well-written book in the emerging area combining both information and economics. We've heard enough times that data/information is an asset without any proper blueprint but this book outlines clearly how to measure, manage, and monetize information as an asset. This will be the new "Tesla" concept book in the new information and economics arena.

—Vijay Thiruvengadam, Executive Director for
Decision Support and Analytics, University of Michigan

Laney was one of the first experts to identify and call out the power of Big Data. Now, in *Infonomics*, Laney issues a call to action. This book is a welcome addition to the emerging body of serious literature on the power of data in an Age of Information.

—Randy Bean, CEO and Founder of NewVantage
Partners LLC, and thought-leader and contributor to *Forbes*,
MIT Sloan Management Review, *Harvard Business Review*,
and *The Wall Street Journal*

This book is essential for any CDO or aspiring CDO. More importantly it should be read by all CEOs who wish to lead a data driven business. The ideas, concepts, and examples are well thought through and are rigorous. This will be perpetually on my shelf and on my recommended list.

—Peter Jackson, Head of Data, Southern Water, UK

I've seen how hard this is first hand to transform a business from a product/feature based organization to one that is not only data driven, but competes based on data assets. *Infonomics* is a great, comprehensive view on how to approach this change and all the considerations to account for through the journey.

—Corey Ferengul, Executive-in-Residence,
Hyde Park Venture Partners

INFONOMICS

INFONOMICS

How to Monetize, Manage, and Measure
Information as an Asset for Competitive
Advantage

DOUGLAS B. LANEY
Gartner, Inc.

bibliomotion
inc.

First edition published in 2018
by Bibliomotion, Inc.
711 Third Avenue New York, NY 10017, USA
2 Park Square, Milton Park, Abingdon, Oxon OX14 4RN, UK

Bibliomotion is an imprint of Taylor & Francis Group, an informa business

No claim to original U.S. Government works

Printed in Canada on acid-free paper

International Standard Book Number-13: 978-1-138-09038-5 (Hardback)
International Standard eBook Number-13: 978-1-315-10865-0 (eBook)

Library of Congress Cataloging-in-Publication Data
Names: Laney, Douglas B., author.
Title: Infonomics : how to monetize, manage, and measure information as an asset for competitive advantage / Douglas B. Laney.
Description: New York, NY : Routledge, 2018. | Includes bibliographical references and index.
Identifiers: LCCN 2017011754 (print) | LCCN 2017032587 (ebook) | ISBN 9781315108650 (ebook) | ISBN 9781138090385 (hardback : alk. paper)
Subjects: LCSH: Business intelligence. | Commercial statistics. | Information technology.
Classification: LCC HD38.7 (ebook) | LCC HD38.7 .L347 2018 (print) | DDC 658.4/038—dc23
LC record available at https://lccn.loc.gov/2017011754

Visit the Taylor & Francis Web site at www.taylorandfrancis.com

To Susan and Ethan

Contents

Acknowledgments

Writing a book is at once a release and a burden, and paradoxically a solitary journey that cannot be accomplished alone. As Charles Dickens penned, "No one is useless in this world who lightens the burdens of another." This infonomics concept and book idea has been percolating inside me for nearly two decades, and it took an army of people to exact it from me. I'm indebted to so many friends, family, and colleagues who have come to my side in lessening the burden and enabling its release. These individuals include, but are hardly limited to the following:

Heather Pemberton Levy, my editor, for her unremitting support, guidance, counsel, patience, writing assistance, coordination, and occasional "author therapy" sessions. This book is an order of magnitude better and more approachable because of your talents.

Andrew Spender, Gartner's head of global communications, for his encouragement of developing the book idea since its inception years ago, and his sponsorship of the project that allowed it to move forward.

Michael Sinocchi and his team at Taylor & Francis Group publishers who magically turn electrons into paper and ink, and Erika Heilman and Jill Friedlander at Bibliomotion for originally accepting the proposal.

Tom Davenport for his inspiration and support over the years, and writing the book's foreword.

Many Gartner colleagues and other collaborators who wittingly or unwittingly contributed their brilliant content and ideas, especially: Alan Duncan,

Alan Dayley, Alexander Linden, Andrew White, Ankush Jain, Brian Lowans, Charlotte Patrick, Christine Yuan, Dale Kutnick, David Newman, Debra Logan, Dimitris Geragas, Doloris Ianni, Ehtisham Zaidi, Frank Buytendijk, George Heyman, Hank Marquis, Hung LeHong, Ian Oppermann, James Price, Jamie Saunders, Jennifer Park, John Cox, John Ladley, John Wheeler, Jorge Lopez, Kristian Steenstrup, Kurt Schlegel, Laura Craft, Lisa Kart, Mark Beyer, John Davis, Heather Pesch, Mark Raskino, Mike Pedersen, Michael Patrick Moran, Mike Rollings, Michael Smith, Nick Heudecker, Nina Evans, Olive Huang, Paul Haskins, Rick Howard, Rita Sallam, Robert Hetu, Saul Brand, Saul Judah, Thomas Oestreich, Ted Friedman, Valerie Logan, Victoria Barber, Yefim Natis. And thank you to all my colleagues in the Gartner Data & Analytics research community, along with Gartner's editing team who have helped to improve my content one presentation and research note at a time.

John Mancini at AIIM for holding an invaluable Executive Leadership Council Summit on Infonomics, and the summit's participants, including: Thornton May, Ben Levitan, Hanns Köhler-Krüner, John Bondi, John newton, David Horrigan, Rich Howarth, Randy Krotowski, Jeff Quiggle, Reynold Leming, Dennie Heye, Jaspar Roos, George Parapadakis, Andreas Rindler, Stephane Croisier, Kjeld Stipsen, and Hans van Hoof.

The many professionals who gave of their valuable time to be interviewed for the book, including: Leandro DalleMule, Brendan Smith, Mary Adams, Della Shea, Scott Zager, Brian Ehlers, Tom Linsmeier, Martin Spratt, Joel Spenadel, John Ladley, Paul Adams, Steven N. Miller, Steve Schaumberger, Bruce Weininger, Paul Sonderegger, Tom Redman, Nolan Miller, Paul Magelli, Blackford Middleton, Rich Wagner, Kevin Barnicle, David Lee, Rob Freeborn, Tom Hogan, John O'Rourke, Sanjay Parthasarathy, Randy Shumway, John Wheeler, Dan Maycock, Roger Pilc, Jim Emmons, J.T. Sison, Stan Rosenthal, Venkat Subramanian, Matt Cordner, Rick Crabbe, Larry Grossman, Isaac Silver, Chuck Devries, Christina Clark, and Gokula Mishra. And to Wenjing Fei who tirelessly transcribed hours and hours of these interviews.

Those who squeezed in time over holidays, on airplanes, or at bedtime to provide invaluable manuscript reviews including: Alan Duncan, Alberto Sutton, Benjamin Taub, David Newman, Della Shea, Ed Porter, Ian Oppermann, James Kobielus, James Price, Jenny Sussin, John Ladley, Kelle O'Neal, Paul Schindler, Richard Hunter, Roger Williams, Sergio Topfstedt, Stewart Buchanan, Svetlana Sicular, Tom Fountain, Victoria Barber, Frank Buytendijk, Jamie Popkin, Valerie Logan, Mike Rollings, Andrew White, Saul Brand, Debra Logan, Mario Faria, and Joe Bugajski.

Other colleagues and information professionals who offered invaluable support and encouragement along the journey, including: Anthony Bradley, Brian Burke, Chris Howard, Daryl Plummer, Dale Kutnick, Graham Waller, Hank Barnes, Ian Bertram, Joe Bugajski, John Davis, Ken McGee, Mario Faria, Mark Raskino, Mike Harris, Rebecca Scragg, Regina Casonato, Richard Hunter, Roger Moore, Tom Redman, Val Sribar, Nick Caffarra, the late great Hayward Schwartz, and many Gartner account executives and client service professionals.

Gartner graphic artists Jessica Bower and Kathleen Losche, who turn PowerPoint graphics into pop art.

Gartner's secondary research services professionals, especially Somendra Tripathi, Sindhu Jayakumar, and Sharma Shubhangi, who helped unearth and encapsulate many of the stories and data points found throughout the book, Kirsten "The Analyst Whisperer" Sharrock, our research team's project coordinator extraordinaire who helped keep me sane and out of trouble (mostly) performing mysterious tricks with my schedule this past year to maximize writing time.

And a very special thank you to my family and friends, especially Susan and Ethan for their unfailing support and patience during their many months of suffering with a shadow of a husband and father; my mother, brother, and many friends who understood when I just couldn't be there the past year; "Moose," who kept me powered up with chocolate chip cookie dough and Tony's Subs; and Kugel, my constant furry writing companion who stayed up with me countless late nights.

I am forever grateful to each and every one of you for helping me on this pilgrimage.

You have not lived today until you have done something for someone who can never repay you.
                    —John Bunyan, author of *The Pilgrim's Progress*

Foreword

It's often remarked in passing that information is an asset, but the conversation doesn't go much beyond that. But this book and the many useful examples it contains are evidence that assessing and optimizing the monetary value of information should go well beyond casual commentary. Information has become like oil, timber, precious metals, or buildings—even endowed with certain economic characteristics these others do not. Information is worth big money, and those who don't exploit its value are leaving valuable resources on the table. Strategists and business leaders must become fluent in the economics of information, and they've come to the right place to do so.

You'll find more content herein than from any source about this important topic, and Doug Laney has been thinking clearly about it for many years. But let me condition your expectations: don't expect a magic formula for converting information to money. Conversion of an item of information to a specific monetary value has always been difficult and highly situational. The value of information depends heavily on the context—the buyers and sellers, the time and place, and the multiplicity of ways to evaluate it. Information is worth what someone will pay, is worth more to some than others, is worth less as it ages, and so forth. Peter Drucker once famously defined information as "data endowed with relevance and purpose," and those attributes are notoriously subjective.

In other words, information is shifty stuff that is difficult to pin down in an economic sense. And as Laney points out early in the book, it can be easily copied and distributed. As economic assets go, it's one of the tougher types from which to extract value. Nonetheless, this book makes it clear that the effort to do so is worthwhile.

You may also be thinking that determining the value of information is most important when you are selling it outright. But that is only one of many ways to think about information value, and as Laney points out, an often problematic one. Companies that sell entirely different types of products or services often find it difficult to begin selling information. Fortunately, this volume is replete with examples of other valid ways in which companies can make money or make themselves more valuable by harnessing their own—or in many cases, others'—information.

The book also exposes and delves into a glaring oversight of the information profession, one that has plagued the industry and businesses for decades: the lack of an accepted set of standards for information management. Laney explores several other disciplines for which such methodologies exist, from physical asset management to library science, and posits how data leaders should heed and adopt a similar set of formal practices—starting with his clear-cut set of "Generally Accepted Information Principles."

No matter what difficulties pop up in the field of infonomics, even more opportunities pop up alongside them. The great thing about this book is that it takes a multi-faceted and interlaced approach to the economic value of information—monetizing, managing and measuring its value (perhaps the "3Ms" of infonomics will take their place alongside the famous "3Vs" of Big Data—*volume, variety*, and *velocity*—a tripartite alliteration that Laney also coined). There is scarcely an organization (or even an individual) that can't benefit from embracing and adopting these concepts.

Those infonomics adopters might make information more valuable in a wide variety of ways. Perhaps they will add insight and context to their data by mixing in other information. They may add value through analytics—describing what's already happened, predicting what will happen next, or prescribing what the next step should be. Some organizations will embed information and analytics into products and services. Or they may simply better portray the value of their organization through information, increasing its market value. The possibilities are almost endless.

I view this field of infonomics as being in its earliest stages. You can't yet get an academic degree in the topic, and you won't find many "infonomics departments" within organizations at this point. Most IT people have been too technical in their focus to consider these issues in any detail, and most strategic thinkers haven't focused enough on the specific economic value of information to pursue the topic effectively.

This is good news for you, dear reader. If you give this book the careful attention it deserves, you'll become a scarce and valuable commodity—an expert on the business and economic possibilities of information. Information is probably going to become an even more valuable asset over time, and you too will only become more valuable as a creator, explainer, and maximizer of that value.

Thomas H. Davenport
President's Distinguished Professor of IT
and Management, Babson College
Research Fellow, MIT Initiative on the Digital Economy
Author of *Competing on Analytics* and *Only Humans Need Apply*

Introduction

When I was a young boy, one sweltering night in Deerfield, Illinois, just as I was falling asleep my father burst into my room, "Douglas. Get up. It's time. You need to see this." Normally my mother would have protested, but not for this.

I followed my father down to the family room where we sat in silence in front of our 12-inch black-and-white Zenith television. He turned to me and said, "Don't ever forget you saw this."

We watched for several minutes while my father continued to adjust the rabbit-ear antennae. Eventually on our tiny TV, a little white blob emerged from a bigger grayish blob, descended a bit, and a crackly voice announced: "That's one small step for [a] man, one giant leap for mankind."

I'm sure my dad was choked up. I just thought this was neat, really neat, but of no surprise. Most nights I went to sleep in spaceman pajamas beneath solar system bed sheets, fully anticipating this moment.

Several hours earlier, the world had watched Neil Armstrong override a lack of sufficient information on the lunar landing site to avoid a field of boulders. With only seconds of fuel remaining he touched down the Eagle safely on the surface of the moon.

Dad worked for a global medical device manufacturer. With his black horn-rimmed glasses, flat top haircut, and white short-sleeve button down shirts often sporting a pocket protector, it occurred to me he could pass for a NASA mission control specialist. Instead, he was a world-class engineer with several patents to his name. In that moment, our excitement wasn't because of the technology. Dad would have been able to coolly tell you how all of the transistors, circuitry, activators, compressors, and other electromechanical components in the lunar lander worked.

"Isn't it incredible that we can see and hear this as it's happening?" he exclaimed. What truly thrilled my father was not the fact that mankind had the technology to land a man on the moon but that multimedia *information* about it was streaming into our family room for his son, for him, and for a billion others around the world to witness—live.

Since then, it seems that information—a fascination with it, the pursuit of it, and ultimately a career producing and delivering information about information—has been a common thread for me. I have never been all that fascinated with technology or even software, but more so by what fuels them.

As a kid I memorized gravitational, size, and distance fact tables about the planets, and devoured books on and tried my hand at cryptology. As a teen I got into coding, developing table-based approaches to video game development, and at the University of Illinois, a differential equations class frightened me out of the mathematics program and into developing an independent degree in software engineering and business administration. This despite the protests of the engineering school administration: "Why would anyone want to use computers for business?"

As an IT industry analyst, first with Meta Group and now Gartner, I have a front row seat to witnessing and advising organizations in their ongoing tussle with the unrelenting onslaught and infinite opportunities of information. Technologies and techniques seem to be perpetually a half-step behind the increases in the volume, velocity, and variety of information. More disconcerting to me is that the overall perception of and approach to information has not kept pace with its economic significance.

Sure, many senior executives *talk* about information as one of their most important assets, but few behave as if it is. They spend more money tracking their company's office furniture and PCs than their information assets. They report to the board on the health of their workforce, their financials, their customers, and their partnerships, but almost never the health of their information assets. They squeeze every drop of value out of employees, budgets, and raw materials, while allowing most information assets to languish.

Much of this oversight has to do with what is deemed to have meaningful value to the standard bearers of corporate measurement: the accounting profession. But in today's Information Age, an antiquated regulatory prohibition against formally recognizing information on your balance sheet is a poor excuse for failing to monetize, manage, and measure information as a true asset.

This book is a call to such executives—for chief executive officers (CEOs) and business leaders to more fully wield information as a corporate asset, for chief information officers (CIOs) to improve the flow and accessibility of information, and for chief financial officers (CFOs) to help their organizations measure the actual and latent value in their information assets. More directly, this book is for the burgeoning force of chief data officers (CDOs) and other information and analytics leaders in their intrepid struggle to help their organizations become more *infosavvy*. This book is a set of new ideas, frameworks, evidence, and even approaches adapted from other disciplines to help them transform their organizations.

Infonomics is a broad concept I conceived and first mentioned around the turn of the millennium to express information's increasing behavior and importance as an economic asset. Over the years I have continued to research and develop the concept—exploring, relating, and integrating the disciplines of information theory, accounting, asset management, property ownership and rights, measurement, innovation, and economics. This has taken me from working with and interviewing clients, colleagues, information consultants, valuation experts, accountants, economists, and academics on these topics—to the depths of reading hundreds of pages of accounting standards body discussion papers on the recognition, and valuation and reporting of intangibles.

As such, infonomics is at once a conjecture and a construct. Each of these above ideas I have endeavored to recast in the context of information itself, and render practicable. Whatever your role, I hope you find each of the three parts of this book (*monetizing, managing, measuring*) beneficial to you. Certain readers will find one part more useful or interesting to them than another. Regardless, I appreciate you joining me on this infonomics journey. And a journey it is. I'm anxious to learn about the new ideas, methods, and achievements this book inspires.

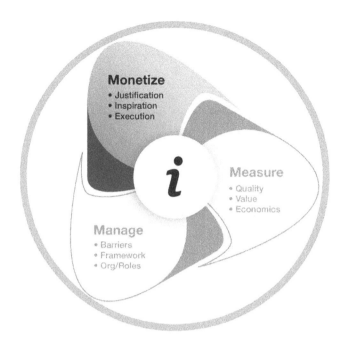

Part I: Monetizing Information as an Asset

CHAPTER 1

Why Monetize Information

Take the A1081 heading towards Harpenden and St. Albans. After about two miles you will come to a mini roundabout, carry straight on towards Harpenden. Take the first turn on the left after a quarter-mile, signed "Thrales End Lane." After another quarter-mile the road takes a sharp right hand-bend, just before this corner there is an entrance on your left hand side signposted "Thrales End Business Centre."[1]

You are now at the farm of Ian Pigott somewhere in Hertfordshire, England. This wheat, oats, and barley farm may be at the "end of Thrales," but it's at the forefront of monetizing information.

Pigott watches as his autonomous 11-ton John Deere tractor thunders across two thousand acres of farmland every week or so. It is guided by information coursing back and forth from a satellite—directed by information from weather forecasts, soil readings, pesticide use, and plant samples—and streaming nutrition and other information to the farmer's tablet. From a comfy chair in his office, Pigott can monitor and manage the entire operation, in real time, down to the square meter. Other similarly tricked-out farms use drones to survey for crop stress or flooding, sense and locate underground aquifers, precisely portion out animal feed, and use infrared cameras to identify flock fevers indicative of bird flu.[2]

Due to information-fueled analytics and information, farming has become just another white-collar desk job. Sure, kicking back, putting up your feet, and running a farm may be cool—but let's "follow the money," as they say.

Despite the 800 percent increase in the cost of these sensor-loaded, intelligent combines and other ag-gadgetry, farms also like Tom Farms in Indiana benefit from a 50 percent increase in profits. The ability to farm twenty thousand acres today versus seven hundred acres in the 1970s with the same number of employees no doubt is a major contributing factor. How about eliminating the need for crop diversification to hedge against weather, disease, and market conditions? Information about markets, soil, and weather, combined with precision information-driven efficiencies enable the farmer to grow whatever will be most profitable.[3]

Moving up the economic food chain, do you think the farm equipment manufacturers like Deere and Caterpillar simply are profiting from their computerized crop creators? Hardly. They're capturing data from them to help maintain and service them, get smarter about conditions and operations, design the next generation of equipment, sell more of it, and license to seed and fertilizer companies like Monsanto and Archer Daniels Midland. In turn, these companies use the information to develop new agricultural products, and even to identify farms illegally using them. And ultimately grocery stores, restaurants, and consumers benefit from higher quality products and lower prices.

Looking across several levels of this agricultural supply chain, we can identify a parallel *information supply chain* in which information is used to:

- Improve operational efficiencies,
- Improve maintenance,
- Improve production,
- Improve quality,
- Improve sales,
- Improve product development, and
- Improve business relationships.

Each of these capacities represents a discernible, discrete economic benefit in which information can be monetized, managed, and measured. And when any of these go unattended, you're leaving money on the table. This is what infonomics aims to solve.

Monetize, Manage, and Measure Your Information

Infonomics is the theory, study, and discipline of asserting economic significance to information. It provides the framework for businesses to monetize, manage, and measure information as an actual asset. Infonomics endeavors to apply both economic and asset management principles and practices to the valuation, handling, and deployment of information assets.

As a business, information, or information technology (IT) leader, chances are you regularly talk about information[4] as one of your most valuable assets. Do you value or manage our organization's information like an actual asset? Consider your company's well-honed supply chain and asset management practices for physical assets, or your financial management and reporting discipline. Do you have similar accounting and asset management practices in place for your "information assets?" Most organizations do not.

When considering how to put information to work for your organization, it's essential to go beyond thinking and talking about information as an asset, to actually valuing and treating it as one. The discipline of infonomics provides organizations a foundation and methods for quantifying information asset value and formal information asset management practices. Infonomics posits that information should be considered a new asset class in that it has measurable economic value and other properties that qualify it to be accounted for and administered as any other recognized type of asset—and that there are significant strategic, operational, and financial reasons for doing so.

Infonomics provides the framework businesses and governments need to value information, manage it, and wield it as a real asset. Aptly, the topic coincides with the objectives and responsibilities of one of the hottest roles in businesses today: the chief data officer, or CDO. Most of the thousands of CDOs appointed in the past few years have been chartered with improving the efficiency and value-generating capacity of their organization's information ecosystem. That is, they've been asked to lead their organization in treating and leveraging information with the same discipline as its other, more traditional assets. This book is for them.

This book also is for CEOs who want to guide their organizations from just using information to weaponizing it. It is for CIOs who want to transform their organizations from regarding information as "that stuff IT manages" into a critical *business* asset. It's also for the CFO who is heads-up to the economic benefits of information, but is looking for ways to better understand, gauge, and financially leverage these benefits. And this book is also for the enterprise architect who wants a new set of tools to create novel information-based solutions for the organization, and for academics in business and computing sciences forming and shepherding the next generation of leaders into the Information Age.

This book is structured in three parts to provide a comprehensive guide for how to *monetize, manage, and measure* your information (Figure 1.1). First, we'll examine why information affords unique opportunities to monetize it both directly and indirectly and give you a range of examples to help justify the business case for monetizing your organization's information. This first section on monetizing information as an asset provides the justification, inspiration, and execution methods and closes out with an examination of advanced analytics and how to exploit Big Data for monetizable insights.

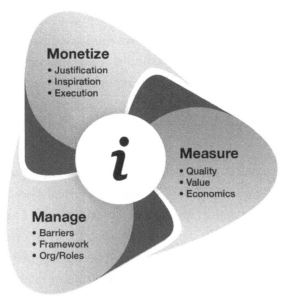

Source: Laney, Faria, Duncan, "Seven Steps to Monetizing Your Information Assets," Gartner Research G00291622, October 7, 2016

Figure 1.1 *Infonomics*

In part II, we'll tackle the challenges and best practices for managing your internal and external information as an asset and how to structure your organization and roles to build an *infosavvy* organization. This section on managing information as an asset addresses the barriers to doing so, provides new ways to approach information asset management, and suggests a set of "Generally Accepted Information Principles" for doing so. Part III breaks down the current limitations to measuring information as an asset while offering new tools to measure the various benefits and costs of information. It also provides specific information valuation models and adapts key economic principles to help you begin quantifying and maximizing the benefits of your information assets.

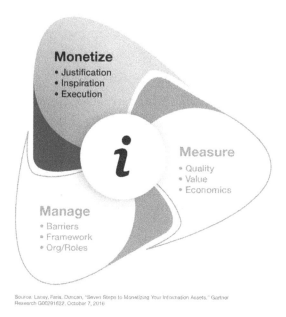

Source: Laney, Faria, Duncan, "Seven Steps to Monetizing Your Information Assets," Gartner Research G00291622, October 7, 2016

Figure 1.2 *Infonomics—Monetize Information*

The Possibilities of Information Monetization

Let's dispel the notion right away that information monetization (Figure 1.2) is just about selling your data. It's much broader than that. In today's information economy we see a range of possibilities: information is used as legal tender (or at least in place of legal tender in many kinds of transactions); information most certainly is used to generate a profit—and not just by Google, Facebook, and the rest of the digerati, but by just about every business in every industry today with even just a copy of Excel—and information is regularly converted into money by a growing marketplace of household-name data brokers such as ACNielsen, Bloomberg, and Equifax, and by upstarts like Tru Optik, AULIVE, and hundreds (perhaps thousands) of others.

The imperative to monetize information in traditional businesses in all industries has become palpable. A 2015 Gartner study found that among the top ten Big Data challenges, respondents cited "how to get value from Big Data" as the number one challenge three times more often than any other challenge. Value challenges are cited five times more often than staffing related, leadership, or infrastructure/architecture challenges, and three times more often than risk or governance issues. By 2016, the same survey revealed a shift from how to get value to "determining value" as the biggest challenge—an indication of the need to *measure* the outcomes (which we'll deal with in chapter 12).

The range of ways for *any* organization to monetize information is nearly endless. In chapter 2 we'll examine several inspirational real-world stories of information being monetized across industries and business functions. The remainder of this chapter challenges the common myths that prevent information monetization within an organization, and presents opportunities to leverage information's unique characteristics for real economic benefit.

Top Information Monetization Myths

Even with many well-publicized stories, several information monetization myths create cognitive roadblocks that hinder business leaders from realizing anything near the full promise of information:

- Information must be sold to be monetized,
- Monetization requires an exchange of cash,
- Monetization only involves your own information,
- Monetized information typically is in raw form,
- One must be in the information business to monetize information,

- Few others would want our information, and
- It's best for us just to share our information with our suppliers and partners.

As a way to cleave through the cerebral fog of these myths, let's first explore some key reasons why monetizing information is not only an excellent idea, but an increasing imperative for businesses.

Endless Economic Alternatives for Information

The first mental roadblock to monetizing information is a failure to think beyond selling it. It's best not to get painted into that corner, lest you limit the economic potential of your information assets. Instead, think more broadly about "methods utilized to generate profit." These methods can range from indirect methods in which information contributes to some economic gain, to more direct methods with which information may generate an actual revenue stream.

Indirect methods of information monetization can include using data to reduce costs, improve productivity, reduce risks, develop new products or markets, and build and solidify relationships.

Indirect methods for monetizing information abound, and we do them daily and for most processes. The problem is that most organizations don't measure the information's economic impact. So how can they claim they're monetizing it? They can't, really. In part III, I'll describe how to measure the economic impact of information. An inability to measure information's top or bottom line impact shouldn't stop you from using it, but in reality it probably does limit how well, how broadly, and how creatively you deploy it. So let's put a stake in the ground: *You are indirectly monetizing information only if you are measuring its economic benefits.* This may not quite be an aphorism, but it's certainly useful.

Consider March 5, 2015, when Citigroup added $9 billion in market capitalization and a dividend increase of 500 percent. That morning the U.S. Federal Reserve had released the results of the second phase of its annual

Comprehensive Capital Analysis and Review (CCAR) stress tests on major banks.[5] Citigroup had passed with flying colors—the cleanest test of top U.S. banks—by correlating and analyzing 2,600 macroeconomic variables with revenue streams from dozens of business units with the help of machine intelligence technology from Ayasdi.[6] They had uncovered variable permutations which were difficult to identify using basic business intelligence approaches, and reduced this process from three months to two weeks. In using information to demonstrably reduce risk and improve compliance, Citigroup had added billions in market value.

Or consider how the Carolinas-centered mid-range upscale department store chain Belk is monetizing information to measurably optimize merchandising, marketing, and real estate investments. By blending and analyzing data from its millions of customers across thirteen different databases, along with census, ethnicity, and population migration data, with the help of self-service data integration and analytics software from Alteryx, it developed attrition models to analyze customers by spend level, purchase history, and other dimensions to identify and target high-value multi-channel customers. In doing so, Belk has increased diverse and non-diverse spend, increased the number of multi-channel customers, optimized assortment plans and store format, and improved store opening and closing decisions. As a result, it has almost doubled the number of online and in-store customers.[7]

Just as monetizing any other kind of asset doesn't necessarily involve selling it, monetizing information doesn't mean selling or licensing it, either. In fact, the opportunities for indirectly monetizing information arguably are broader than those for monetizing it directly. You are only limited by your imagination . . . and your ability to measure and attribute the benefits.

Get More Than Cash for Your Information

Cash may be king, but the bad news is that the king himself knows you have it. In other words, it's taxable. Exchanging your information for monetary remuneration—that is, selling or licensing it—may seem the easy way to go about transacting with information, but it is rarely the best method. Not only are cash transactions highly visible on income statements, but money is a mere proxy for or derivative of other kinds of value. Instead, consider getting what you really want in return for the information. With the right trading partner, you will end up receiving more economic benefits from your information than you would from having them write you a check.

Primarily, look for opportunities to get favorable terms and conditions, or discounts, from suppliers in return for information about how you or your customers are using their products.

Grocery stores have been facilitating both sides of this for decades.

Most of us regularly swipe our loyalty cards at the grocery store and watch as the register automatically discounts certain items. But is it really a discount? Of course the grocer advertises that we will receive discounts by signing up for and using a loyalty card. But is it really because we're loyal? Do we get bigger discounts the more often we shop? No. Perhaps the loyalty card is encouraging loyalty, but we can obtain one from any and all major grocers, then use them whenever we want. Therefore, it seems there's something more going on here than just a loyalty-based discount.

In reality, "loyalty-based discount" is secret retail code for "free stuff in exchange for information about you and your purchase." More than your loyalty, grocers and other merchants with similar programs are after your data.

Over three decades ago FedEx's CEO Fred Smith proclaimed that "The information about the package is just as important as the package itself."[8] Since then, this realization and mindset has swept across every corner of commerce. Recently, we see companies purely in the business of accumulating and selling data with stratospheric valuation multiples. The grocer "loyalty" example has been around for decades, but it is a business-to-consumer (B2C) model. Some businesses leaders today are realizing that this model can be extended to business-to-business (B2B) scenarios, as well. Indeed, I have consulted to businesses in nearly every sector from telecommunications to energy to manufacturing to financial services on forming internal efforts to package, productize, price, and promote their own information assets. To extend Fred Smith's proclamation, in some situations *perhaps information about the customer is just as important as the customer himself.*

Tax advantages or not, bartering with (or for) data opens up new avenues of commerce, even for traditional businesses. Information has evolved from being a business byproduct to a business performance fuel, and now to a new legitimate accepted form of legal tender. Leaders who cultivate, manage, and are prepared to leverage this new-age currency will increasingly have an increasing array of revenue streams and commercial options available to their organizations.

Think Beyond Your Own Data

Most business and IT leaders I speak with who are interested in "monetizing our information" unwittingly squeeze in that unfortunate and limiting word: "our." Ownership implications aside, which I address in chapter 12, you should be thinking about how to collect data from external sources— particularly sources devoid of commercial restrictions. This is as true or more so for business analytics initiatives as it is for information monetization. The incremental value of exogenous data is largely untapped by most organizations.

You may not have noticed, but in the previous examples (i.e., Citigroup and Belk), they weren't just using their own data. Rather they were ingesting, integrating, and incorporating exogenous data with their own data. Citigroup snags hundreds or thousands of macroeconomic variables, while Belk pulls in census and other population data.

Insights using just your own data are just that, "*in*sights." They fail to put your operations, your situation, or your future into the global context where it belongs. Even more valuable are "*out*sights." Microscopes are great for diagnosing, but telescopes provide the ability to anticipate and plan.

In chapter 3 I discuss how to understand and curate the range of exogenous information sources that can be valuable for both direct and indirect monetization, such as open data, syndicated data, social media data, and others. It isn't easy. Just knowing what information is out there is difficult enough, even before you try to sort out which data is potentially useful, then integrate it. Data scientists are gaining these *information curation* skills, but specialists are in desperate need by many organizations. Do you have a dedicated information curator? If not, perhaps you should.

Uncover Your Hidden Treasures

Another objection we often hear about monetizing data is, "Who would want our data? It's proprietary to our business operations." Most of your partners, suppliers and customers are either in a similar business to yours, or no more than one industry removed, as it were. Take a look up and down your supply chain. Why wouldn't they find some of your information valuable in some way or another? In raw form, it may not be immediately usable. But sitting idly in your databases it's of no benefit to anyone else whatsoever.

Later on I'll cover data preparation, ownership, and privacy as part of the information monetization method, but suffice it to say, *where there's a will there's a way* to share information in some form with someone else who wants it. The bigger issue is that they may not know you have information useful to them, and even if they did, they wouldn't know how to use it. You may have to help develop the market for it. No disrespect, but you probably don't even know yourself what information you have throughout your organization. Unfortunately, very few organizations have anything near a comprehensive inventory of their information assets.

Regardless, your enterprise architects or CDO, if you have one, should initially be tasked with identifying external opportunities for monetizing your information assets.

Although government organizations in the U.S. are prohibited from selling data outright due to the Freedom of Information Act, they're getting better all the time at helping others monetize it in ways that benefit the public. The City of Chicago, for example, compiles data on vacant buildings for various reasons including compliance, public safety, and taxation. But the city also makes this data available via geographic and other overlays like neighborhood so real estate developers can identify prime locations to consider for renovation. It's an economic win for the city, for the developers, and for the city residents.[9]

Stop Giving It Away

Many business and IT leaders admit their companies have established an unfortunate precedent. Over the years, they have offered up their data to business partners, suppliers, or even industry associations—all for naught, or for very little in return.

"We've slid so far down that slippery slope of freely sharing our data with suppliers, I don't know how we could ever climb back up," one retail executive confided to me. "We're leaking data, which in today's world means we're leaking money."

Of course you want to be in the good graces of those throughout your business ecosystem. But you have something they want or crave, and yet you have been giving it away all these years.

The good news is that most business have started amassing ever more information—more granular or detailed information on sales, customers, processes, and so forth—which presents an opportunity to demarcate what you're willing to offer gratis versus the information you extract a premium for in return.

Take Advantage of Information's Unique Characteristics

The unique economics of information offer another set of reasons why information is ripe for monetization. Information has certain characteristics not found in other kinds of assets that render it able to generate value in new and interesting ways.

When compared to other kinds of assets, information has a variety of unique characteristics making it a resource ripe for monetization:

- Information is highly reusable,
- Information is liquid in a wide variety of contexts,
- Information is not considered a capital asset,
- When bartered, information isn't taxed,
- Information is easily replicable,
- Information can be transferred easily and instantly, and
- Information has exponential benefits.

Information's Reusable Nature

Order a pizza. Then eat it. Unless maybe you have had too much beer with it or the sausage was undercooked, you will never see it again. If you want another pizza, you have to order or make another one. Not so with information. When information is consumed it doesn't disappear. In fact it remains unaltered. It is *non-depletable*.

Certain purpose-built mechanisms such as those in the popular messaging app Snapchat delete information by design after a period of time. And business systems can be architected to move or archive or delete data based on some heuristics. But generally, when viewed or searched or otherwise processed—as is its nature—information remains perfectly intact.

Similar to other kinds of intangibles, particularly patents, this makes information especially reusable or re-monetizable. Why license or barter with or analyze information just one way or just one time when it is practically begging to be deployed over and over, and simultaneously by multiple individuals or processes? Economists call this kind of asset *non-rivalrous*.

This is the foundation of the economic models for publishers, news organizations, data brokers, and even research companies like Gartner.

In chapter 13, I will deal with the economic concept of diminishing marginal utility in the context of information assets, but for most practical purposes it makes perfect sense (and dollars) to monetize your information in a variety of ways. Unfortunately, since information is not yet considered a balance sheet asset, most business leaders don't think of it as an asset with this incredibly unique characteristic. Therefore they forego much of its value potential.

Let the Information Flow

True, most information generated or collected by your business is confidential, proprietary, and specially structured for your business, your applications, your employees, and perhaps your customers and select business partners. As it should be. But increasingly, much information has a certain degree of *liquidity*. While not as liquid as cash, and it never will be, certain kinds of information from individual's preferences and demographics to internet of things (IoT) sensor or operational data has a viable market—or at least holds value for some organizations somewhere. A Temple University student studying statistics and economics, Isaac Silver, put it succinctly to me: "Information is more versatile because it's more contextual," meaning it can be applied in a wide variety of contexts. With money you can buy things; with information you can attain insights, relationships, performance, *and* things.

Identifying information licensees or developing a market, and preparing information for use by others, may not be your core business, but it shouldn't be overlooked. Even data you capture or generate which you may not find particularly useful in the context of your own business may be economically beneficial to others. And as you develop future applications and business processes, it's not a bad idea to consider what ancillary information you could capture which might be valuable to others as well.

But don't just think about external monetization. Information can be a form of capital useful to your own business units or departments beyond that which generated or captured it initially. Tear down the silos and eliminate the inhibiting notion of "data ownership" within your organization, as

I assert in chapter 11. Then you'll find information can be deployed in even more high-value ways.

A Capital Offense

It may offend one's sensibilities that information isn't considered a capital asset by current accounting standards and regulatory bodies—e.g., generally accepted accounting principles (GAAP), American Institute of Certified Public Accountants (AICPA), and Financial Accounting Standards Board (FASB). But instead of whining about it or scratching their heads why information is *non-capitalizable*, business leaders should be taking advantage of the obfuscation it offers and incorporate this "feature" into their business models.

Only under rare circumstances do the public or your competitors get purview into what information you collect, generate, barter for, license, or otherwise share with or receive from others. Nor can they gather how you are putting that information to work without reverse engineering observable or reported business activities. This gives information a unique property in relation to other kinds of assets, and a comparative beneficial posture in obscuring the intricacies of your business from competitors. For the most part, even as a public company, you can publish an entire annual report without disclosing anything about the information assets you're collecting, generating, or using.

How much is Google's, Facebook's, Uber's, or even Walmart's or Monsanto's information worth? No one really knows.[10] And exactly what information do they have and what are they doing with it? Other than for privacy regulation compliance reasons, they don't have to disclose that to anyone.

A Taxing Situation

As discussed earlier, barter transactions are recorded by both parties separately based on the value of the good or service received. According to generally accepted accounting principles (GAAP), discounted transactions are recorded at the value of the money exchanged, not the cost of goods. Cash is king in these transactions. Yet there's no requirement that both parties perceive the same recorded value for what they have received. However, if we presume or demonstrate that the grocer in the example earlier is monetizing the incremental data received by virtue of a personally identifiable loyalty card being used, then the transaction (or part of it) ostensibly becomes a barter transaction.

So here's where it gets interesting: information has no value, according to the accounting profession. That's right, despite what 80 percent of business executives surveyed by Gartner contend,[11] a company's information assets are not assets at all—at least and quite conveniently by neither the accounting profession nor government revenue services (e.g., the U.S. Internal Revenue Service [IRS]). Even for companies such as ACNielsen, S&P, and D&B that long have been purveyors of data, and more recent ones such as Google, Facebook, and Twitter, any valuation of their vast storehouses of information assets is nowhere to be found on their balance sheets.

Therefore, if companies receive information in return for providing any good or service, arguably the value of the transaction for accounting and tax purposes could be recorded as zero or non-existent altogether. Since information has no balance sheet value, in barter transactions it may be considered *non-taxable* by the receiving party. Now you may not want to find yourself in a position of arguing this in front of a revenue service auditor or tax court, but on the other hand, you may want to consider using information as a form of currency in certain situations. And companies in the business of licensing information (e.g., credit bureaus, data brokers, news outlets, social media companies, research firms, etc.) of course formally book these transactions. Tax advantages or not, as I contended earlier, bartering with or for data opens up new avenues of commerce, even for traditional businesses.

Endless Copies

Just as information isn't depleted when consumed, for better or worse, information is easily *replicable*. Not only does it not disappear when consumed, endless copies of it can be made to use for an infinite array of purposes, again without affecting the original. Moreover, copies are generally indistinguishable from the original. Yes this causes endless heartburn for chief security officers and chief data officers, but it also affords opportunities well beyond those of physical or financial assets.

Imagine if the information in a book or magazine could only be sold once and in the possession of only a single individual at a time. Thanks at first to scribes, then the printing press, then moveable type, then punch cards, then floppy disks, and now the internet, information can be duplicated and made available to multiple parties with effortless ease. When considering how to realize the potential value of your information assets, perhaps it's a hindrance to think of them as a single dataset. Instead, think of them as the contents of a book or magazine and how making copies of it for others (both those inside and outside your organization) could be mutually beneficial.

This is the basis of the business models of real estate and automobile sales aggregators like Zillow and AutoTrader. And its how the New York Stock Exchange was able to introduce an entirely new line of business to monetize its information: its Market Data Analytics Lab, which makes available market data and analytic tools for curious quants.

A History of Transferability

Along the lines of information's replicability is how easily it can be transferred. Making copies and transporting it are different but certainly related. In the era before electronic data, information was heavy. It was printed on stone tablets, then wood and paper. And yes, some types of tacit information were "transported" orally.

One Reddit contributor with a bit too much time on his hands estimated the Library of Congress and its millions of books, manuscripts, photographic images, sheet music, vinyl records, magazines and comic books, maps, and government publications at about 16,000 tons of information. But he also estimated the informational contents of the library at about 20 terabytes of uncompressed text requiring an optical drive of only about 15 pounds today.[12]

The point is that information today has marginally low information carrying costs and transportation costs. And these costs are plummeting continuously—not just the storage costs, but also the bandwidth costs for sending information anywhere on the planet (or beyond) at any time. Compare this to the inventory and distribution cost of almost any kind of physical asset. Indeed, invisible transistors have replaced bulky vacuum tubes, but most physical assets—from machine tools to automobiles to oil refineries to raw materials like concrete or iron ore—haven't realized the order of magnitude reduction in storage and transportability expense that information has over any time horizon.

Yet, many business models and operating models still fail to capitalize fully upon, or be architected around, the low and rapidly lessening costs of storing and transporting information. This characteristic of information represents a significant challenge for many established and entrenched companies. However, it's a tremendous opportunity for business leaders who are looking to invent new disruptive business models, or entrepreneurs looking to invent new digital businesses.

Netflix is a classic example of this awareness and opportunism: first identifying the low storage cost and high transportability of DVDs via the postal system, then capitalizing on the improved storage and transportability of streaming films over the internet. Where's Blockbuster today? Disintermediated by data. The only store I have seen in the past five years is in Anchorage, Alaska, where internet access is still unavailable or spotty for some in the surrounding area.

New Business Models and Profitability

The long-term value of IT with respect to business investments lies not in the features and functions of a proposed technology or solution, but in the value of the information that the technology or solution creates to drive new business models and profitability. Most information assets have significant potential utility well beyond the application that produces, captures, and/or initially consumes them.[13] Even if their future uses and value are unknown, their potential ancillary value likely outweighs the cost of generating/collecting and managing it. Also keep in mind that information's realized value may grow exponentially, via what's known as the "network effect."[14]

This principle implies that the value of the original business or IT investment is potentially greater than its core benefits. It should also include the value of the data it generates as well. Therefore, project justification/return on investment (ROI) models should consider the derivative or alternative potential value of these information assets across an extended lifecycle.

Because information has this definitive derivative value (along with the aforementioned diminishing carrying costs), enterprise architects should make it their business to ensure new or upgraded solutions maximize the volume, variety, and volume of information collected or generated. Yes, even if the immediate benefits are only speculative. Only occasionally, as in the collection of personally identifiable information (PII), will the risks of collecting additional information possibly outweigh its potential benefits.

The CDO of a major financial services firm shared with me this principle in action:

> As we plan our ERP [enterprise resource planning] implementation, we take a look at every data element in the design, to determine the future benefits of being able to analyze or monetize that data. We also look at every data element not in the plans that we could be capturing, to see what potential benefits we're sacrificing.

Data management and governance expert, and head of services delivery with First San Francisco Partners, John Ladley, acknowledges that the general failure to do just this has been a "foundational flaw in IT and data management for years." He proclaimed to me, "As long as I see development teams cranking out hundreds of apps and services without considering the ancillary uses of data, I will have full employment!"[15]

Organizations that monetize their information assets outstrip their rivals by using it to reinvent, digitalize, or eliminate existing business processes and products. Yet 50 percent of 249 respondents in an online Gartner poll said their company is not monetizing information in any way. 31 percent said they are doing so indirectly by measuring the economic benefit of data through better decision making. However, in an indication of executive disconnect on the topic, another study revealed that 60 percent of senior executives claim they are "already generating revenue from the information they own."[16]

As you consider how to combat the myths discussed in this chapter and leverage information's unique capabilities, next let's dive into examples of how organizations across industries are monetizing information for a range of business benefits. Chapter 2 is designed to inspire information-driven innovation, and help you build a business case to monetize information in your own organization.

Notes

1. "Thrales End—Find Us," Thrales End—Find Us, accessed 09 February 2017, www.thralesend.co.uk/find.html.
2. Adam Satariano, and Alan Bjerga, "Big Data Technology Is Boosting Farmers' Productivity," Bloomberg.com, 09 June 2016, accessed 09 February 2017, www.bloomberg.com/news/articles/2016-06-09/big-data-technology-is-boosting-farmers-productivity.
3. www.nytimes.com/2014/12/01/business/working-the-land-and-the-data.html.
4. Throughout this book I will use the term "information" to refer to any and all forms of data or content, structured or unstructured, raw or processed. However, tacit information (a.k.a. "knowledge" or "wisdom") is a different topic altogether as it does not meet the conditions of a true asset, and therefore cannot be monetized, managed, or measured as one. Also, in most circumstances I consider the "data versus information" argument to be pedantic, and phrasing like "turning data into information" to be trite marketing speak. As I'll discuss, information's potential value is more of a continuum. That said, you certainly will be able to use some of the concepts herein to put some meat on any "data versus information" notions, should you wish.
5. "Citigroup Has Cleanest Fed-Test Pass of Wall Street Rivals," Bloomberg.com, 11 March 2015, accessed 09 February 2017, www.bloomberg.com/

news/articles/2015-03-11/citigroup-has-cleanest-stress-test-pass-of-top-wall-street-banks.

6. Ayasdi, "After Yesterday, CCAR Less Stressful for Citigroup," Ayasdi, 16 October 2015, accessed 09 February 2017, www.ayasdi.com/blog/bigdata/yesterday-ccar-less-stressful-citigroup/.

7. Alteryx Follow, "Dial Up Loyalty and Experience with Multi-Channel Customer Analytics," Share and Discover Knowledge on LinkedIn SlideShare, 14 January 2014, accessed 09 February 2017, www.slideshare.net/Alteryx/dial-up-loyalty-and-experience-with-multichannel-customer-analytics.

8. Gerald Hampton. "Business Management—Perfect Package," *Business Management*, 01 June 2007, www.busmanagement.com/issue-9/perfect-package/.

9. "Vacant and Abandoned Building Finder—Chicago," Vacant and Abandoned Building Finder—Chicago, accessed 09 February 2017, http://chicagobuildings.org/.

10. Well, actually I'll show you how to calculate the value of Facebook's information in chapter 10.

11. My informal discussions with executives at Gartner events from 2011–2015.

12. "DAE Know the Weight of the Library of Congress If Not This May Be It! • /r/DoesAnybodyElse," Reddit, accessed 09 February 2017, www.reddit.com/r/DoesAnybodyElse/comments/dd90n/dae_know_the_weight_of_the_library_of_congress_if/?st=ivuf553s&sh=34087f7e.

13. The concept of how the future value of information can be used to fund current initiatives is explored in "How CIOs and CDOs Can Use Infonomics to Identify, Justify and Fund Initiatives," Douglas Laney and Michael Smith, Gartner, 29 March 2016. www.gartner.com/document/3267517.

14. The network effect is a phenomenon in which a product or service gains additional value as more people use it. It's also called a network externality or demand-side economy of scale in economic parlance.

15. John Ladley, email to author, 17 December 2016.

16. "The Business of Data," The Economist Intelligence Unit Ltd., 2015.

CHAPTER 2

Prime Ways to Monetize Information

As discussed in chapter 1, the first mental roadblock to monetizing information is a failure to think beyond selling it. Painting yourself or your organization into that corner limits the economic potential of your information. Instead, think more broadly about the broad-brush "methods utilized to generate profit."

The trend to see and use information as an asset is still in the "early adoption" phase, making doing so a competitive differentiator for leading organizations. But even when information leaders have embraced this idea, there's an array of challenges to transform the idea of value into a reality that benefits the organization.

Information has economic value that organizations can "turn into money" in two essential ways:

- By exchanging it for goods, services, or cash, and
- By using it to increase revenue, or reduce expenses or risks.

Yet most information and business leaders lack the experience and tools to monetize information. Why? Perhaps we have a collective mental block due to the value of information itself being largely unrecognized on balance sheets, even as the value of other intangibles such as copyrights, trademarks, and patents are measured and reported. Or perhaps it's for any of the excuses just mentioned.

The reasons to monetize data are quite varied. The following twelve drivers of data monetization should be more than enough to help you craft a business case:

1. Increasing customer acquisition/retention,
2. Creating a supplemental revenue stream,
3. Introducing a new line of business,
4. Entering new markets,
5. Enabling competitive differentiation,
6. Bartering for goods and services,
7. Bartering for favorable terms and conditions, and improved relationships,
8. Defraying the costs of information management and analytics,
9. Reducing maintenance costs, cost overruns, and delays,
10. Identifying and reducing fraud and risk,
11. Reducing maintenance costs, cost overruns, and delays, and
12. Improving citizen well-being.

Increasing Customer Acquisition and Retention

Job number one of most companies, certainly from an economic standpoint, is to sell more and sell better. So it's no surprise that some of the leading ways organizations are monetizing information assets are focused on their sales and marketing functions. Many of these methods involve learning more about their customers and prospects, and doing more with this information. We are also starting to see an increased interest in gathering and leveraging a broader spectrum of information about markets and trends derived from external sources.[1]

Georgia Aquarium Dips Into Data to Increase Ticket Sales

In its first year of operation in 2005, the Georgia Aquarium hosted more than 3.5 million visitors. With 120,000 animals across sixty habitats in more than 8 million gallons of water, it was the largest aquarium in the world. Senior vice president (SVP) of marketing Carey Rountree commented, "We didn't have to do any marketing at all. It was a case where you're closing the doors and they're coming in through the windows." Ticket demand was so intense that patrons had to wait six months or more to get reservations.

Yet within a few years attendance had dropped precipitously, to about two million annual visitors. The stream of first-time visitors slowed, as did repeat visits. To bolster attendance, the aquarium added theme parks and new exhibits, to little avail. Then, at the urging of one of its board members, Mark Becker, himself a trained statistician and president of Georgia State University, the aquarium invited Georgia State marketing professor V. Kumar to assess and tackle the attendance problem. Kumar looked at various constraints including customer satisfaction versus crowds, and spend versus profits. Then he concluded, "The question is not simply, 'How do you bring in more customers?' It's 'How do you bring in the *right* customers and keep them coming back?'" After determining who these kind of people are, the aquarium was able to develop a media plan to attract them.

First, Kumar and his team analyzed the top postal codes of visitors and the highest revenue season pass holders to create demographic profiles of the highest-spending season pass holders. Then they identified postal codes with concentrations of similar residents and households, and predicted which kind of media would be most effective in reaching those potential visitors. Armed with this media targeting model, and only a $700,000 increase in media spend (up from $2 million), the aquarium saw attendance grow 10 percent, revenue grow 12 percent, and season pass renewals increase 10 percent over projections. The aquarium had converted detailed visitor and demographic information plus $700,000 in additional media spend into a tidy $8 million gain.[2]

Walmart Helps Searchers Find the Right House

During the week of October 3, 2011, if you visited Walmart.com and searched for "house" you would have been presented with a list of items including seldom-purchased dog houses and a random assortment of housewares. Just as any other week. At the time, Walmart's search engine was state of the art—crunching, matching, and monetizing data from its massive clickstream of forty-five million monthly visitors along with historical purchase data on billions of sales and descriptions of hundreds of thousands of products, then optimizing the search results for any term a site visitor entered.[3] Or did it?

Enter a small team of only fifteen people from Kosmix, which Walmart had acquired a year earlier. They were the foundation of @WalMartLabs, now the engine of innovation at Walmart which has acquired over a dozen companies as of this writing. Within ten months they had extended the company's search engine to incorporate machine learning–based semantics (or what they called the "social genome")[4] which also took into consideration products and topics trending on Facebook, Twitter, Pinterest, and other social media platforms. What Walmart's search capability had been lacking was an awareness of what was happening in the world at any given moment, and how this factored into people's searches. By the week of May 10, 2012, when television viewers were saying goodbye to their favorite characters at the fictional Princeton-Plainsboro Teaching Hospital, Walmart's upgraded "Polaris" search engine had figured out site visitors were looking for the boxed DVD set of the medical drama series *House*, not home goods or a place for their puppies.[5]

Within the year, according to @WalMartLabs vice president at the time, Sri Subramaniam, who oversaw the project, the number of sales resulting from consumers searching for products had jumped almost 15 percent including a reduction in shopping cart abandonment. At Walmart scale, that's monetizing information to the tune of an additional *billion dollars* per year in online sales.[6]

The big "ah-ha" moment and lesson here is to stop fixating inwardly on your own information. The wealth of external information, especially when juxtaposed with yours, can yield monumental monetization opportunities.

Creating a Supplemental Revenue Stream

Packaging up and licensing data is the most direct form of information monetization, but there are other ways to generate revenue from information by infusing it into products and services, or using it to develop new goods or services. In these forms of monetization, information is contributing right to the top line.

In most industries, from retail to telecommunications to manufacturing and of course in social media companies, information about customers, processes, and products is being licensed as a supplemental source of income. Most notoriously, retailers and grocers such as Dollar General, Rite Aid, and Kroger have made certain datasets commercially available to partners, suppliers, and others for a fee or other considerations.[7][8][9] Retail industry experts place Kroger's incremental information windfall at an impressive $100 million annually.[10]

Sometimes selling information is a preferable alternative to no revenue at all. The CEO of a midsize U.S. manufacturing company of sonic buoys and other inertial sensors shared with me how, instead of simply losing business to lower-cost manufacturers in Mexico or elsewhere, it licensed its well-honed expertise in the form of detailed manufacturing and testing processes to those who would otherwise undercut them. Competitors become partners, and a new revenue stream materializes!

Often directly monetizable information is hidden in plain sight. This unutilized or underutilized "dark data" takes on several forms. Often it is captured during the course of doing business, but somewhat overlooked for ancillary purposes. Most frequently you will find it in the form of unstructured content. For example, the real estate aggregator Trulia discovered that 90 percent of its web traffic is from people clicking on photos of homes. But Trulia had no information about what was in the photos. The photos had no descriptions or tags. So Trulia's data science team trained a one-billion-node neural network to learn what is depicted in them. Now, according to Todd Holloway, who started Trulia's data science program, "The system can find you a home in the Hamptons with photos of wine cellars."[11] Helping a buyer find a home is one thing, but now Trulia can correlate sales data with what site users are looking at, and license this information and insight to realtors, homebuilders, appliance manufacturers, and any type of company within the periphery of the real estate market.

Too often organizations fixate not only on their own information, but on a subset of it. Admittedly, structured data can be much easier to leverage analytically, but the untapped economic potential in unstructured content can readily eclipse it.

Introducing a New Line of Business

As you become more proficient at and serious about marketing your or others' compiled information assets, this may warrant establishing a specific business unit to do so. Communications and medical companies such as Juniper Networks, Orange, Verizon, Sprint, Telefonica, Teva Pharmaceutical Industries, and Nordic Wellness Products already have established business functions dedicated to productizing information.

In fact, you may find your core business isn't the ideal line of business at all.

In 2012 when I first spoke with the budding entrepreneurs of Tru Optik, Andrew Swanton and Alex Geis, they gushed about the new file system they had developed for managing Big Data. These two budding entrepreneurs told me how they had proved the system's capability by capturing high-velocity, high-volume BitTorrent traffic on the millions of videos, music, software, games, and other content being bootlegged (mostly) via this peer-to-peer communications protocol. Instantly, it occurred to me that this information was as or more valuable than their technology, and I suggested as much to them. Today, Tru Optik collects and monetizes Internet Protocol (IP)-specific—that is, geo-locatable—details on which content is being shared via BitTorrent and other plat-forms by more than five hundred million people across 150 countries.[12]

This real-time historical data and other data integrated from YouTube, Instagram, Facebook, Twitter, Last.fm, IMDB, Spotify, and SoundCloud is available via their application program interfaces (APIs) or dashboards to help its customers such as production houses, media labels, advertisers, and networks identify unmonetized demand for entertainment content. Swanton even hinted that his system can predict Nielsen television ratings a week before Nielsen publishes them.

No, you may not want to pivot as much as Tru Optik did, but don't overlook the possibility of introducing a new information-based revenue stream out of an incremental technology advance.

In the telecommunications sector alone, the global market for monetized data, estimated at $24 billion in 2015, is expected to grow to close to $80 billion by 2020.[13] As the CEO and co-founder of Vistar Media commented, "If I was a CEO of any telecom operator in the U.S., I would be saying to myself I can do the same. That's going to be something these guys are talking about in the boardroom."[14] Multiply this across all industries and the market opportunity for externally monetizing information, excluding data brokers and those primarily in the information product business, could be in the trillions of dollars.[15]

Yet again, due to mostly unrealistic privacy concerns among consumers, Gartner's communication service provider industry expert, Charlotte Patrick, contends the market for information operates in some respects like a black market—with secret deals, devoid of publicity, off-balance sheets, and generally off the radar. As SAP Mobile President John Sims commented at an industry conference, "The mobile operators don't want to reveal this. They are fearful people will take this and twist it into something that it isn't"—no matter how much these companies stress that the data is anonymized and summarized.[16]

Yes, the ethical "creepy line" (as my colleague Frank Buytendijk calls it) for information monetization can be toed or even crossed, and legally so. But be sure to do so in a way that does not draw too much attention—and if it does, that customer benefits are front and center.

Entering New Markets, Quickly

Whether it's introducing a new product into an existing market or an existing product into a new market, monetizing available information can mean the difference between success and failure. And it can open up new options when other kinds of investment vehicles may not be possible.

Throughout 2011 and 2012, Noam Bardin was looking to expand the presence of his company's mobile mapping app throughout South America. He met with various providers of mapping information to get access to their proprietary geographic data. But he wasn't about to pay with the precious limited cash he had. Instead, he bartered with the data his app collected on automobile traffic, roadwork, accidents, and police locations. Eventually a company called Multispectral went for the deal, and within the year Waze became available to Brazilian drivers. As Bardin said, "It would have taken us a year and a half to get there on our own."[17]

Entering megamarkets like China requires an understanding of its cultural nuances and needs, a bit of interesting data, and some innocent ingenuity. And sometimes it's a bit of understanding and ingenuity only a kid can muster. In Gloucestershire, United Kingdom, a sixteen-year-old girl has named over a quarter-million Chinese babies—or rather the online service she's developed has. Beau Rose Jessup visits China regularly with her family where she says she is frequently asked to help family friends and even strangers select English names for their children. Choosing an English name is a common and serious practice that can make it easier for Chinese to assimilate when they study and work in Western countries. Jessup realized that many Chinese select English names from pop culture, because they do not have access to Western baby naming sites. This results in some embarrassing names. "I have heard of someone called Gandalf and another called Cinderella," she says. For a mere 60 pence, her site, Specialname.cn, enables parents to select key attributes they wish for their child and have a list of easily pronounceable, socially acceptable candidate English names generated. Special Name also shares the list with family and friends over the WeChat social network to help with the selection process. And after the name is chosen, a printable certificate is generated with the name, its meaning, and examples of famous people with the same name.[18] [19]

In short, don't overlook the benefits of information-based bartering arrangements to get new offerings off the ground more expeditiously, or the simplicity of creating an external information flow as a means to generate new revenue streams in new geographies.

Enabling Competitive Differentiation

Monetizing information can separate your products and services from those of others in the marketplace. In the examples of Dollar General and Kroger, consumer packaged goods (CPG) companies and other suppliers may find they prefer doing business with these retailers because of the transparency and value afforded by the sales and other data made available. And maybe Amazon's new brick-and-mortar store will outmaneuver grocery giants by using cameras, sensors, deep learning, and automatic payments to track what shoppers are selecting and eliminate the checkout process altogether. This information is monetized also by eliminating the cost of checkers and point-of-sale systems, saving shoppers time during which they're likely to shop more, and licensing or generating insights from the data.

Intuit's TurboTax is another classic example of a service differentiated by both extracting and inserting information into its product. Intuit compiles data from the millions of tax returns prepared using its software. As more and more U.S. taxpayers migrate to its online software-as-a-service (SaaS) version, Intuit is able to collect more and more data on the usage of its product, but also details of its users' tax returns. This *deinformationalization* of the product along with information it compiles on tax audits enables Intuit to *informationalize* its product further with information and analytics on tax audit risks and probabilities—thereby rendering its product differentiated from others. Human tax preparers by comparison can only guess at tax audit red flags based on their limited personal experience. Even if Intuit could monetize this information more directly, baking it into the offering instead creates a more valuable product—one which Intuit can defensibly raise the price of each year.

And if it isn't already obvious to you, Intuit isn't just monetizing our tax returns through the core TurboTax functionality, Intuit is monetizing the U.S. tax code itself. The U.S. tax code is a veritable mountain of information, having grown from about 500 pages in 1800 to 1,000 pages after President Franklin Roosevelt's New Deal, to 8,200 pages following World War II, to 26,300 pages in 1984, to nearly three times that length today. Intuit and others have brilliantly capitalized on an iconic scourge of U.S. capitalism and congressional recrement—the continually burgeoning 74,608 pages of United States tax code.[20]

My colleagues Mark Raskino and Graham Waller would call these examples being "digital to the core" (coincidentally the name of their groundbreaking book on digitalization). Baking information deeply into business processes or reinventing processes by leveraging available information assets isn't just a way to go digital—it's another clever way to "level up" the economics of your business model.

Bartering for Goods and Services

Sometimes you want something someone else has but are unwilling to or cannot pay the cash price they're asking. Or maybe you want to keep the exchange off-book for reasons of privacy, reputation, or taxation. In these cases, it makes perfect sense to revert back to the most ancient form of commerce: bartering.

As explained in chapter 1, "loyalty-based discount" is code for "free stuff in exchange for information about you and your purchase." More than your loyalty, grocers and other and merchants with similar programs are after your information.

Exchanging information for goods and services is the basis of the upstart business HERE Life that affords students at the Universities of Illinois and Kansas special iPads, shared automobiles, and swank apartments in a new building in which their every movement (well, almost) is tracked and recorded. In turn, HERE Life markets analyses of this information to major consumer brands.

Recently, we see companies purely in the business of accumulating and monetizing information benefit from stratospheric valuation multiples. But why should they be the sole purveyors of information? Retailers, mobile and internet service providers, energy and utilities companies, and financial transaction processors are on the leading edge of bartering with information. This is because most information bartering examples today involve customer data. But other kinds of business information are becoming accepted currency as well, such as the retail product categorization and basic market data IRI trades with its customers in return for their transaction feeds. In industries like manufacturing and shipping, making operational data available to others throughout the business ecosystem is becoming more commonplace, and expected by business partners.

Bartering for Favorable Terms and Conditions, and Improved Relationships

While bartering with information for goods and services may make sense in a consumer product–oriented ecosystem, in the B2B world, discounts frequently are prearranged or based on volume. Sometimes however, it's easier to win favorable contract terms in return for sharing information. Moreover, the liquidity and regulatory conspicuousness of money can make information a preferable form of currency. Traditionally, favorable terms and conditions are offered to customers in good standing or based on guaranteed purchase volumes. More often however, they're based on the exchange of information. In the case of at least one major airline manufacturer, detailed visibility into its suppliers' operations, processes, inventory, and other business dealings gives it increased supplier confidence which it rewards with favorable contract terms.

Contract terms aside, the exchange of information among trading partners facilitates improved relationships. Transparency breeds trust, and nothing embodies transparency better than the flow of information among businesses. However, other than for contract negotiations, most companies just don't have anyone in an "information product" role, nor anyone particularly proficient at making these kinds of deals with their information or for another's information. You should, though. Abe's Market hired one.

Abe's (now part of Direct Eats) was an upstart Israeli-founded online marketplace for healthy living food and other products. A few years ago, its Chief Revenue Officer, Kimberley Grayson, and her team capitalized on the opportunity to provide their multitude of mostly small suppliers with invaluable information from and about buyers. In a classic win-win-win triple play, she and her team devised a mechanism for capturing feedback from consumers in return for discounts (i.e., free stuff). This data and comparative insights were made available to suppliers in the form of a custom scorecard. *Who bought the products? When and how many? When did they consume them? When do they intend to buy more? How were the product's taste, value, and nutrition?* Various dietary, demographic, and psychographic information was also gleaned from the transactions and surveys. In return, suppliers didn't pay cash for this information. Rather they offered free products and deeper discounts just to get their hands on these invaluable insights to help them develop better or different products and optimize inventory levels and shipping. But Grayson didn't stop there. She realized that this data in aggregate would also be valuable to major manufacturers of snacks (e.g., Kraft, Mondelez, Nabisco, etc.) to understand the emerging market for healthy snacks and lifestyles.[21]

This triple-play "everybody wins" relationship model should be part of just about every company's business. You win through higher customer satisfaction and increased revenues; your suppliers win via improve products and increased sales; and consumers win via better products at lower prices—all by riding the same wave of information.

Defraying the Costs of Information Management and Analytics

In addition to top-line gains, monetizing information also can involve the expense side. Remember, monetization is about any kind of *economic gain attributable to one or more information asset.*

In just one year, discount retailer Dollar General realized a net income increase of 121 percent with a 9.5 percent increase in same-store sales. Part of these results were due to an intriguing project headed by senior VP and CIO, Ryan Boone. Despite the anxieties of externally exposing forty-five terabytes with seventy billion rows of data about $12 billion in sales from 8,800 stores, Boone engaged cloud-based data warehouse and analytics provider 1010data (now part of Advance/Newhouse) to consolidate data from a variety of databases. This provided deeper and more rapid insights into sales and other activity. Almost immediately, Dollar General discovered its stores were not open at the right times. Sales data indicated some of its outlets had heavy sales near closing time, implying they probably should be extending their hours.[22]

But this isn't where the story ends. Dollar General wasn't the only company interested in this information. As an astute marketer of hundreds of thousands of products, it saw one more product to sell: its information. Soon Dollar General started generating dollars from the aggregate and analyzed data by selling it to retailers like Pepsi and Unilever. Not only could these CPG companies see how well their goods were selling, but for a premium they could benchmark themselves against competitors. Ultimately, one of the industry's first data warehouses in the cloud started paying for itself. As 1010data's CEO recounted, "This data is so valuable . . . that their data infrastructure becomes a profit center rather than a cost center."[23]

Another retailer found that just by updating its infrastructure to better handle Big Data processing, it shaved hundreds of thousands of dollars off its annual processing expense. The volume of sales data Sears had was bringing its mainframe and its competitiveness to their knees. With eight billion rows of sales data on eleven million Stock Keeping Units (SKUs), nearly two billion rows of inventory data, and about four thousand stores, it was only able to calculate item price elasticity quarterly, and only on a 10 percent subset of data. The business simply was unable to react to market conditions and new product launches. According to the project executive, Phil Shelley (now CEO of Datametica), moving this processing off the mainframe and into Hadoop reduced six thousand lines of batch code to four hundred lines of PIG, providing up to one hundred times improved performance, delivering $600,000 in annual savings, and enabling Sears to calculate price elasticity on a weekly basis using all available data.[24] [25]

Unfortunately, the vast majority of information and analytics leaders think and act only intramurally about their data warehouses or other data stores. Yet, the expanded economics of availing this data to others outside your four walls can be significant. Even worse, too many organizations shortchange the economic benefits possible from their information assets because of deficient infrastructure.

Reducing Maintenance Costs, Cost Overruns, and Delays

Whereas information monetization focused on sales and marketing is most often oriented toward top-line economic gains, organizations (including those in public sector) also drive financial performance gains through improved operational efficiency.

Lockheed Martin supplies $46 billion of aeronautics, information systems, missiles and fire control, mission systems and training, and space systems to government organizations and some companies. With over 125,000 employees in nearly six hundred facilities in every state and seventy nations and territories working on thousands of highly technical, complex, and largely taxpayer-funded projects, Lockheed Martin's leadership is extremely conscious about issues leading to cost overruns and program delays.[26] Delays can result in milestone payments, payment withholdings, write-offs, de-bookings, and a reduction in awarded contracts—each directly impacting cash flow.

But let's back up to the hidden potential of monetizing "dark data." Dark data is how some refer to unutilized or underutilized data—typically data that was collected and used for a single purpose, then forgotten about and often archived. Sometimes it's jokingly referred to as "zombie data" in how it resembles the living dead, or as "digital exhaust," or "digital debris," or even "digital detritus" by those etymologically and alliteratively inclined. At a presentation I gave in 2011 at a Microsoft event, the CIO of one of the Big Four systems integrators asked, "We're a consulting firm, what dark data could we possibly have?" I suggested that his firm likely is sitting on twenty years of archived emails and project communications that, if mined and correlated to projects which had suffered from certain kinds of issues (e.g., as scope, budget, personnel/staffing, technology, and so forth), could yield leading indicators of similar project issue for current client engagements.

This is precisely what Lockheed Martin did with the help of Ayasdi's machine intelligence platform and analytics services. As Prakash Sesha, senior corporate engineering manager with Lockheed Martin's Technology and Operations Group, recounted at a Gartner event, "A program manager considers three things important: Are we delivering what we said we were going to deliver? Are we on target in terms of schedule? And are we at or below cost?"[27] The challenge was that Lockheed's current metrics were trailing indicators, not leading indicators.

Only experienced program managers could tell "by their gut" that a program was going south, said Sesha, but they didn't have the data to anticipate that degradation. In analyzing hundreds of variables including text analysis of project communications and documentations, Lockheed was able to detect specific signatures of programs predicted to degrade in performance with manageable false-positive rates, while decreasing the amount of historical data required to do so from six months to just two months. By monetizing project information in this way, Lockheed Martin now has 300 percent improved foresight into program assessments, saving potential losses in the hundreds of millions of dollars.

Although information assets regularly are deployed to assist with product maintenance, rarely are they deployed for *project* maintenance as effectively as Lockheed Martin has done. Yet the information for doing so is there. It may be hidden in emails or other project documentation, but don't let that deter you.

Cashing In on Improved Business Performance

Thirty thousand hours. This is how much time customers had been inconvenienced while empty Automated Teller Machines (ATMs) were waiting to be reloaded throughout Singapore. DBS Bank handles twenty-five million transactions a month from its four million customers across the country's more than 1,100 ATMs. "It's important for us to place customers at the heart of the banking experience across all our touch points," says David Gledhill, managing director and head of group technology and operations with DBS. "Any downtime in a single ATM would mean inconvenience for our customers. Hence, we have to continually improve the efficiency of our ATM network and operational process."[28]

To do so, DBS partnered with SAS to forecast withdrawal activity and optimize machine reloading. Gledhill shared that previously ATMs often would either run out of cash prior to the scheduled reload, or the ATM reloading personnel would show up at machines during a peak usage period like during lunch hour in the business district.

Here, a focus on customer experience led to banking improvements. But instead of merely leveraging information to improve its next best offer, DBS monetized its process-related information to improve monetary disbursement. It developed a solution that incorporated manufacturing and logistics concepts along with operations research techniques such as forecasting and queuing theory to optimize its ATM cash loading process. Nimish Panchmatia, executive director and head of Singapore consumer banking operations, recounts "We set out to accurately assess customers' withdrawal patterns across the entire network for each machine. Using these forecasts, we were able to generate an optimized schedule that achieved minimum cash-outs and trips while being operationally realistic and robust."[29]

As a result, cash-outs at DBS ATMs have been reduced 90 percent, 20 percent of replenishment trips have been eliminated, the amount of leftover cash returned to the bank following replenishment trips is down 40 percent, and the number of customers affected by the ATM reloading process has been reduced by 350,000.[30]

Too often, business leaders take for granted the inefficiencies in basic business processes like scheduling, but as DBS shows, there can be significant hidden economic value realized from attacking them with available information assets, a bit of analytics, and the willingness to change an accepted process.

Identifying and Reducing Fraud and Risk

Indirect forms of information monetization can include exposing and limiting fraudulent activity. While not selling or licensing or productizing information directly, using it to limit these kinds of unwarranted expenses certainly represents a measurable economic benefit.

In the U.S., Medicare and Medicaid fraud costs taxpayers $70 billion. So in 2015, the Health and Human Services Department hired a chief data officer and put in place aggressive plans to attack this problem. The result: the largest health care fraud takedown in history. In early 2016, 301 individuals were indicted in schemes totaling $900 million. But the key to the crackdown wasn't just manpower. "Data can be the unsung hero," commented HHS chief data officer, Caryl Brzmialkiewics. And even though this represents a fraction of the overall fraudulent activity, HHS metrics show this bust has had a deterrent effect on the order of another $1 billion in reduced fraudulent payments.[31]

But sometimes fraudsters are "slimier" even than those scamming the health care system. The City of New York has seven thousand miles of water mains, tunnels, and aqueducts delivering water to homes and businesses throughout the five boroughs. Accordingly, it also has 7.400 miles of sewer lines which return the wastewater from these locations and street sewers through ninety-six pump stations to fourteen treatment plants. Commercial businesses are required to install grease interceptors to separate oil, fats, and grease from wastewater and prevent grease from entering the city's sewer system. Periodically these interceptors must be manually cleaned out and the grease carted away by licensed haulers. Increasingly, city inspectors had been discovering sewer pipes clogged with hardened grease which restricts the flow of wastewater, leading to flooding and backups. The city estimates over 60 percent of sewer backups are caused by improperly dumped grease, particularly from restaurant fryers.[32]

Instead of pulling up every manhole in the city, the health department enlisted the Office of Policy and Strategic Planning, a "geek squad of civic-minded number-crunchers working from a pair of cluttered cubicles across from City Hall."[33] They unearthed data from an obscure agency which certifies restaurant grease-carting services. Layering the geospatial data of restaurants without a current grease-carting contract to that of nearby sewers, the team was able to give inspectors a list of suspected derelict restaurants and clogged sewers. Sure enough, this simple integration of disparate data sources yielded a 95 percent success rate in tracking down grease dumpers. The result: an increase of 2 million gallons of sewer capacity by removing 30 million pounds of debris, and a more efficient deployment of city health and water department workers.[34]

As the City of New York shows, fraud can be tackled by adeptly overlaying various information assets, and real economic benefits can be found in almost every corner in (or under) your organization.

Improving Citizen Well-Being

While corporations are beholden to their shareholders, governments are accountable to and responsible for their citizens. In the U.S., the Freedom of Information Act (FOIA)—along with similar "open data" directives at a national and local level in the U.S. and many other countries—establishes an overarching mandate for the usage and availability of non-sensitive government information just for that purpose. But just to be sure, FOIA sets up a further roadblock prohibiting the monetization of that information by U.S. agencies. Information is considered part of the public trust. Although FOIA specifies how government agencies may be reimbursed for the cost of searching, preparing, and copying requested information which is not already available on government open data portals, lately some government organizations such as the Department of Commerce are testing the edges of FOIA by charging exorbitant fees for simple information requests.[35]

But ultimately the government sharing of information usually is for the purpose of improving citizen safety, security, health, and opportunity. The ultimate monetization of this information takes the form of reduced government costs and economic growth.

Recently, I met with the Federal Aviation Administration (FAA), where Larry Grossman, its deputy chief security officer, recounted how the FAA is improving what information it makes available along with its format and structure.

"We already release tons of flight-related data based on formats and time intervals meaningful to us," said Grossman, "But this isn't the most efficient for external entities who are developing consumer products. It's inhibiting innovation." He went on to describe how its "External Data Access Initiative" benefits the FAA, pilots, and passengers: "Currently, we spend a lot of time and money producing these charts and other aggregate data products. But the plan is for the FAA to focus more on the data itself and make it more consumable, thereby encouraging the industry to produce innovative data products from it. Collaborating with the aviation industry in this way could save taxpayers the millions of dollars it costs us to produce these charts, and help spur greater innovation targeted at efficiency and safety."[36]

Grossman shared a specific example of how improved real-time information products produced by private enterprise using FAA data could save pilots money and improve passenger safety:

When there's a presidential movement or stadiums filled with more than 30,000 people, the FAA issues temporary flight restrictions (TFRs) over that airspace. But of course they're not displayed on the standard charts pilots use. Similarly some flight control towers are staffed on a part-time basis, and this information is in separate chart the FAA publishes and subject to change. Since the FAA doesn't want to prosecute pilots for violating closed airspace or put aircraft and passengers into danger flying into airports with un-staffed towers, the FAA is encouraging private enterprises to use its data to create dynamic charts with multiple overlays. Similarly, the FAA is encouraging companies like LiveATC that pays people who live near airports to put antennas on their homes that collect and transmit real time air traffic control (ATC) signals, then makes them available to pilots via a $0.99 iPhone app.

These are just a couple of examples from a single government agency. Across national and local government organizations throughout the world, similar initiatives have or are taking shape, such as with national postal services:

- Poste Italiane, the Italian postal service, has kicked off a project to have postal carriers collect and certify street numbers to make them available to mapping companies such as Google who still only have imprecise locations for many addresses, and
- Post Malaysia has a booming courier business along with its regular mail business. It is looking into having postal carriers observing and reporting on infrastructure issues such as potholes, damaged or missing signage, and construction problems. Other government organizations would fund this data collection to improve citizen safety and defray some postal service expenses.

Another increasingly common way local governments are monetizing information is through public-private partnerships. In 1876, the City of Los

Angeles installed its first electric street lamp. Installing and maintaining street lighting is a significant expense for municipalities. Today, L.A. has over two hundred thousand streetlights, consisting of four hundred different models installed across 7,500 miles of roads and freeways. At night, crews patrol the streets to detect outages, and the city gets forty thousand calls from residents each year reporting issues. Recently L.A. and other cities have started installing smart, IoT-based LED streetlights that handle cellular and WiFi traffic. The city receives $1,200 per year in rent for each "SmartPole" and nets nearly $9 million per year in energy savings alone. The poles can also capture information on outages, nearby accidents, and traffic patterns—saving on maintenance and saving lives.[37]

Assessing the economics of information in the public sector can be a bit trickier than with commercial organizations. Rather than a profit motive, government organizations are driven more by the economic and other benefits to citizens and businesses. Still, the opportunities to deploy information in measurably improving economic opportunity, safety, and well-being are endless, and just starting to be realized by national and local governments.

You're Definitely in the Information Business, or Should Be

These examples highlight that every business is, can be, or should be an information business, monetizing information in a spectrum of ways. According to the CapGemini EMC Big Data Report, 63 percent of respondents consider that the monetization of data could eventually become as valuable to their organizations as their existing products and services.[38] But consider that a recent Gartner survey indicates fewer than 20 percent of organizations are either licensing or exchanging their information for goods and services from others, and a scant 31 percent are even measuring the economic benefits of using their information assets themselves.[39]

Even if your information won't ever become as valuable as your existing products or services, it is unconscionable to forgo an opportunity to monetize it in one or more ways. Whether it's getting into digital business, digitizing your offerings, licensing your data to suppliers or partners, baking your information assets into existing products or services to extend their value, or measuring and leveraging the economic benefits of deploying information internally, you had better get your organization into the information business, or suffer the consequences of becoming a casualty of the Information Age. To get started, the next chapter presents a step-by-step process to monetize your (or even others') information assets.

Notes

1. The examples below are part of a library of hundreds of information innovation "art of the possible" examples I have compiled. As I fully expected the Big Data "boo birds" and naysayers to start coming out of the woodwork at some point, I started collecting these real-world examples of organizations around the world generating significant economic value from available information assets. I hope you are inspired by them.
2. "Boosting Demand in the 'Experience Economy'," *Harvard Business Review*, January–February 2015 Issue, https://hbr.org/2015/01/boosting-demand-in-the-experience-economy.
3. "Our Retail Divisions," Walmart News Archives, http://corporate.walmart.com/_news_/news-archive/2005/01/07/our-retail-divisions.
4. Sarah Perez, "In Battle with Amazon, Walmart Unveils Polaris, a Semantic Search Engine for Products," TechCrunch, 30 August 2012, https://techcrunch.com/2012/08/30/in-battle-with-amazon-walmart-unveils-polaris-a-semantic-search-engine-for-products/.
5. "List of House Episodes," Wikipedia, https://en.wikipedia.org/wiki/List_of_House_episodes.
6. Zak Stambor, "Wal-Mart Factors Popularity into Site Search Results," Internet Retailer, 30 August 2012, www.internetretailer.com/2012/08/30/wal-mart-factors-popularity-site-search-results.
7. Stacey Vanek Smith, "Data Is the Economy's New Oil," Marketplace Podcast, 01 May 2013, www.marketplace.org/2013/05/01/tech/data-economys-new-oil.

8. Alex Samuely, "Rite Aid Exec: Quick App Technology, Data Offer Predictive Capabilities," *Mobile Marketer*, 20 January 2016, www.mobilemarketer.com/cms/news/database-crm/22092.html.

9. Matthew Boyle, "Kroger's Secret Weapon," *Fortune*, 27 November 2007, http://archive.fortune.com/2007/11/21/magazines/fortune/boyle_datamining.fortune/index.htm.

10. Gary Hawkins, "Will Big Data Kill All but the Biggest Retailers?," *Harvard Business Review*, 18 September 2012, https://hbr.org/2012/09/will-big-data-kill-all-but-the.

11. "CDO Executive Forum 2014," *DataDriven Business*, 12 November 2014, www.datadrivenbiz.com/cdoforum/conference-agenda.php.

12. Steve Ellwanger, "Tru Optik Goes Over the Top to Track Media Consumption of 500 Million People," Beet.TV, 02 August 2016, www.beet.tv/2016/08/andre-swanston-summit.html.

13. Kate Kaye, "The $24 Billion Data Business That Telcos Don't Want to Talk about," *Ad Age*, 26 October 2015, http://adage.com/article/datadriven-marketing/24-billion-data-business-telcos-discuss/301058/.

14. Ibid.

15. Ibid.

16. Ibid.

17. Mark Milian, "Data Bartering Is Everywhere," Bloomberg, 15 November 2012, www.bloomberg.com/news/articles/2012-11-15/data-bartering-is-everywhere.

18. "A 16-Year-Old British Girl Earns £48,000 Helping Chinese People Name Their Babies," BBC Newsbeat, 06 September 2016, www.bbc.co.uk/newsbeat/article/37255033/a-16-year-old-british-girl-earns-48000-helping-chinese-people-name-their-babies.

19. Isabelle Khoo, "Special Name: Teen Earns Ridiculous Amount of Money to Name Babies," *The Huffington Post Canada*, 08 September 2016, www.huffingtonpost.ca/2016/09/07/baby-naming_n_11892178.html.

20. Jason Russell, "Look at How Many Pages Are in the Federal Tax Code," *Washington Examiner*, 15 April 2016, www.washingtonexaminer.com/look-at-how-many-pages-are-in-the-federal-tax-code/article/2563032.

21. Kimberley Grayson, interview with author, 14 August 2014.

22. Joe Skorupa, "What's in Your Market Basket?," RIS News, May 2010, www.1010data.com/media/1078/1010data_risnews_casestudy_dollargeneral.pdf.

23. Smith, "Data Is the Economy's New Oil."

24. Rachael King, "How Sears Uses Big Data to Get a Handle on Pricing," *The Wall Street Journal*, CIO Journal, 14 June 2012, http://blogs.wsj.com/cio/2012/06/14/how-sears-uses-big-data-to-get-a-handle-on-pricing/.

25. Dr. Phil Shelley, "Hadoop in the Enterprise: Legacy Rides the Elephant," SlideShare, 09 July 2012, www.slideshare.net/Hadoop_Summit/hadoop-in-the-enterprise-legacy-rides-the-elephant-13587064.

26. "Who We Are," Lockheed Martin Website, accessed 08 February 2017, www.lockheedmartin.com/us/who-we-are.html.

27. Prakash Sesha, "Ayasdi: How Machine Intelligence Uncovers Hidden Insights in Complex Data," Gartner Business Intelligence & Analytics Summit, 30 March 2015, http://www.gartnereventsondemand.com/session-video/BI13/SPS38.

28. "Forecasting ATM Cash Demands: DBS Bank Has 80% Fewer Cash-Outs, Improves Process Efficiency by 33%," SAS.com, accessed 08 February 2017, www.sas.com/en_ie/customers/dbs.html.

29. "DBS Awarded Most Innovative Use of Infocomm Technology," DBS Newsroom, 24 November 2014, www.dbs.com/newsroom/DBS_awarded_most_innovative_use_of_infocomm_technology.

30. "Innovative Use of Advanced Analytics Prevents Cash-Outs at ATMs," Informs, accessed 08 February 2017, http://analytics-magazine.org/innovative-use-of-advanced-analytics-prevents-cash-outs-at-atms/.

31. "Better Data Just Saved Taxpayers $900 Million in Medicare Fraud," Nextgov, accessed 08 February 2017, www.nextgov.com/big-data/2016/06/better-data-just-saved-taxpayers-900-million-medicare-fraud/129357/.

32. "New York City Business Integrity Commission, Department of Environmental Protection, and Mayor's Office of Policy and Strategic Planning Launch Comprehensive Strategy to Help Businesses Comply with Grease Diposal Regulations," NYC Business Integrity Commission and NYC Environmental Protection Press Release, 18 October 2012, www.nyc.gov/html/bic/downloads/pdf/pr/nyc_bic_dep_mayoroff_policy_10_18_12.pdf.

33. Alan Feuer, "The Mayor's Geek Squad," *The New York Times*, 23 March 2013, www.nytimes.com/2013/03/24/nyregion/mayor-bloombergs-geek-squad.html?_r=0.

34. Press Release, NYC Business Integrity Commission.

35. David Yanofsky, "I'm Suing the US Government for Its Data on Who's Entering the Country," Quartz, 20 May 2016, http://qz.com/685956/im-suing-the-us-government-for-its-data-on-whos-entering-the-country/.

36. Larry Grossman, discussion with author, 15 June 2016.

37. "Los Angeles First City to Install SmartPole Street Lighting Technology Developed by Philips and Ericsson," TheClimateGroup.org, 12 November 2015, www.theclimategroup.org/news/los-angeles-first-city-install-smartpole-street-lighting-technology-developed-philips-and.

38. "New Global Study by Capgemini and EMC Shows Big Data Driving Market Disruption, Leaving Many Organizations Fearing Irrelevance," PR Newswire, 10 March 2015, www.capgemini.com/news/new-global-study-by-capgemini-and-emc-shows-big-data-driving-market-disruption-leaving-many.

39. "Methods for Monetizing Your Data," Gartner Webinar, 20 August 2015.

CHAPTER 3

Methods for Monetizing Information

A few years ago, my family decided to move from one of the western suburbs of Chicago to one of the northern townships about 30 miles away. As with anyone who sells a house via a realtor in the U.S., the listing in the multiple listing service (MLS) database is more-or-less public information available from real estate company or real estate aggregator (e.g., Zillow, Realtor.com) websites. If you have experienced the dreaded process of selling a home lately, you will recall being inundated with mailings from real estate companies, mortgage brokers, moving companies, and other businesses looking to latch onto your move. It seemed every local business related to moving or home buying had contacted us, except one: our own bank.

Think about that for a moment. What is one of the top milestones compelling people to change banks? When they move, of course. Surprisingly, our bank never contacted us to offer any number of services to ensure we remained customers, such as:

- Offer us a mortgage or home equity line,
- Introduce us to a new local branch and banker,
- Update our address information on file,
- Send a reminder to move the items in our safety deposit box, or
- Print us new checks.

In fact, over a year after we moved and I sorted out all these items on my own, I received a call from my private banker at the old location who still didn't know we had moved. By then, this bank even had subsumed the mortgage from the originator! Yet they still were unable to make the connection internally.

How simple would it be for even just a high school kid to write an app that matches homes in the MLS with the bank's customer database? Probably one long night's worth of coding, an energy drink, and a protein bar. At most.

Well, even if my global bank hasn't figured out how easy it is to monetize customer information, there's a prime example of one that has. Westpac Bank in Australia has five customer-facing divisions serving some thirteen million customers. Its consumer bank operates a network of over 1,400 branches, third-party distributors and call centers, and nearly four thousand ATMs, along with internet banking services.[1] And whereas my bank's mission statement starts with something hackneyed about "client service," the number one company value listed on Westpac's corporate website is "Delighting Customers—by deeply understanding and exceeding expectations."[2]

It's here where Westpac decided to put its money (and information) where its mouth is. But at the time, Westpac only was able to accurately suggest particular services for less than 1 percent of its customers. It just didn't have a complete picture of who each customer was. But under the leadership of Karen Ganschow, general manager of customer relationship marketing, Westpac launched a "KnowMe" program to centralize and analyze all of customer activity—including bank website browsing history, ATM and call center usage, and so forth. "We want to make sure that every time we interact with a customer there is something that is personalised for them," Ganschow said. "We are trying to use data so that customers will stay engaged with the bank forever." But she also acknowledged the information-related challenges and opportunities: "Our data sources are growing very fast and customer interactions are growing very fast. We know who you are paying. We know where you are shopping and what you are buying. There is a lot of data pouring into our data warehouses."[3]

In just the first nine months of the "KnowMe" initiative, Westpac more than recouped its investment, monetizing all this information for an AU$22 million increase in revenues. Within a couple of years, "Next best offers" had reached 37 percent of customers, and 60 percent of those engaged signed up for additional banking products.[4]

Traditionally, information managers have had a limited view of how they can help business leaders generate value from information, mainly focusing on operational and analytical benefits. Information leaders rarely have the knowledge or experience to manage their organization's information as an asset. Business leaders increasingly see others in their own or adjacent industries monetizing their information in various ways, but don't know how to get started doing this themselves. Conversely, information leaders typically lack the most basic capability for information asset management: an accurate and current information inventory, including internal and external information with the potential for economic benefits. In many organizations, information sharing is rare because of turf wars or difficulty arising from poorly administered standards that hamper information leaders' efforts to create and carry out an organization-wide information monetization strategy. But when organizations fully embrace information as an economic asset of benefit to the entire enterprise, data hoarding subsides and principled behavior takes shape.

The Steps to Monetizing Information

Not to oversimplify the many challenges and tasks involved in monetizing information, these seven basic steps, if executed well, should reap significant rewards. As the central theme of this book is about treating information as an asset, it should come as no surprise that the monetization approach follows somewhat familiar research and development (R&D) and product management/marketing approaches for monetizing other kinds of assets or raw materials. Variations on this approach will be based on which monetization method you have in mind. For example, a full information product management function may not be necessary if your focus is on indirect monetization methods only—although one sure would be helpful for most organizations. As with any approach, of course, adapt these steps to your particular needs and culture:

1. Establish an information product management function tasked with generating measurable economic benefits from available information assets,
2. Develop and maintain an inventory of possible information assets from throughout the organization, as well as from second- and third-party sources,
3. Evaluate alternatives for both direct and indirect information monetization,
4. Identify, adopt, and adapt high-value information monetization ideas from other organizations, especially those in other industries,
5. Test information monetization ideas for feasibility,
6. Prepare and package information for monetization, and
7. Establish and cultivate a market for the information asset.

Establish an Information Product Management Function

Although you may already have an information leader such as a chief data officer (CDO) or an analytics leader, I recommend a designated individual or team tasked with *identifying and pursuing opportunities for and generating demonstrable economic benefits from available information assets*. They may report to a data and analytics executive, into the enterprise architecture group, or perhaps even a business unit head.

Creating a distinct, dedicated information product management role is vital when business and information leaders agree on directly monetizing information by generating revenue or other financial benefits from exchanging it. Organizations typically already have a defined approach for managing and marketing products. Analogously, if you are considering licensing information in any form, you need someone whose job is to define and develop the market for the information asset and to productize it.

Finding qualified talent for this kind of role can be difficult. Traditional product managers may have an advantage over other candidates, but why not consider hiring individuals with experience at a data broker such as Experian, Equifax, D&B, IRI, LexisNexis, Nielsen, or J.D. Power?

Ideally, the information product manager reports to the CDO (itself an emerging role for information-savvy organizations, to be discussed in chapter 8) or into a new information product line of business head. This chain of command, askew to the IT organization, underscores that information is a business asset, not an IT asset. Moreover, an information product manager is a good counterweight to people (such as some data scientists) who can get carried away by interesting problems that may be tangential to the business objectives.

The information product manager can leverage existing product management disciplines for:

- Conceiving and planning new ways to monetize information,
- Identifying or developing information markets among partners and others, and
- Coordinating with IT, marketing, finance, legal, and other product management groups to execute information productization objectives.

Pythian CEO Paul Vallée said Pythian executives recently spoke about the company's experience in taking more of a product management approach. They determined a committee approach wasn't getting things done, and that the company required a single owner to drive the process:

We needed somebody who understood exactly how the business works. We needed someone who had been with the business a long time and had been involved in establishing our practices. That was what we needed to do in order to break through that inertia and to get rid of the committee for day-to-day decisions. Although, a group of stakeholders should always be consulted throughout the project, at the end of the day, one person needs to be a leader.[5]

Similarly, Samir Desai, CIO at Equinox Fitness Clubs, said the key is getting just the right individual into the role: "Not everybody is cut out to be an innovator. I think you need to choose someone who understands the business and the technology, and who has the right kind or personality fit to play that role."[6]

This year, Qantas announced it is searching for someone to "lead the development of innovative data products over the Data Republic[7] platform, driving internal value for the Qantas Group and value for other participants on the platform." This individual will be expected to use their "data industry expertise to generate business for the platform" by "seeking out internal and external leads and developing and proposing value optimising data use cases to help solve various business issues."[8]

Even though information product managers may not be developing "products" in the same sense as a typical product company, they take a product management approach and embody the same skills as successful product managers. These skills include:

- **Thinking big.** This is not about how to deliver interesting information to eyeballs, but how to deliver important information to business processes in a way that transforms them.
- **Identifying and understanding customers.** Information product customers may be internal or external to the organization, and they may be partners or suppliers. And in most cases, they will need help conceiving of themselves as potential information product customers or appreciating the economic opportunities bound up in information they perhaps didn't even know existed.
- **Swimming upstream and across the current.** An information product manager needs to be able to navigate cross-functionally, and up and down throughout the organization, especially among IT, business, finance, legal, and marketing leadership.
- **Being Experimental.** Information product management also involves a smattering of R&D. Most organizations don't do information

research and development, so it's up to the information product manager to set up and lead this function.

- **Evolving.** Information product managers must be able to evolve their ideas and evolve the information product itself. Technically, information products are easy to develop, meaning yours will have to improve rapidly to keep ahead of competitors—external or even internal.
- **Measuring and communicating.** Information product managers should welcome being gauged solely on the economic benefits of their solutions. These goals should be well established and communicated along with projections and ongoing results.

Identify Available Information Assets

Organizations that don't know what information they have or could acquire, are unable to leverage it as an asset. As one CIO for a large insurance company recently admitted to me: "It's silly that someone around here has an inventory of our office furniture, but nobody in the company has an inventory of what data we have."

When Netflix decided to get into the content business, producing its own original content, it took a look at what information it had that other production houses did not. At the time with twenty-seven million subscribers in the U.S. and thirty-three million worldwide, Netflix had information on thirty million viewer "actions" per day including when a viewer pauses, rewinds, or fast-forwards; three million searches; four million ratings; and information correlating demographics with the time of day shows were watched and on what devices.[9] This information, correlated with viewer-created metadata on the actors, action, genre, and other descriptors, gave Netflix a solid confidence that a U.S. adaptation of the British version of *House of Cards* would be a huge hit. Not only that, but this unique pool of Big Data helped Netflix tweak the production, right down to the color palette used on set, to the language and dialog, to the duration and frequency of sex scenes, and that releasing the season all at once would generate greater buzz.

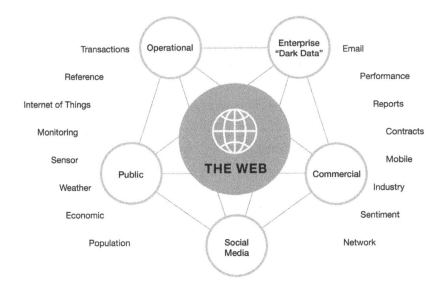

Source: Laney, Faria, Duncan, "Seven Steps to Monetizing Your Information Assets." Gartner
Research G00291622, October 7, 2016

Figure 3.1 *Information Asset Inventory*

So the first job in monetizing information is to know what information
you have or could get, and where it is. Start by identifying specific sources
of information that could be leveraged (Figure 3.1).

As you are inventorying your information assets, and ideally cataloging
external information sources of potential relevance, be sure to keep an eye
out for those with monetizable characteristics, including:

- Information that originates within your organization, for which you
  have some claim of provenance and control,
- Information that is proprietary in nature. That is, others do not have
  it or are restricted in how they can use it,
- Information that is secure. Monetizing information that is easily
  accessed or hacked can result in a black market for it which may can-
  nibalize your own efforts,
- Information that is not subject to restrictive privacy limitations,

- Information that is known or proven to be of sufficient accuracy and precision,
- Information that is complete, in that it represents a solid slice of the known universe of such activities or entities, and for which any given record is complete (e.g., without missing fields),
- Information that is of a general or accepted context, rather than information that may not be meaningful outside your organization or industry, and
- External information collections with liberal terms and conditions such as most open data published by government organizations, or information that can be harvested and repurposed without restriction.

In chapter 12, we'll look at ways to measure an information asset's potential, even monetizable, value.

Operational Data

This is information about customers, suppliers, partners, and employees that is readily accessible in online transaction processing and/or online analytical databases. It typically includes transactional data, contact data, process data, and reference data such as master data. Enterprises often have the opportunity to collect even more information during the course of business via sensors or process monitoring such as:

- Log data,
- Smart meters,
- Internet-connected devices (e.g., IoT),
- Voice/phone,
- Security camera feeds,
- RFID, and
- Wireless signals.

For example, XO Communications now analyzes 500 discrete customer data elements including call patterns, late or delinquent payments, and other vital signs. After just a four-month implementation, XO reduced customer churn by 47 percent, protecting $15 million in revenue.[10] And Memorial Healthcare System integrated information from eight hundred disparate databases for greater visibility into vendor activities, resulting in a 40 percent reduction in vendor invoice cycle times that led to vendor discounts totaling over $2 million.[11]

Dark Data

This is information collected during the course of business that remains in archives, is not generally accessible, or is not structured sufficiently for analysis. It can include emails, contracts, documents, multimedia, system logs, or other intellectual property. Parsing, tagging, linking, or otherwise structuring or extracting usable information from these sources is the greatest immediate opportunity for most businesses among all types of information.

From chapter 2, Lockheed Martin's analysis of project documentation to anticipate issues, along with new-age lenders like Kreditech that use a customer's browser and phone histories to determine lending risk, are both classic examples of dark data in action. Similarly, SJV Criminal Data Specialists uses Connotate's web content extraction technology to scour court records from some 1,500 U.S. jurisdictions, resulting in the reduction of eleven million hours of annual cumulative records research, over $1 million in annual savings, and a 55 percent growth in business attributable to these new efficiencies.

But dark data doesn't have to be in the form of textual documentation. It also can include how much beer is left in a perfectly opaque keg. Bars and restaurants typically waste 15 percent of their beer by replacing kegs too early, thereby losing sales from running out of a brand before they realize it. SteadyServ has found a way to monetize this dark data about how much beer is remaining in a keg. With a system that tracks the keg contents via sensors, the company provides real-time insights to all supply chain stakeholders such as the retailer, brewer, distributor, and brand managers via a mobile app.[12] [13]

In the rarest of circumstances, even dark data can be in the form of oral history. The forty-thousand-year knowledge base of the indigenous people living on the Fish River pastoral property in Australia's Northern Territory has been monetized, in compliance with the Kyoto Protocol treaty on climate change, into almost AU$600,000 in payments for carbon offset credits. With the support of the Indigenous Land Corporation, the indigenous peoples' vast experience in land management is generating credits from low-carbon emissions dry savanna burning which have been purchased by Caltex.[14]

Commercial Data

For many years, industry-specific data aggregators (D&B, IMS, Equifax, Nielsen, and Experian, for example) have offered syndicated credit, real estate, postal, household, and other information by subscription. Today, marketplaces are emerging for almost any variety of information. Examples include, Data Republic, Dawex, Apervita, Datastreamx, Quandl, and ProgrammableWeb. And black markets for personal and commercial data are rampant. Even among business partners, information assets are being used in private bartering where once only financial and material assets were. Data and analytics leaders, along with business leaders and enterprise architects, all need to be aware of commercial information sources that relate to their market and assess their potential, as well as work with business partners to encourage the availability of their information.

The managed network service provider, DSCI, typifies the way many companies leverage syndicated data. At the tail end of a marketing automation implementation project, DSCI's marketing communications manager, Stacey Corbin, was trying to determine which data should be imported into the sales system, and employed Dun & Bradstreet to help cleanse and enrich its customer data with nearly four dozen additional fields of information. Doing so enabled DSCI to monetize this combined information by improving email deliverability by 42 percent and more than doubling conversion rates from 5 percent to 11 percent.[15]

Public Data

Many governments have also begun opening their information coffers as a matter of principle or dictum. Open government initiatives for economic development and for health, welfare, and citizen services are in various stages of implementation throughout the world. This information can also have real commercial value—especially when mashed with other sources—to understand and act on local or global market conditions, population trends, and weather, for example.

Public data even can be used to create new (ahem) *high*-value businesses such as Potbot, a virtual cannabis "budtender." At its core is a recommendation engine that uses information on strains, cannabinoids, and medical applications aggregated via semantic web technology. Potbot also incorporates data from cannabis seed DNA scans along with recordings of brain activity in clinical tests. It monetizes this information, not just in the form of a consumer app, but also in helping growers improve their yields for the most popular or beneficial strains.[16] [17]

Public data is most monetizable when integrated with your own proprietary information. Consider the example of one of the largest brewers in the world. Its attempt to enter the Chinese marketplace had produced less than stellar margins. With only about 75 percent forecast accuracy, it was stocking and thereby wasting too much inventory, while also failing to accommodate market demand in some areas. To solve this problem the brewer correlated its internal forecast information against a wide swath of global and regional economic information from weather to jobs to population to the sales and prices of other kinds of products. In doing so, it identified which of these factors were leading indicators (alone or in combination) for its business. As a result, the business increased its forecast accuracy almost instantly to about 95 percent.

Social Media Data

Individuals and businesses blogging, tweeting, yammering, instagraming, Facebook posting, and LinkedIn updating have created a fast-growing, potentially precious source of information about preferences, trends, attitudes, behavior, products, and companies. Posts, trends, and even usage patterns themselves increasingly are used to identify and forecast target customers and segments, market opportunities, competitive threats, and business risks, and to select job applicants.

The U.S. Center for Disease Control estimates nearly fifty million Americans are sickened by foodborne disease every year. Researchers at the University of Rochester developed a system to provide indicators of health-related issues among New York City's twenty-five thousand restaurants. Using a combination of machine learning and human crowdsourced "Mechanical Turk" approaches, its experimental nEmesis application can identify likely eatery culprits based on the location and content of diners' tweets. As the research paper explains:

> These users make up an "organic" sensor network—a dynamic mesh of sensors interconnected with people facilitated by Internet enabled phones. A single status update often contains not only the text of the message itself, but also location, a photo just taken, relationships to other people, and other information.[18]

The system analyzed 3.8 million tweets over a four-month period within 100 kilometers of NYC, identifying 479 "sick" tweets within 100 hours of when a user was at a particular restaurant during operating hours. Tweet GPS tags, check-in data if available, and restaurant location data were used to pinpoint restaurants with potential health issues. nEmesis' predictions correlated well with official health department restaurant grades. In the future, the system could be used to focus health inspections—thereby saving resources and health care costs along with improving citizen well-being.

Web Content

Scraping content from competitor, partner, or industry websites can turn the web itself into your company's biggest database. Software companies such as Connotate, BrightPlanet, and Mozenda specialize in harvesting this type of content.

One such company taking advantage of this freely available web content is the multinational life science and biotech company, Sigma-Aldrich, now part of Merck. With over 180,000 products, pricing them optimally within the marketplace was an impossible manual task. Today it collects, aggregates, and structures competitor product pricing information in real time using web data collection agents, then feeds this information directly into its SAP data warehouse.[19]

Information leaders have two roles in this phase:

- Helping business leaders understand the range of information available so they can put this information into the context of organizational goals, and
- Refining the raw information by using various technologies such as information governance, data profiling, and metadata management.

In chapter 11, I will discuss and illustrate how to zero in on the information assets that offer the greatest economic potential, using Gartner's information value models.

Evaluate Alternatives for Both Direct and Indirect Monetization

As discussed in chapter 1, methods of monetizing information can be classified into two broad groupings: direct monetization in which information generates explicitly attributable economic benefits, and indirect monetization in which information contributes to economic benefits more circuitously or obliquely. Organizations could adopt both, depending on their information product strategy.

Direct monetization usually is in the form of a transaction. It ranges from exchanging information in return for goods and services, to incorporating information into existing or new products or services, to outright selling it (more often licensing it, actually) in one form or another (Figure 3.2).

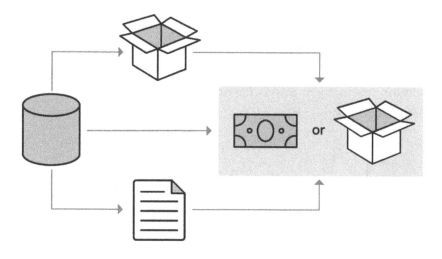

Source: Laney, Faria, Duncan, "Seven Steps to Monetizing Your Information Assets." Gartner Research G00291622, October 7, 2016

Figure 3.2 *Direct Information Monetization*

The methods of direct monetizing include:

- Bartering or trading with information,
- Information-enhanced products or services,
- Selling raw data through established data brokers or other third parties,
- Developing and offering data/report subscriptions (either predefined or custom), and
- Selling analytics solutions using data (customer and third party) as a component of the overall solution.

When monetizing information directly, you must decide to what degree the information will be enhanced through integration, analytics, or reporting; and how the information will be made available and by whom.

One typical practice of successful direct monetization programs is publishing a branded index, which is a data aggregation that is made publicly available. Examples of branded indexes include the Nielsen television ratings, the J.D. Power automobile awards, the ADP employment index, and even

Gartner Magic Quadrants. A branded index advertises your expertise in this area and signals that you have additional information available to license.

Indirect monetization is about optimizing the business. It entails using information internally to improve a process or product in a way that results in measurable outcomes, such as income growth or cost savings (Figure 3.3).

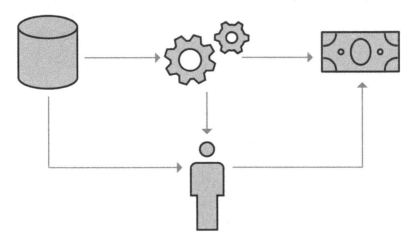

Source: Laney, Faria, Duncan, "Seven Steps to Monetizing Your Information Assets." Gartner Research G00291622, October 7, 2016

Figure 3.3 *Indirect Information Monetization*

Examples of indirect monetization are about using information to:

- Improve efficiencies,
- Measurably reduce risks,
- Develop new products and markets, and
- Build and solidify partner relationships.

The important aspect of indirect monetization is to measure the accrued economic benefits. Without this measurement, it is difficult at best to claim that information is actually being monetized. In chapter 13, I detail several methods of measuring information's economic benefit that can be used to justify and prove indirect information monetization ideas.

Adapt High-Value Monetization Ideas from Other Industries

Understanding, evaluating, and adapting what other organizations are doing, especially outside your own industry, can jump-start your monetization efforts. Clients often ask me, "What are others in our industry doing?" I suggest that unless they want to be in second place, they should also look beyond their own industry for ideas to adopt and adapt. Chapter 2 provides multiple examples across industries to get you thinking about the possibilities for your own organization.

Looking beyond a single industry is increasingly important not just to find good ideas, but also as a kind of early warning system of how other companies are evolving their information monetization initiatives, which could encroach on your own market in unexpected ways.

Public case studies, professional organizations and industry conferences can all be sources of inspiration, new ideas, and new thinking about monetizing information. They can also be important sources of understanding potential problems, obstacles, and risks.

Curating such examples can take some time and effort. Over the past five years, Gartner has been compiling examples of what we call the "art of the possible with information and analytics." This compilation includes hundreds of examples from every sector, every major geography, and the majority of business domains and information types. It is useful in helping to spur the imagination clients. Or as one business executive told me, "These examples of what other companies have done has shamed us into action. We now have an information R&D function in addition to the research and development we do for our core products."

Test Ideas for Feasibility

Ideas for monetizing information have to be realistic. So put them to the test using this feasibility checklist (Figure 3.4). This checklist delineates feasibility into nine dimensions that should be assessed with a scoring method such as a Likert scale. Each dimension has a starting question to crystallize and

Type of Feasibility	Feasibility Indicator
Practical	Is the idea something that is utilitarian, or merely interesting/cool? Is it usable?
Marketable	Is the idea something with sufficiently broad appeal, internally or externally?
Scalable	Is the idea something that can be developed and implemented to the extent required or intended?
Manageable	Do you have the skills to oversee the development and implementation of the idea?
Technological	Do you have the tools and skills to design, build, test, roll-out and maintain the idea?
Economical	Is the idea something that will generate sufficient return on investment?
Legal	Does the idea conform to industry regulations and local laws where it will be used or implemented?
Ethical	Will the idea be something that has the potential for customer, partner, or public backlash?
Ecological	Will the idea cause undue impact on the environment?

Source: Laney, Faria, Duncan, "Seven Steps to Monetizing Your Information Assets." Gartner Research G00291622, October 7, 2016

Figure 3.4 *Feasibility Checklist*

focus the evaluation process. More questions will emerge for each dimension as the discussion gets into specifics relevant to the organization.

The scoring for each feasibility indicator should be ruthless: there's no room here for wishful thinking. A thorough, open, clear-eyed discussion and assessment is the best preparation for selecting a score. Below we'll look at each feasibility dimension:

Practical

Is the idea utilitarian, or merely interesting or "cool"? Is it usable? Some ideas are just clever, perhaps generating interest or being merely a publicity stunt. This is fine in the short term, but is the effort worth it in the long haul? Will people (including you) or businesses (including your own) actually use it? What is it a substitute for, and do you really see that product or service being subsumed?

Marketable

Would the idea have sufficiently broad appeal, internally or externally? Some information monetization ideas are too highly targeted or focused on a narrow market. Perhaps this makes sense if that market is willing to pay sufficiently, or your costs are low enough.

Scalable

Can the idea be developed and implemented to the extent required or intended? Most information and analytics solutions can be scaled without much difficulty and sublinearly. But be sure yours is. Once your pilot must accommodate a wider variety of information sources of varying quality or timeliness or completeness, and users of the solution become more demanding of certain functional or performance features, will it scale?

Manageable

Do you have the skills necessary to oversee the development and implementation of the idea? Prototypes and pilots don't require nearly the operational overhead full-blown implementations do. Especially if your monetization idea involves exchanging or licensing information to others outside your organization, be sure to consider the sales, legal, operations, accounting, and customer support requirements.

Technological

Do you have the tools, information and skills to develop and roll out the idea? Some information monetization ideas may be too complex for your organization to implement beyond a prototype. Are you prepared to invest in additional computing resources and/or consultants to make it a reality?

Economical

Will the idea require too much investment or generate sufficient return on investment? Most organizations don't have any experience at all in calculating or even estimating the ROI for information monetization initiatives. Nor do they even know the cost basis for their own information assets. Although productizing information is not as costly, and typically scales better than physical products or human-delivered services, expect to spend far more time and expense than you expect developing the market for it.

Legal

Does the idea conform to local laws where it will be used or implemented? Industry regulations, and national and local laws regarding the collection and use of information, are shifting continuously, and in many cases are still ill-formed. Are you prepared to push the envelope, identify loopholes, and lobby or respond quickly to proposed regulations or laws affecting your idea? Or is your organization more conservative and willing to wait for others to blaze the trail?

Ethical

Will the idea be something that has the potential for customer/user/public backlash? Be sure to brainstorm all the ways someone could misuse, misconstrue, mishandle, or misappropriate the information you are making available to them. What are the worst-case scenarios, and what are the various ways other organizations have been tripped up ethically? Is your idea only "doing good," or are there others who could suffer unwittingly because of it? Ask your customers and partners for their thoughts on the idea from an ethical standpoint. This question should not be an afterthought: reputational slipups can sink a company faster than technological or organizational ones.

Often it is best to stay well within the current norms of what is socially accepted and legal, but be forewarned that seldom are such ideas groundbreaking. At other times, you may want to push social boundaries while remaining within legal ones. Conversely, you may want to push the boundaries of what is legally accepted, when social norms are changing faster than the laws can keep up. Finally, you may want to experiment with revolutionary ideas that challenge both social norms and established regulations. Many laws have loopholes—especially where information uses are concerned. Maybe you've found one to monetize.[20]

Prepare Data for Monetization Use

How are you going to gather the information, and from where? Then, what are you going to do to enhance its utility and potential economic value? Again, think of how physical production processes use raw materials to eventually create finished goods.

At the most basic level, many of these are tasks with which most information management organizations are familiar:

- Aggregating and/or sub-selecting information into more meaningful forms and formats,
- Integrating information into new derivative forms,
- Supplementing information with additional sources,
- Analyzing information to expose certain insights,
- Cleansing information to improve its validity,
- De-identifying information to protect against exposing personally identifiable or other sensitive content,
- Packaging the information in various ways to appeal to different kinds of markets and users,
- Determining and developing information access methods such as APIs, publish-subscribe, file transfer protocol (FTP), etc., and identifying or deploying a marketplace platform for hosting or distributing the information, and
- Setting up an information product maintenance function.

Establish and Cultivate the Market for the Information Product

Finally, for externalized information products (and yes, internal customers as well), there's the whole marketing aspect, starting with packaging the information product, determining how it's going to be made available, positioned, priced, promoted, and sold, and what the terms and conditions for its use might be.

This is where a dedicated information product marketing role really pays off. But these tasks, at least initially, could leverage existing corporate or business unit marketing expertise:

- Field testing the information product,
- Documenting and promoting use cases and proof points,
- Segmenting the market and determining sales and marketing channels,
- Establishing information product positioning, messaging, and collateral,
- Establishing licensing fees and terms,
- Setting up sales enablement,
- Setting up a customer support and satisfaction function,
- Determining how to package the content,
- Deploying or selecting a marketplace platform,
- Implementing the technical means to distribute the information, and
- Establishing licensing fees and terms.

What Information Monetization Success Looks Like

It's good to be able to claim you've monetized information, not just used it for operational or reporting purposes. This can lead to increased budgets for further similar initiatives, the means to impress investors or potential investors, or even professional gains for those involved. You know you've been successful, and can point to your successes when you have achieved one or several of the following:

Revenue Gains, Cost Savings, or Risk Reduction

Ideally, you know you've succeeded in monetizing information when, of course, you can attribute some measurable economic gain to the information—regardless of how it was applied. Again, some of these gains may come in the form of direct revenue gains, indirect revenue, and attributable cost savings or reduced risks. It isn't always easy to connect the dots from some realized economic benefits back to the specific information assets involved (or vice versa), but it is critical to do so, or at least attempt to do so even if (well documented) estimates and assumptions are involved.

Economic Attribution

As you measure the economic gains achieved, you are also in a position to measure the net value of the information assets used themselves. As I illustrate in chapter 11, the value of the information for any given use must be considered in the context of other resources employed as well. These will typically include computing resources and labor.

Productization

From an offering perspective, you may have *productized* some information or *informationalized* a product. In the former, information is licensed to others in some form, sometimes as raw data or in some cases as summarized information or construed insights. In the latter, information is used to enhance the use, performance, salability, or other qualities of an existing product or service.

Information Management Improvements

A typical, almost unfailing byproduct of information monetization efforts is the improved management of information—from its data governance and data quality, to its storage and protection. Once your organization realizes and communicates the economic benefits of any given information asset, attitudes about and attention to its care and feeding will improve significantly.

Internal Scuttlebutt

Most clients I speak with about embarking on information monetization strategies recount how certain individuals in their organization are uneasy about the prospects of "selling our data." Of course I have shown how rarely if ever is an organization's information actually "sold"—rather, it is licensed. Still, the point of contention is around externalizing information in some fashion and the accompanying manifest risks thereof, especially with personally identifiable information (PII). Remember however, monetizing information takes many forms, only a few of which involve externally sharing it. Expect this unease to continue from some, even after the project is proven successful. Other individuals will have quite the opposite reaction: they will be invigorated by leveraging your own (or others') information assets in uniquely innovative ways.

Market Reaction

As with any business model advance or innovation, expect competitors to follow or react in some way. Some competitors may attempt to question your company's integrity for "selling customer data" even if you're only licensing aggregate point-of-sale (POS) information devoid of PII. Others may quickly do the same, perhaps devaluing the market information for which you have been the sole proprietor. Other competitors may expand on your monetization scheme, perhaps creating joint ventures or new external ventures which are not subject to the same compliance regulations of your industry. Already, I have seen these moves being made among some companies in highly regulated industries such as banking and insurance.

Investor Awareness

Investors and equity analysts have begun recognizing and rewarding information-savvy moves being made by companies. I have heard them ogle over companies, referring to them as "becoming more like Google or Uber" in the way they amass and monetize information. Regardless of whether accountants deem information a recognized balance sheet asset any time soon, investors most definitely have begun taking note.

Analytics: The Engine of Information Monetization

Most methods for and examples of information being monetized in part are based on an organization's ability to make sense of, find patterns within, or produce nuggets of insight from available information assets. As information's volume, velocity, and variety continue to reach new extraordinary levels, the human eye and human brain increasingly are insufficient tools for generating economic value from it.

We have become accustomed and attuned to reading tables of data along with eye-popping charts and other visualizations. But despite how fanciful these two-dimensional (or simulated three-dimensional) data derivations have become, they are starting to lag significantly compared to the power of analytic computing. Moreover, human cognitive and physical reaction times now pale in comparison to those of integrated analytic-operational technologies. While there yet may be room for human creativity in how to monetize information, the mechanisms for doing so are being subsumed by technology, especially analytics and AI technology.

In the next chapter, we'll look at the critical part that analytics plays in monetizing information. Not just for classic decision making, the role of analytics beyond basic business intelligence (BI) is critical to realizing the new economics of information.

Notes

1. "Our Business," Westpac.com, accessed 12 August 2016, www.westpac.com. au/about-westpac/westpac-group/company-overview/our-businesses/.
2. "Our Strategy and Vision," Westpac.com, accessed 12 August 2016, www.westpac.com.au/about-westpac/westpac-group/company-overview/ our-strategy-vision/.
3. Stuart Corner, "Westpac Using Big Data to Woo Customers with Offers Made to Measure," *The Sydney Morning Herald*, 04 March 2014, www.smh.com.

au/it-pro/business-it/westpac-using-big-data-to-woo-customers-with-offers-made-to-measure-20140303-hvfx5.html.

4. Corner, "Westpac."

5. Lynda Partner, "4 Factors for Digital Transformation Success," Pythian.com, 12 July 2016, www.pythian.com/blog/4-factors-digital-transformation-success/.

6. Partner, "4 Factors."

7. Data Republic is an online data marketplace in which Qantas recently invested.

8. Ry Crozier, "Qantas to Extract All It Can from Data Exchange Investment," iTnews.com.au, 13 January 2017, www.itnews.com.au/news/qantas-to-extract-all-it-can-from-data-exchange-investment-447220.

9. David Carr, "Giving Viewers What They Want," *The New York Times*, 24 February 2013, www.nytimes.com/2013/02/25/business/media/for-house-of-cards-using-big-data-to-guarantee-its-popularity.html.

10. "XO Communications," ibm.com, accessed 05 June 2016, www.ibm.com/smarterplanet/global/files/us__en_us__leadership__xo_communications.pdf.

11. "Florida Hospital Network Deploys IBM's ECM Solution to Prevent Vendor Fraud, Reduce Operating Costs," hospitalmanagement.net, 06 November 2013, www.hospitalmanagement.net/news/newsflorida-hospital-network-deploys-ibms-ecm-solution.

12. "Steadyserv iKeg Beer Analytics for Bars," Inc.com, accessed 05 June 2016, www.inc.com/doug-cantor/steadyserv-ikeg-beer-analytics-for-bars.html.

13. accessed 05 June 2016, www.steadyserv.com.

14. "First Indigenous Carbon Credits Sold," Australian Government Indigenous Land Corporate Press Release, accessed 15 January 2016, www.ilc.gov.au/IndigenousLandCorporation/media/Items/Content/Media/Media%20Releases/First_Indigenous_Carbon_Credits_Sold.pdf.

15. "DSCI Improves Targeting & Segmentation Driving 2X Increase in Online Conversion," Dun & Bradstreet, 22 July 2016, www.dnb.com/perspectives/marketing-sales/dsci.html.

16. Chris Weller, "Tech Startups Bring Science to Marijuana Dispensaries," *Newsweek*, 30 July 2014, www.newsweek.com/2014/08/15/tech-startups-bring-science-marijuana-dispensaries-262096.html.

17. accessed 09 February 2017, www.potbot.com.

18. Adam Sadilek, Sean Brennan, Hery Kautz, and Vincent Silenzio "nEmesis: Which Restaurants Should You Avoid Today?," University of Rochester, 2013, www.cs.rochester.edu/u/kautz/papers/Sadilek-Brennan-Kautz-Silenzio_nEmesis_HCOMP-13.pdf.

19. "Sigma-Aldrich Corporation Uses Connotate to Fuel Competitive Pricing Program," Connotate Press Release, 21 March 2012, www.connotate.com/press-releases/sigma-aldrich-corporation-uses-connotate-to-fuel-competitive-pricing-program/.

20. For further guidance, see Frank Buytendijk's work on digital ethics, including "Digital Ethics, or How to Not Mess Up with Technology," Gartner, www.gartner.com/document/2853620.

CHAPTER 4

Analytics
The Engine of Information Monetization

Mobilink is Pakistan's leading provider of voice and data services, based in Islamabad, with thirty-eight million subscribers communicating over nine thousand cell sites and 6,500 kilometers of fiber optic backbone. But as with most telecommunication providers, and many other kinds of businesses, its leadership is as concerned about customer churn as it is about gaining new customers. Faced with fierce competition in an exploding market, it was compelled to generate improved economic value from the data on its millions of subscribers and two hundred thousand retailers across ten thousand cities, towns, and villages. More specifically, how could it answer the age-old but increasingly important question: How can we offer the right services to the right customers at the right time? How can we monetize all of this information, including social media data, in building customer trust, improving loyalty, and decreasing churn while maintaining profit margins?

To answer these questions, Mobilink deployed SAP's InfiniteInsight[1] predictive modeling solution against its storehouse of Big Data, resulting in better targeted and more effective promotions and campaigns, which increased customers' usage of high margin, value-added services like text messages, ringtones, and music. The results of this effort included an eightfold increase in the uptake of customer retention offers (from 0.5 percent to 4 percent), a 380 percent boost in campaign response rates (mostly from social network analysis), and a predictive modeling approach that enables Mobilink to deploy new predictive models in less than a day.[2]

Unless you are licensing information directly or trading it for goods and services, it's more likely you are monetizing it indirectly via some form of analytics or digitalization. Even with the latter, most licensed or bartered information has some degree of analytics applied to it before it is shared. And even when licensing information, most organizations will add value to it by generating and selling the insights or analysis instead of or alongside the raw information itself.

However, evolving from traditional business intelligence (BI), represented by enterprise reporting or end user query tools, has been slow to materialize in many organizations. Not only have lagging organizations lost out on the opportunity to understand their businesses and markets better, but they have squandered opportunities to generate measurable economic benefits from (i.e., monetize) their information assets. In this chapter, we will explore the case for reaching beyond business intelligence, and how embracing these ideas can lead to improved economic benefits for your organization.

Beyond Basic Business Intelligence

"From what I have been able to determine, we have over 100 distinct internal BI implementations producing some 15,000 reports, most weekly, some monthly or quarterly," confided the new CIO of a Big-4 systems integrator. "And that's just in the U.S." He went on to question the value these implementations and reports generate for the organization: "I have no idea who is using them, and if they're using them at all, for what purpose. But these systems are costing us millions, so I'm considering just shutting down some just to see who if anyone complains."

This story is repeated over and over in varied vernacular by IT executives I speak with, most often by those who have inherited a gaggle of data warehouses, data marts, and BI applications. Often it's followed by a common proclamation: *I'm desperate to get IT out of the report writing business.* Their real concern isn't the cost or resources required by BI—it's the inability to link it to discernible economic gains. I'm certain that if IT executives could attribute top- or bottom-line value propositions—or any key organizational metrics, for that matter—to these implementations, then they would be clamoring to keep them with in IT.

From Descriptive to Diagnostic, Predictive, and Prescriptive Analytics

Basic BI implementations are everywhere, in every corner of every organization. They range from personal spreadsheets to financial and production reports to executive dashboards. The sprawl of these applications, particularly as a result of commonplace data warehouse implementations over the past twenty years, no doubt has improved enterprise transparency and influenced improvements in productivity, customer and partner relationships, and compliance. But slicing and dicing and reporting on information, in most cases, has fallen woefully short of producing measurable economic benefits. And where these implementations may have been measurable, few organizations have actually measured them other than with poor proxies of value such as "user satisfaction." Ultimately, BI and data warehousing have become a significant IT cost sink, in many instances only with acknowledged soft and unmeasured business benefits. Yet inertia to continue generating hindsight-oriented reports and dashboards is a function of having chased after them the past twenty or thirty years.

Typical BI implementations tend to be far removed from actually monetizing data, or connecting the dots between them and top- or bottom-line value propositions. More advanced analytic capabilities which generate actionable insights, predictions, or explicit recommendations can be connected more readily to economic improvements. Therefore, there's an imperative for organizations to reach for advanced analytics capabilities (Figure 4.1).

However, advanced analytics initiatives tend to be more challenging and vocational—that is, targeted at a particular business problem or opportunity rather than "the enterprise." And because information reporting and exploration continue to serve a valid purpose in organizations (especially with the

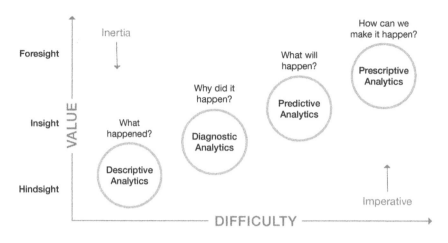

Source: Laney, Kart, "Emerging Role of the Data Scientist and the Art of Data Science." Gartner Research G00227058, March 20, 2012

Figure 4.1 *Gartner Analytic Ascendency Model*

emergence of self-service BI), it can be helpful to consider BI and advanced analytics as distinct entities and initiatives with unique value propositions, staff, and technologies from one another.

The Advanced Analytics Advantage

Fifty years after Coca-Cola acquired the Minute Maid brand in 1965, a customer called to complain about the consistency of orange juice from week to week and from one season to another. Except this wasn't just any customer. It was a popular fast food restaurant with over two thousand locations. They had threatened to switch to another "orange drink" provider.[3]

If there's anything Coca-Cola prides itself on, it's the quality and consistency of its products. Oh, and not losing customers. So this call set into motion a project to determine just how to establish orange juice consistency regardless of the season, supply chain disruptions, or regional orange prices and availability. Our job was to "take Mother Nature and standardize it," said Jim Horrisberger, director of procurement at Coke's massive juice packaging plant an hour south of Disney World. "Mother Nature doesn't like to be standardized."[4]

But that's just what Coke did. With the help of Revenue Analytics, a consultancy that also helped Delta Airlines maximize its revenue per mile, "We basically built a flight simulator for our juice business," said Doug Bippert, Coke's VP of business acceleration. The so-called super-secret methodology called "Black Book" analyzes a quintillion decision variables including weather patterns, anticipated crop yields, and cost pressures, plus the six hundred flavors Coca-Cola scientists determined comprise an orange. Then the algorithm dictates how to blend and batch oranges, based on their flavor analysis, for consistent juice.[5]

Now, Bippert said, "If we have a hurricane or a freeze, we can re-plan the business in five or ten minutes because we've mathematically modeled it." So the next time you drink orange juice, remember you're drinking an algorithm.[6]

Whereas BI implementations are appropriate typically for informing business managers of performance indicators, advanced analytics implementations can provide far-reaching organizational benefits over basic BI. The requisite BI tool/platform features of data aggregation, summarization, selection, slicing, drilling, and charting are tuned for presenting information *interesting* to users, but not necessarily information *important* to optimizing business processes. Today, only strategic decisions (and not even all of them) may be made at a rate slower than the speed of business. Tactical and operational decisions increasingly must be made at a rate faster than that of which humans are capable.

Despite continued corporate reliance on spreadsheets, now analytics is a core competency in most organizations. However, most implementations—particularly enterprise implementations—entail basic decision support solutions for business managers and executives. In addition, much information is still left to interpretation, pockets of analytics result in information clashes between departments, and many users choose not to rely on analytic output to guide their decisions and behavior, or at least limit their reliance on it. Resolving this demands producing analytic results beyond simple summarizations, and involves delivering those results direct to business processes–not necessarily to people. Directing analytic output merely at eyeballs continues to be one of the great fallacies and limitations of BI.

However, advanced analytics in all its variety of instantiations (for example, data mining, prediction, artificial intelligence, complex-event processing, visualization, and simulation) can be not only difficult to implement, but also difficult to articulate and coordinate. This is why even the most well-intentioned analytic initiatives can too easily devolve into a pedestrian presentation of lagging and loosely relevant performance indicators.

Ultimately, the keys to generating measurable economic value with information involve implementing forms of advanced analytics focused upon:

- **Exploiting Big Data.** Increases in the volume, velocity, and variety of information assets are a boon for data monetization. Analytic capabilities have struggled to keep up with the size, speed, and range of available information. But organizational capabilities are just as important.
- **Improved and actionable decision making.** Analytic technologies and solutions can drive improved and actionable decision making, leading to increased business performance. Solutions for decision making tend to embrace complexity, including sophisticated scenarios. And they frequently involve improving or automating business processes, or reducing risk.
- **Identifying monetizable insights.** In addition to classic decision making and automation, monetizing information through advanced analytics can be achieved through deeper understanding of processes, people, and markets; improved foresight; and innovating products and services.

While many of the ideas you conceive will overlap some of the above, each of these should be a starting point for exercises in identifying ways to generate improved economic benefits available information. Ask yourself and others in your organization: *How can we exploit the characteristics of Big Data? How can we use information to make better/faster decisions? What questions can we ask now that couldn't be addressed earlier?* The answer to each of these most certainly will lead to opportunities for monetizing your (and others') information assets.

Exploiting Big Data

At the beginning of the millennium, I started to notice a set of rising information management challenges among clients. These challenges related to the emergence of e-commerce, an increasing number of documents, images, and other unstructured data types, and electronic interactions among business. While many clients were lamenting and many vendors were seizing the opportunity of these fast-growing data stores, I also realized that something else was going on. Sea changes in the speed at which data was flowing mainly due to electronic commerce—along with the increasing breadth of data sources, structures, and formats due to the Y2K-centered ERP application boom—were as or more challenging to data management teams than was the increasing quantity of data. I defined these three-dimensional challenges as a confluence of a rising *volume* of data, increasing *velocity* of data, and widening *variety* of data.[7] These "three Vs," as they're known, formed the basis for understanding and defining what today is known as "Big Data."[8] While most information management professionals and nearly all vendors obsess over the size (volume) of information, this represents only one facet of magnitude (i.e., bigness). And additional "Vs" which others have cleverly (?) posited, such as "veracity" or "value" or "vulnerability," are neither measures of magnitude nor defining characteristics of bigness.[9]

Regardless how one defines Big Data, it represents a fertile resource for monetizing, sometimes by licensing it to or trading it with others, but more often by analyzing it and executing on these insights. Not just reporting on it, but actually analyzing it. By merely reporting on Big Data, the result is the same pie charts and bar charts and tables as you would get by analyzing a sample of smaller data—albeit with perhaps some improved confidence. Increased data volumes can improve analytic accuracy, increased data velocity can improve analytic precision, and increased variety can improve analytic completeness.

Monetizing the Increased Volume of Information

With regard to Big Data volumes, basic BI solutions tend to be challenged. But advanced analytic solutions, particularly data mining, machine learning, and predictive applications, flourish with large datasets. The larger the dataset, the easier it is to uncover hidden subtle patterns and trends, and therefore, opportunities which are likely to evade the competition.[10] In addition, the subtle signals are magnified by large datasets, and a larger breadth of dimensions can be established to discern business monetizable correlations. If the goal of a business process is to increase the probability of a customer transaction happening, then having a wealth of data about, for example, that customer, similar customers, market/shopping conditions, and product and upstream supplier inventories, along with *subtransactional* data[11] about the customer's real-time shopping behavior (online or in-store), can be used by advanced analytic applications.

One excellent example of a company taking advantage of massive volumes of data is Vestas. Founded in 1898 as a blacksmith shop in western Denmark, Vestas has breezed into a global leadership position in the wind turbine business with over 75 gigawatts worth of generating capacity worldwide.[12] To optimize the placement of wind turbines Vestas thus far has collected about 20 petabytes of weather data. This includes information on temperature, barometric pressure, humidity, precipitation, and wind direction and speed from altitudes of ground level up to 300 feet at the tip of the blades. Feeding this information into an IBM supercomputer has enabled Vestas to reduce wind forecast modeling from three weeks down to fifteen minutes, and precisely optimize the placement of turbines within a 10-square-meter grid—whereas previously it could only optimize placement within a 27-square-*kilometer* grid. With the ability to develop turbine sites one month faster, Vestas installs one turbine every three hours somewhere around the world, passing along these savings and margins to customers, employees, investors, and product development.[13][14]

Monetizing the Increased Velocity of Information

As with the earlier Lockheed Martin project insights example, the increased velocity and variety of project information made available enables it to anticipate complex design and development program issues much earlier, thereby saving millions of dollars in cost overruns and rework.

Typical BI solutions where analytic output is directed at people not processes can falter as the speed of data inputs ratchets up. Increased information velocity implies an increased speed of business. At even low levels of velocity, humans become incapable of ingesting and using information efficiently, at which point business process effectiveness can suffer. This is the point at which advanced analytic applications are required that consume and respond to swift streams of data (think of algorithmic stock trading.) These apps can make recommendations either to users responsible for administering an operational business process or be integrated with the business process applications themselves.

Monetizing the Increased Variety of Information

While many BI solutions can report on information from multiple sources on demand, or make use of integrated data in data warehouses or marts, they don't truly take advantage of this diversity of data. A query tool can readily co-present data from differing sources, but tends to falter at corelating in ways other than standard regression analyses. Advanced analytics technologies, however, specialize in relating multiple data sources to discover unforeseen relationships such as matching employee candidate qualifications to the skill sets and experience of an organization's best employees.

By 2:1 over the issues of information volume and velocity, IT and business professionals contend that the variety of information not only is the greatest information management challenge, but represents the biggest opportunity for generating economic benefits from information.[15] [16]

This is why organizations like Coca-Cola discussed earlier find huge measurable benefits in integrating information on crop yields, cost pressures, GPS data, and the six hundred flavors comprising an orange to optimize orange juice production consistency.

Even public sector organizations can find ways to monetize a variety of information. Pinellas County in Florida implemented the Centers for Disease Control's Youth Risk Behavior Surveillance System (YRBSS) which monitors six types of health-risk behaviors considered leading causes of death and disability among youth and young adults. It integrates data from systems which track injuries and violence, sexual behavior and STD rates, alcohol and drug use, tobacco use, dietary behaviors, level of physical activity, and the prevalence of obesity and asthma. The youth risk index then is used to implement one or more programs within three areas: parental engagement and parenting practices, school connectedness, and/or protective services. Through improved understanding of these issues and the factors which drive them, Pinellas County has been able to make strides in reducing the unfortunate expenses associated with them.[17]

Increased information volume, velocity, and variety characteristic of Big Data can also help magnify, identify—and thereby monetize—hidden nuggets of insight.

Improved and Actionable Decision Making

Analytic technologies and solutions can drive improved and actionable strategic, tactical, and operational decision making, leading to business performance gains that deliver tangible economic benefits. Solutions involving decision making often are targeted at situations in which the number of actors, amount of information, number of information sources, and the potential outcomes and their urgency or importance are great. As such they often involve improving or automating business processes or reducing risk, not merely informing individuals.

Embracing Complexity, Unexpected Activity, and Changing Conditions

In addition to embracing complexity, advanced analytic solutions can handle unexpected data and dynamic business/market conditions more effectively. Machine learning algorithms, and neural networks in particular, make sense of more randomized inputs, adeptly dealing with outliers or information that doesn't fit otherwise prescribed formats, categories, or time frames.

Until recently, an Australian insurance company had segmented customers on six dimensions using an off-the-shelf BI tool. This led to insurance products and marketing campaigns which failed to differentiate the company or gain market share. After supplementing its BI implementation with an initial deep analysis of customer data, resulting in an awareness of more than one hundred significant dimensions (including artificial derived ones), the company was able to identify and target gaps in the market quite easily.

One of the most dynamic activities in any business is the configuration and evolution of complex products. At some point NCR business leadership realized its ATMs were offered with tens of thousands of configuration options. Dealing with this kind of SKU proliferation on top of increasing product complexity adversely affected the sales cycle. Across the value chain, NCR experienced a lack of alignment between customer demand, solutions management, operations, and sales. So with the help of analytics software from Emcien, it produced a demand-shaping pattern analysis for determining the optimal number of product configuration options, resulting in a $110 million bump in revenues and a 5 percent increase in sales efficiency.[18]

Optimizing Business Processes

Ultimately, any form of information monetization is the result of some business process or combination of business processes. BI tools generally are standalone with respect to the business processes that they support. Even when embedded into business applications, they tend to present charts or numbers in an application window. Ideally, output is updated to reflect the user's activity and needs, but less often is it used to affect the business process directly. Evolving to complex-event processing solutions, recommendation engines, rule-based systems, or artificial intelligence (AI), combined with business process management and workflow systems, can help to optimize business processes more directly, either supplementing or supplanting human intervention.

Case in point: a company formed from a collection of shopping stalls in 1919 by an English trader named Jack Cohen today has hardwired its thousands of refrigeration units to a data warehouse. By 1996, Cohen's company would become the United Kingdom's largest retailer, collecting £1 of every £7 spent in the U.K.[19] Tesco now has over 3,100 stores across the U.K., Europe, and Asia.

"Ideally, we keep our refrigerators at between -21 and -23 degrees Celsius, but in reality we found we were keeping them colder." said John Walsh, Tesco's energy and carbon manager for Ireland. "That came as a surprise to us." In a project collaborating with IBM Dublin's research laboratories, Tesco worked with refrigeration manufacturers to collect data from in-store controllers and feed it into a dedicated data warehouse. The system takes unit readings twenty times per minute and overlays the analytics on a Google map illustrating their performance. Each unit produces seventy million data points per year. With sophisticated statistical processing and machine learning, the system can identify refrigeration units which are performing suboptimally, even when knowing nothing about how refrigerators should perform. As a result, upon complete rollout, Tesco expects to deliver €20 million per year to its bottom line via a 20 percent reduction in refrigeration energy expense, and eliminate 7,000 tons of CO_2.[20]

Automating Governance, Risk, and Compliance

Even before mandatory governance, risk, and compliance (GRC) reports are produced—typically with BI or corporate performance management platforms—organizations should have the means to identify potential, imminent issues before they occur. Advanced analytic applications, tied to data streams consisting of leading GRC indicators, can make business process owners aware before trailing indicators.

Deeper analytic capabilities are needed to uncover the ultimate source of discovered GRC or fraud issues through the forensic examination of transactions and other business activity, including contrasting those activities with an understanding of written contracts. Additionally, as a matter of course during prescribed audits, robust analytic tools can go beyond the manual sampling still done by most auditors today to assess every record fully.

One of the biggest risks anywhere is driver fatigue, especially for those driving big rigs. "Trucking and logistics is an extremely challenging and competitive industry," explains Lauren Dominick, Predictive Modeler at FleetRisk Advisors, a 25-person commercial fleet consultancy based in Alpharetta, Georgia. "These companies need to be able to deliver goods reliably and on schedule, while ensuring driver safety and avoiding accidents that can cause delays, damage cargoes, and even cost lives." Dominick also describes how the work environment is stressful with an average employee turnover rate exceeding 100 percent annually.[21]

The idea behind FleetRisk Advisors is one of pure information monetization: that companies have a mountain of unused information (dark data) about their drivers and vehicles. Originally, FleetRisk's process suffered under the strain of manual calculations and basic types of reporting. Today, it automatically compiles near real-time telematics data from each driver's electronic logbook and integrates it with employee information from other systems. With this integrated information asset, FleetRisk analyzes drivers' pay versus one another and industry averages, and combines this with other stress factors and employment history. As a result, it has been able to help reduce employee attrition by more than 30 percent saving on training and other hiring-related costs. More important, explains Dominick, "Across our client-base, we're seeing a minimum of 20 percent reduction in the overall accident rate, and an 80 percent reduction in severe accidents such as rollovers, driving off the road or rear-end collisions. By identifying the risk factors—especially those that contribute to fatigue—we help our clients to intervene before accidents happen."[22]

Enhancing Scenario Planning

Even beyond forecasting and other kinds of prediction, advanced analytic capabilities can include comparative risk-reward assessments (for example, Monte Carlo simulations). This is the realm of sophisticated economic modeling. Yet most business leaders are barely aware of such methods, let alone trained in them. Increasingly it is becoming critical for organizations to embrace advanced analytical solutions like scenario planning that can be used to drive optimal organizational strategies and performance.

One planning process we all know could use some improving is the efficiency of airline gate and ground personnel. But the problem isn't with the personnel themselves—rather, it's with their scheduling. It's a little known fact that estimated times of arrival (ETAs) are provided by pilots themselves. 10 percent of the time these estimates are off by more than ten minutes, and 30 percent of the time they're off by five minutes. Pilots may know their speed, altitude, direction, and distance to the airport, however they lack other detailed information and the analytic capability to provide more accurate estimates.

But a system being installed at airports around the world developed by PASSUR analyzes information about weather, flight schedules, and historical flight data, plus data feeds from its network of passive radar stations installed near airports. This immense multidimensional body of information enables the computation of refined ETAs by evaluating current conditions versus prior "sky scenarios" to model and balance likely outcomes and risks. At airports where this system is in place, the improved efficiency of personnel scheduling and throughput can yield several million dollars per year. And at such outfitted airports, United Airlines claims its fleet is avoiding two to three airport diversions per week.[23] [24] At a cost of up to $200,000 each, sky scenario planning is a significant way to monetize this information.

Identify Monetizable Insights

In addition to classic decision making and automation, monetizing information through advanced analytics can be achieved through deeper understanding of processes, people, and markets; improved foresight; and innovating products and services.

Understanding Unstructured Information

BI technologies and implementations are inherently hard-coded to accept certain kinds of data from known sources in understood formats. Advances and extensions in BI technology have made it possible to perform rudimentary analysis on unstructured text. But when it comes to truly analyzing it using language and syntactically aware algorithms, graduating to advanced analytic technologies which specialize in this is required. And beyond written text, sources of enterprise intelligence and performance increasingly are in even more complex formats, such as audio and video. As discussed in chapter 2, much of this unstructured information lies dormant in the form of what's called "dark data." Much like the dark matter of the universe, we know dark data is there because it has a gravitational effect on our business and operations as it remains unused and unmeasured.

As I have long advised clients, there are only three ways to generate economic benefits from unstructured information (or *content*) before you structure it: you can read it, search it, and sell it. But the process of extracting most forms of value from unstructured information, even the process of categorizing or parsing content, implies some form of pre-processing. Maximizing the economic value of most content involves analyzing it in some way, either to identify patterns or structure it so as to render it as input to some automated process.

This is just what the Birmingham, Alabama-based insurer Infinity Property and Casualty did to identify indicators of fraudulent insurance claims. Infinity's senior vice president of claims operations, Bill Dibble, doesn't believe in "silver bullets"—but he had this idea that insurance claims could be scored using predictive analytics in much the same way as credit applications. While Infinity already had a rudimentary system which screened questionable claims based on "red flags," it still required quite a bit of manual intervention, thereby slowing down the claims process, and affecting customer service. Moreover, its hard-coded flagging process had trouble catching emerging fraud patterns. However, by text mining the content of previous claims known to be fraudulent, Infinity matches these patterns to the content of police reports, medical files, and other accident-related documents. These patterns of "narrative inconsistency" indicate probable fraud.

With this new predictive claims analytics system in place, Infinity's success rate in pursuing fraudulent claims jumped from 55 percent to 88 percent, and in the first six months of operation the system increased subrogation recovery by $12 million. In addition, it has reduced its cost of claims adjustment, leading to improvements in its Loss Adjustment Expense (LAE) ratio. As Dibble exclaimed, "With predictive analytics, we were basically able to close a hole in our pocket where money was leaking out steadily."[25] [26]

Identifying Faint Signals

Competitive advantage and sometimes saving lives increasingly relies on the ability to identify and monetize faint signals. These are signals that either present themselves with infrequent occurrence (for example, fraud, missing input) or in subtle patterns (for example, supplier quality glitch, inventory leakage, and underserved market subsegments). However, human fingers and eyes clicking through and viewing data with a BI tool can all too easily miss these signals. We are at a tipping point in the evolution of the Information Age. Decision making increasingly is automated and managed by machine-based models far more effectively than any human could manage.

Illustrating these faint signals is the web crawling and analytic technology behind HealthMap, a system that really got on the map in 2014 when it identified a clustester of "mystery hemorrhagic fever" cases in Guinea. It wasn't until ten days later that the World Health Organization, having been notified by the health ministry of Guinea a day earlier, announced an outbreak of Ebola. Developed by researchers, epidemiologists, and software developers at Boston Children's Hospital, HealthMap scours billions of posts from tens of thousands of social media sites, local news, government publications, infectious-disease physicians' online discussion groups, RSS feeds, and other sources to detect, plot, and track disease outbreaks. Every hour the application repeats the process, analyzes the text in fifteen languages, filters out noise such as "an outbreak of home runs" or "Justin Bieber fever," and determines the geographic location referenced in the content. It also incorporates a machine learning algorithm which improves over time—matching confirmed disease outbreaks with the information it collected on them, and learning to anticipate their spread.

"Getting case information and data of very specific epidemiology, of outbreaks, and fit that into disease models, where it might spread to, how bad it might be, then integrate it with climate data or transportation data, all of a sudden it's data you wouldn't necessarily have access to," said John Brownstein, epidemiologist and HealthMap co-founder. The ability to quickly identify outbreaks can help local health organizations respond to and contain them faster, not just saving lives, but also saving these organizations and governments money and resources.

To support the cash-strapped WHO in deploying scarce resources, HealthMap continued to track the disease across nearby West African countries.[27] [28] Currently, HealthMap is helping track and now predict the spread of the mosquito-borne Zika virus outbreak.[29]

Evolving to Insight and Foresight

BI tools are designed to present historical data, not so much assist in looking into the future. Slicing and dicing and drilling data, as is the specialty of BI tools, also can offer users insight into not just *what* occurred but *why* it occurred. But ask any stock trader, for example, which is more monetizable—knowing the past, or anticipating the future. The answer is clear.

True, even commonplace spreadsheet software includes a host of statistical formulae and chart types to expose and illustrate trend lines. As is their exclusive domain, advanced analytic technologies greatly exceed basic BI tools in the types of visualizations, pattern matching, and correlative algorithms, predictive techniques and modeling capabilities, simulation, forecasting, and scenario-planning capabilities available to organizations.

Just ask Mike Higgins, manager of sales, analysis, and strategy at Advanced Drainage Systems, whether it's better to know the past or have a jump on the future. Headquartered in Hilliard, Ohio, Advanced Drainage Systems (ADS) is the world's largest manufacturer of products for stormwater management and sanitary sewer applications. Previously, it would draw upon reports from operational, sales, and marketing systems such as its Oracle ERP implementation to estimate forecasts, do planning, and set budgets. Then it evolved to pulling this data into an Excel spreadsheet.

"We look at how sales and order activity is performing currently, match that with a five-year historic trend of the seasonality of the business on a month-to-month basis, and produce a rolling twelve-month forecast," said Higgins. To supplement and tweak the model, "We seek input from our sales managers, based on what they know and data from field intelligence about different types of business activity," he explained. But that wasn't enough. Forecasts were still less than 80 percent accurate, often either leaving money on the table or product in the warehouse.

The next step of ADS's analytic evolution involved working with the advanced analytics company Prevederé Software to assess over one million external datasets for their relevance in enhancing the forecasts. With this access to weather data, global, and local economic data, along with building and construction industry data, ADS identified external leading indicators for its business, creating over 150 predictive models in six weeks. By stripping the bias out of their forecasting and being heads-up to a multitude of external factors, ADS improved its monthly forecast accuracy to 98 percent, leading to a 26 percent increase in monthly year-over-year revenue and a 20 percent growth in monthly sales.[30]

Instigating Innovation

Beyond basic BI, a market is emerging for analytic solutions that drive business innovation. The advanced analytic capabilities of identifying new patterns, performing simulations, and exposing weak signals previously mentioned can be used to spur novel ways of looking at the business and its operations, strategies, emergent customer needs, and market shifts. As organizations struggle to squeeze yet more cost out of the business, the upside that innovation offers can—and should be—driven by a deeper and more exploratory analysis of available data from within and externally.

Clinical pathways themselves are a fairly recent innovation in the history of medicine. Clinical pathways (or "carepaths") are used by health care providers to ascribe the set or cycle of recommended tests and treatments and waiting or recovery periods for a particular patient or type of medical condition. According to OpenClinical.org:

> Clinical pathways were introduced in the early 1990s in the UK and the USA, and are being increasingly used throughout the developed world. Clinical pathways are structured, multidisciplinary plans of care designed to support the implementation of clinical guidelines and protocols.[31]

As databases of electronic medical records (EMRs) are quickly replacing years of pen-and-paper-based diagnoses, lab results, surgical records, and notes from doctors, nurses, physical therapists, etc., this wealth of data is a fuel spawning additional innovations in health care—particularly mining it to develop new or improved clinical pathways. The imperative is there too. In the U.S., Medicare, Medicaid, and the Affordable Care Act (Obamacare) each incentivize health care providers for the quality of care, and disincentivize repeat visits by a patient for the same ailment.

With this kind of innovating in mind, Mercy Hospitals, one of the top five health systems in the U.S., worked with advanced analytics provider Ayasdi to identify situations in which clinical variation could be narrowed, and narrowed toward protocols which provided better outcomes. The topological data analysis solution, leveraging existing computational biology algorithms and machine learning, surfaces groups of similar patient procedures and generates clinical pathways that result in improved patient outcomes and reduced expense. It pinpoints treatments, nursing orders, patient comorbidities, prescriptions, and even equipment that contributed the most to variations in cost and outcomes. And it can be used to model proactively the impact a care path change will likely have.[32] [33] According to Mercy's VP of clinical informatics, Dr. Todd Stewart, the adoption of clinical pathways increased more than 20 percent by Mercy physicians, clinical pathways are deployed more quickly, and over forty new pathways have been defined covering 80 percent of all clinicians. All told, Mercy is saving more than $18 million per year, and increasing as more pathways are incorporated.[34]

From Information Monetization to Information Management

Throughout this section we have explored ways of understanding, conceiving, developing, and implementing ideas for monetizing information. We have broken down the conceptual barriers to thinking about ways to generate economic benefits from available information assets—yours *and* those of others. We have taken a look at how dozens of organizations spanning nearly every industry and geography are monetizing information. And we have stepped through a basic process for making it happen in your organization.

However, there's one big roadblock to monetizing information at an enterprise level. If you noticed, nearly all of the examples throughout this section are one-off, functionally-targeted ideas and implementations. No doubt some new businesses during the past 10–20 years have been based on an economic architecture of monetizing information. As Gartner analysts Saul Brand and Dale Kutnick wrote about the novel concept of economic architecture, "Enterprises must find new digital business opportunities, driven by macroeconomic and microeconomic forces. These will enable them to modify their income statements and balance sheets to improve capital deployment and, ultimately, to restructure their businesses."[35]

But few other organizations have been able to complete the transformation from a fixation on the tired triumvirate of *people-process-technology* to a digital, information-driven business. Why is this? Because they yet fail to manage their information with the same discipline as their traditional assets—those assets represented in black and white on their financial statements. Many IT and business executives talk about information as an asset, and maybe even have the phrase "information is an asset" included in their data strategy documents or data governance principles. But for the most part, such declarations are just a meme, lip-service, or—at best—a whiff of a vision for information. To me, increasingly they're a clarion call to hire a chief data officer.

In the next section we'll examine why organizations are so challenged with managing information well, and how they can overcome this by adopting some new and reclaimed ideas rooted in economics and traditional asset management practices.

The next step in your infonomics journey is to become adept at managing information as an *actual* asset. If you're an experienced information professional or CDO, this may require you to cast aside some traditions. On the other hand, this may be just what you've been looking for. And if you're a CEO, CFO, or business executive experienced with managing other kinds of assets, it's likely you will ask, *Why haven't we been doing this all along?*

Notes

1. Formerly KXEN.
2. SAP.com Customer Successes, accessed 05 June 2016, www.sap.com/bin/ sapcom/fi_fi/downloadasset.2014-08-aug-27-15.predictive-analytics-customer-successes-pdf.html.
3. Coca-Cola executive, interview with author, 13 October 2015.
4. Duane Stanford, "Coke Engineers Its Orange Juice—with an Algorithm," Bloomberg, 31 January 2013, www.bloomberg.com/news/articles/2013-01-31/ coke-engineers-its-orange-juice-with-an-algorithm#p1.
5. Ibid.
6. Ibid.
7. Doug Laney, "Deja VVVu: Others Claiming Gartner's Construct for Big Data," Gartner Blog Network, 14 January 2012, http://blogs.gartner.com/ doug-laney/deja-vvvue-others-claiming-gartners-volume-velocity-variety-construct-for-big-data/.

8. It is believed that James Mashey, a scientist at Silicon Graphics, Inc., or perhaps Michael Cox and David Ellsworth in a 1997 ACM article, were first to publicly use the term "Big Data" in the mid-1990s, not I.

9. For further thoughts on additional Big Data "V"s, see my blog "Batman on Big Data," Gartner Blog Network, 13 November 2013, http://blogs.gartner.com/doug-laney/batman-on-big-data/.

10. Presuming the dataset is of sound accuracy, completeness, timeliness, and other quality characteristics I detail in chapter 13.

11. "Subtransactional data" is a term I began using in the 1990s to refer the lower level of detail beneath business entity, customer-related, and transaction data. It is data reflecting activities between discernible business events. Examples include log data, website clicks, IoT device communications, and video feeds.

12. accessed 05 June 2016, www.vestas.com.

13. "Vestas Wind Systems Turns to IBM Big Data Analytics for Smarter Wind Energy," ibm.com, 24 October 2011, www-03.ibm.com/press/us/en/pressrelease/35737.wss.

14. "Vestas, Turning Climate into Capital with Big Data," ibm.com, 2011, www-01.ibm.com/common/ssi/cgi-bin/ssialias?htmlfid=IMC14702USEN&appname=wwwsearch.

15. Douglas Laney, "Methods for Monetizing Your Data," Gartner Webinar, 22 August 2015, www.gartner.com/webinar/3098518.

16. Information *variety* represents a greater challenge than *volume* or *velocity* because it cannot be solved simply by scaling or swapping infrastructure.

17. Sue Hildreth, "Data+ Awards: Florida Youth Welfare Agency Pinpoints Aid with BI," *Computerworld*, 26 August 2013, www.computerworld.com/article/2483944/enterprise-applications/data--awards--florida-youth-welfare-agency-pinpoints-aid-with-bi.html.

18. "Cashing in on Improved Profitability through Pattern Detection and Big Data Analytics," emcien.com, 2015, http://emcien.com/wp-content/uploads/2015/10/NCR-Success-Story.pdf.

19. Denise Winterman, "Tesco: How One Supermarket Came to Dominate," *BBC News Magazine*, 09 September 2013, www.bbc.com/news/magazine-23988795.

20. "Data Analytics Solution Used to Optimize Refrigerators and Reduce Energy Costs in Grocery Stores," ibm.com, www-03.ibm.com/software/businesscasestudies/mx/es/corp.

21. "FleetRisk Advisors Helps Clients Reduce Accident Rates and Driver Turnover," IBM, accessed 09 February 2017, http://presidionwp.s3-eu-west-1.amazonaws.com/wp-content/uploads/2014/09/FleetRisk.pdf.

22. IBM, "FleetRisk Advisors."

23. Andrew McAffee, and Erik Brynjolfsson, "Big Data: The Management Revolution," *Harvard Business Review*, October 2012, http://hbr.org/2012/10/big-data-the-management-revolution/ar/2.

24. Passur.com, accessed 09 February 2017, www.passur.com/success-stories-airlines.htm.

25. "IBM Enables Infinity Property & Casualty Insurance to Combat Fraud," youtube.com, uploaded 05 May 2011, www.youtube.com/watch?v=qoFYo60rlC0.

26. James Taylor, "Putting Predictive Analytics to Work at Infinity Insurance," JT on EDM, 15 September 2009, http://jtonedm.com/2009/09/15/putting-predictive-analytics-to-work-at-infinity-insurance/.

27. Lyndsey Gilpin, "How an Algorithm Detected the Ebola Outbreak a Week Early, and What It Could Do Next," TechRepublic, 26 August 2014, www.techrepublic.com/article/how-an-algorithm-detected-the-ebola-outbreak-a-week-early-and-what-it-could-do-next/.

28. Zoe Schlanger, "An Algorithm Spotted the Ebola Outbreak Nine Days before WHO Announced It," *Newsweek*, 11 August 2014, www.newsweek.com/algorithm-spotted-ebola-outbreak-9-days-who-announced-it-263875.

29. "2016 Zika Outbreak," healthmap.org, accessed 09 February 2017, www.healthmap.org/zika/#timeline.

30. "Case Study | Improving Forecast Accuracy with Prevederé Software," prevedere.com, 2013, www.prevedere.com/wp-content/uploads/2016/03/CaseStudy-ADS.pdf.

31. "Clinical Pathways," openclinical.org, accessed 09 February 2017, www.openclinical.org/clinicalpathways.html.

32. "The Journey from Volume to Value-Based Care Starts Here," ayasdi.com, accessed 09 February 2017, www.ayasdi.com/applications/clinical-variation/.

33. "The Science of Clinical Carepaths," ayasdi.com, 11 February 2015, www.ayasdi.com/blog/bigdata/the-science-of-clincial-carepaths/.

34. Dr. Todd Stewart, email to author, 13 January 2017.

35. Saul Brand and Dale Kutnick, "Digital Business Success will be Driven by Economic Architecture," Gartner, 04 December 2015.

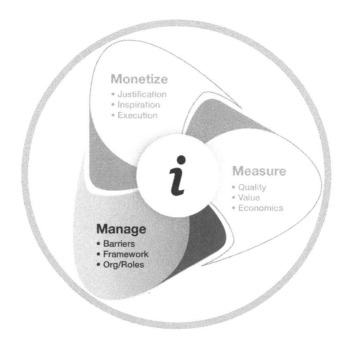

Part II: Managing Information as an Asset

CHAPTER 5

Information Management Maturity and Principles

Imagine a retail manager with no record of his store's inventory. Or consider a CFO who has no general ledger that records her company's financial assets. Or an HR executive with no company directory, employee ratings, or compensation data. Ridiculous or even impossible, right? Well, a lack of inventory about what information assets exist throughout the organization epitomizes the unfortunate state of information management in most organizations today.

Business leaders and IT executives increasingly wax about how their company's information is one of its most important assets. Research from Gartner and others has shown how significantly investors and financial analysts favor information-savvy and information-centric companies. However, information is not recognizable as a balance sheet asset, and therefore never managed like one.

This lack of formal accounting recognition manifests in most organizations that collect, manage, deploy, and value their information with far less discipline than they manage traditional balance sheet assets. Valuation experts and even accountants lament the challenges in valuing a company today without any data on its data. Recently, the head of information strategy for a major government military institution proclaimed to me, "We have a better accounting of the toilets throughout [this building] than our information assets. And for the 'business' we're in, that's a really, really sad state of affairs."[1] In fact the head of data management at one energy client I visited claimed, "We don't have a data directory because we only track our major assets like our generators and transformers." Yet after the meeting there they were: inventory tags on each precious "porcelain asset" in the men's room.

Many companies have information management practices that pale in comparison to the rigor and process and discipline with which actual balance sheet assets are managed. Only in the past few years have we seen the emergence of an executive role specifically for tending to information: the chief data officer. It is now sixty or seventy years since the rise of the chief financial officer, thirty or so years since chief human resource officers started appearing, and about twenty years since chief risk/security officers started being installed. Yes, chief *information* officers have been in place for decades, but their purview has been tilted toward the management of enterprise technologies. Information's role seemingly has been relegated to an input and an output—at worst a byproduct, and at best a resource.

Digital business and the information's emergence as a real economic asset, however, makes information ever more vital to the organization, intensifying the need for effective enterprise information management (EIM) initiatives. Yet data and analytics leaders such as the chief data officer (CDO) struggle to improve the organization's EIM maturity—that is, the capabilities that make possible a program for continuous EIM improvement.

As James Price, managing director with the Australian information strategy firm, Experience Matters, said to me, "We absolutely must take the justification for information management initiatives out of a case-by-case mentality and IT purchases, and put it into the domain of a diligent program of measurable long-term improvement."[2]

The rapid rise and proliferation of the CDO role is an indication that organizations are getting serious about just this. It's also an indication that within the framework of EIM exists a need for approaches to information asset management (IAM). Still, CDOs like Charles Thomas at Wells Fargo see their biggest challenge as data evangelism. And Stan Christiaens, co-founder of the data governance solution provider Collibra, claims he sees a significant "grass roots movement to bubble-up a data authority, even where no CDO yet exists."[3] Indeed I also see CIOs, data architects, non-executive heads of information management, data scientists, business analysts, and even CFOs, CEOs, and other business executives, assuming increased levels of business authority—as scattered and siloed as they may be.

The fatuousness and ignorance of some executives seems to be rooted in a refusal to recognize the importance of information as a legitimate economic asset. Tom Hogan, former director of data architecture and Big Data for a major health insurance company, recounted how when he was making the case regarding the importance of valuing the company's information assets as a precursor to managing them better, one executive argued, "We don't need to know the value of our data. We don't need to concentrate on the data. It's just data." Fortunately for Hogan, he is now with a new company whose management is asking instead, "What else can the data provide?"[4]

Stewart Buchanan, Research VP covering IT finance and workforce management at Gartner, believes that this is because other senior executives and business leaders have a vested interest in IT and the information it provides, but would rather be a beneficiary of its business benefits than acknowledge information's value as an asset in its own right. He contends this is a fundamental enterprise governance issue.[5] Ultimately, nobody in the organization is rewarded or punished based on changes in the return on information the way they are for the return on other assets.

If information were held with the same regard as other traditional assets, we wouldn't see the epidemic of nonchalance and negligence in caring for it, enabling it, and leveraging it. The epidemic infects every industry, companies of every size, and organizations in every geography. It's true that several organizations are innovating with information, as we saw in part I. Often these are pockets of success, targeted functional advances in decision-making or operational performance, and pseudo-accidental innovations. Very rarely do enterprise information assets beget enterprise transformations and a move towards a more structured approach to infonomics. More often these transformations manifest in new industries and are instigated by upstarts.

This disconnect between senior executive understanding versus the nonexistent formalized practice of information accounting is perhaps at the core of the problem. Until senior executives, and boards, go beyond merely talking about information as a key corporate asset, information will continue to be a second-class business resource. Ultimately what this comes down to is the question: *Why don't organizations manage their information with the same discipline as their other, formally-recognized enterprise assets?* After considering this for a minute, seriously ponder another question: *What if a company managed its other assets with the same lack of discipline as our information assets? Answer: The executive team would get sacked and replaced due to gross negligence.*

The Information Management Maturity Model

Enterprise information management cannot be implemented as a single project. Instead, organizations must implement it as a coordinated program that evolves over time.[6] EIM can be adopted in support of a small business unit, where individual data and analytics programs need to be aligned, or it can be adopted across the entire enterprise. Thus EIM is an enterprise-class program model, and maturity can be monitored along various dimensions.

Gartner's EIM maturity model enables organizations to identify what stage of maturity they have reached and what actions to take to reach the next level. The maturity model entails seven dimensions or building blocks Gartner has identified as essential to EIM maturity (Figure 5.1):[7]

- Vision
- Strategy
- Metrics
- Governance
- People
- Process, and
- Infrastructure.

Organizations should assess their level of maturity for each dimension as a starting point for a sustained, systematic effort to improve concurrently in

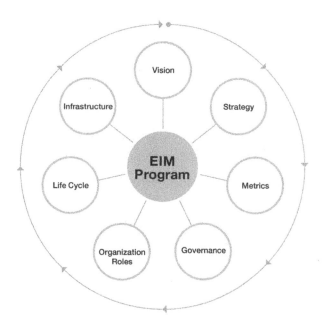

Figure 5.1 *Gartner Information Management Maturity Model*

all seven dimensions in support of an EIM program. Moreover, you should assess their maturity periodically to ensure consistency among different areas of the program and identify successes and lagging areas.[8]

Levels of Information Maturity

The maturity levels and indicators themselves are aligned with current and near-term capabilities of enterprises across industries and geographies:

- **Level 1** organizations are typically in the lower 10 percent of those we advise. They are generally **aware** of key issues and challenges, but lack the budget, resources, and/or leadership to make any meaningful advances in EIM.
- **Level 2** organizations represent approximately 30 percent of those we come across. They generally operate in a **reactive** application-centric

mode, waiting until information-related problems manifest in significant business losses or lack of competitiveness before addressing them.

- **Level 3** organizations represent the approximate 40 percent of those that
  are more or less mainstream today in terms of their information-related
  capabilities. They have become more **proactive** in addressing certain areas
  of information management, and have started to put the "enterprise" in
  information management. Some programs are operational and effective,
  but there is little leverage or alignment across programs and investments.

- **Level 4** organizations represent approximately 15 percent of those that
  are clear leaders in their industry with respect to **managing** and
  leveraging information across more than two programs. They take a
  decidedly managed approach to information management, comprising enterprise-level coordination throughout the organization, with
  effective people, processes, and technologies.

- **Level 5** organizations are few and far between, representing fewer than
  5 percent of those throughout the world. They are typically model
  organizations frequently cited for information-related superiority that
  have **optimized** many (if not most) aspects of acquiring, administ-
  tering, and applying information as an actual[9] enterprise asset with
  high-functioning organization structures, top talent, and using leading-
  edge architectures and technologies.

Just assessing your maturity level won't alone help you improve EIM in
your organization. To develop an effective information management practice
that manages information as an actual asset we'll take a tour of how other
industries and disciplines manage their assets including supply chains, ecosystems, IT, human resources, and financial asset management methods.
By tapping into their best practices, we can develop a program for bringing
effective information management to every organization. Additionally, using
existing business frameworks can aid in your efforts to obtain leadership and
organizational buy-in, support and funding. In essence, behaving as if information is an asset evangelizes and inspires others to come along for the ride.
Before we explore these auxiliary practices over the next couple chapters,

let's examine the range of challenges in information management that span many of the EIM dimensions.

Impediments to Maturity

When we conducted workshops, the broad concerns of the leaders who participated were about EIM leadership, priorities, resources, and corporate cultures that frustrate EIM advances (a list of all the challenges cited by the workshop participants appears in appendix A). To learn more about how infosavvy you and your organization are, visit gartner.com/infonomics.

These concerns emerged from the attendees' acute awareness of their present EIM capabilities. The vast majority of these leaders described their respective organization as either:

- "Aware"—aware of information availability issues but unable to make significant progress to overcome them, or
- "Reactive"—responding to information problems, with steps toward improved information availability hindered by a range of causes.

In both cases, information leaders are responding to the dictates of circumstances, which repeat themselves because leaders cannot or do not devote the time needed to change those circumstances. In both cases, information leaders can be confused, uncertain, or frustrated in attempting to break free of inertia and habitual approaches.

John Hershberger, VP of enterprise analytics at USAA, recounts how even IT shops traditionally have not been concerned about the things he and his team had to do to identify, extract, repair, format, and integrate data to generate value from it. "It was abundantly clear to me that the constituents I supported were interested in the output but not in the back-end. They wanted to do analytic work but not fund any of the data management necessary to make it happen."[10]

Typically, workshop participants felt more confident in their organizational structure and roles, and quite satisfied (if not overwhelmed) with the level of technology at their disposal. On the other hand, many felt they had not addressed information-related metrics or information lifecycle issues at all. While no organizations represented by these workshops seem to have achieved the highest levels of maturity in any dimension, participants did appreciate the characteristics represented by Level 5 maturity as an aspirational target.

Many challenges with managing information as an asset span multiple EIM dimensions. These typically relate to issues with leadership, priorities, resources, and culture.

Leadership Issues

Leadership issues range across all seven of the EIM maturity dimensions. IT and business leaders, even with the same organizations, are on "different pages" with different strategies, priorities, and goals. There is often no adjudicator for such conflicts. Leadership is lacking to establish initiatives, such as enterprise-level metrics to measure EIM effectiveness and progress, or a common consensus on the importance of measurement. There is no ownership, hence no leadership, of information lifecycle management. Key EIM elements, such as information architecture, remain undefined. The CDO role, which in theory brings information into the heart of business planning and processes, often does not exist. Sometimes, the CIO may actively oppose creating such a role for fear that it exposes their own limitations or lack of authority in managing information as an asset.

Della Shea, head of privacy and data governance with the Canadian financial processing firm Symcor, has witnessed firsthand the difference it makes when those leading both operations and governance are aligned in terms of how to approach information management: "When corporate goals and objectives set by the CEO appropriately connect with the role that information plays in achieving those goals, we are able to move forward with approval and funding for EIM related initiatives."

The absence of leadership is especially felt in the EIM maturity dimensions of vision, strategy, and organization and roles, but it is manifest in the other dimensions, too. Workshop participants link this challenge to other stakeholders' lack of business vision, cultural resistance, competing priorities, clarity and definition of strategy, and high-level support for the CDO role.

IM Priorities Over Which You Have Control or Influence

Effective EIM for the digital business requires clear priorities that have the backing of an array of stakeholders, not just one business function. Priorities derive from an EIM strategy, which in turn derives from the EIM vision. Vision is acquired only through a recognition of the most important outcomes or innovations that the business pursues.

Information leaders repeatedly describe as challenges: competing priorities, lack of business vision, differing and unresolved business unit opinions, fear of losing control, disagreement over approaches, and knowing where to start. Again, this class of challenges spanned all seven of the EIM maturity dimensions. These challenges rob decisions and actions of purpose, direction, and effectiveness, thereby reinforcing a reactive mode of operation where one's environment seems subject to forces over which one has little control.

Resources Needed to Advance EIM Capabilities

The lack of resources for advancing EIM capabilities is both real and perceived. Information and analytics leaders express frustration over a lack of experienced or knowledgeable staff resources, funding, domain-specific know-how, a dedicated CDO (seen as an EIM resource), influence of data architects, and life-cycle processes. These resources are either inadequate or totally non-existent.

Information leaders often cite lack of knowledge as a common challenge, sometimes for these leaders or their immediate organization, but also for the larger organization. They claim knowledge was a scarce resource regarding: what data is available, metrics, the cost of data quality issues, the role of information governance, the importance of IM, when and how to centralize or decentralize key roles, the data lifecycle, and keeping current with technologies.

Negative Cultural Attitudes About EIM

Negative cultural attitudes have a perverse effect on EIM progress, creating enormous (but hard to identify) inertia. Data and analytics leaders repeatedly identify culture as a serious obstacle in many of the EIM maturity dimensions.

Lack of cultural acceptance is an explicit problem for both the EIM vision and strategy dimensions, and for governance. But cultural attitudes, both within the data and analytics organization and the larger organization, are implicit in other dimensions. In EIM metrics, for example, basic concepts such as relating metrics to business processes and tying actions to metrics are proposed as "remedies" precisely because there is no "culture of measurement." In the EIM lifecycle, issues such as lack of lifecycle ownership, lack of understanding of the concept of a data lifecycle and its importance, and unawareness of or ignorance of relevant standards also reflect ingrained cultural attitudes.

Stuart Hamilton, senior hydrologist with Aquatics Informatics in Vancouver, British Columbia, believes the problem is deeper than just attitudinal: "Information neglect is one of those things that you see every day but you don't see it because it is so much like bland wallpaper that covers everything. Once it is explained, so that you can see it as a business pathology, it resonates in many ways."

The Barriers to Information Asset Management

In addition to Gartner's ongoing research on the topic, a few years ago I stumbled across a groundbreaking research paper by James Price, founder and managing director of Experience Matters, and Dr. Nina Evans with the University of South Australia. Price and Evans researched and authored an academic paper, "Barriers to the Effective Deployment of Information Assets: An Executive Management Perspective."[11] Their findings also illustrate how executives readily acknowledge the existence and importance of information assets within their organizations, but fail to put in place hardly any mechanisms for the management or government of information—as an asset.

Price and Evans slot the challenges to managing information as an asset into five broad categories:

1. **Awareness**: no recognition of a problem, lack of formal training, limited on-the-job training, and organizational immaturity.
2. **Leadership and Management**: a lack of executive support, mistake intolerance, tolerance for workarounds, no system of rewards or punishments, a lack of vision, IT seen as a panacea for information asset management deficiencies, and resistance to change.
3. **Business Governance**: a lack of accountabilities and responsibilities, responsibilities assigned at the wrong level of the organization, technology-focused IT leadership, and a lack of measurements.
4. **Enabling Systems and Practices**: imprecise language about information, insufficient accounting practices, technology shortcomings, and poor IT reputation.
5. **Justification**: lack of a catalyst (such as a crisis, business changes, or new compliance requirements); compliance and risk are burdensome; other prevailing priorities; unknown cost, value, and benefits of information assets; intangible and intertwined benefits; a strict process view; rewarding inefficiencies; and information not being an interesting provocative topic (such as digitalization or artificial intelligence).

As a profession, it seems we information management folks have been whining about these barriers and challenges for decades. Long before I met him, one of my mentors and former colleagues, Hayward Schwartz, was on the 1960s IBM team that developed the DB2 database. As "old school" as he seemed to the rest of us in the 1990s, his eye was always on the future: "New generations of information techno-wizardry and techno-wizards come and go," he once said to me. "With all these shiny new technologies and shiny new consultants, do you ever wonder why we've made little advancement in the way information is actually managed?"[12]

It took me years to understand the wisdom and hope embodied in Hayward's question. And it took me years more to realize that all around us are *other* assets which have been managed for centuries or millennia, not perfectly, but certainly with greater mastery than we exert today over our information assets.

Generally Accepted Information Principles

Like a world traveler who gains an appreciation for different cultures, bringing home and embracing the best of each, let's look at what we can "bring home" to the land of information management from the world of asset management. Over the next couple chapters, we'll be exploring asset management standards, principles, and methods we can borrow from a variety of other disciplines, including: physical asset management, supply chain management, IT, and software asset management—and from records management, intellectual property management, and even library science, among others.

For framing a set of information asset management doctrine, let's turn to yet another standard: the U.S. accounting set of Generally Accepted Accounting Principles. The framework includes a set of *principles* based upon basic *assumptions* and tempered by a set of *constraints*. Although GAAP provides guidance for preparing financial statements, I believe the framework provides a useful way to express a concise set of Generally Accepted Information Principles.[13]

So as to not take them lightly, this suggested set of information assumptions, principles, and constraints are gleaned from:

- Key aspects of asset management principles from other domains,
- Reviewing hundreds of information strategy–related documents and speaking with thousands of clients during my tenure at Gartner,
- My years as an information practitioner, and
- The countless luminous publications and ideas produced by my colleagues and other associates.

Assumptions

Assumptions are agreed-upon basic beliefs about information. They guide our understanding about how information assets can and should be perceived, managed, and deployed.

1. Asset Assumption	Information is an asset, because it meets each of the criteria of an asset.[14]
2. Proprietorship Assumption	An organization's information assets include all forms of data and content of discernible identifiability for which it can claim ownership and/or exclusive control.[15]
3. Appraisal Assumption	Information has realized, probable, and potential cost and value.[16]
4. Dominion Assumption	The practice of internal information "ownership" limits its potential value to the organization, and thereby the performance of the organization itself.
5. Benefit Assumption	Information has uses well beyond its original purpose, does not deplete when used, and can be used simultaneously for different purposes.

Constraints

Constraints are generally agreed-upon information regulations, confinements, or bounds. They acknowledge the limits of how well or precisely information assets can be monetized, managed, and measured, and therefore restricts how absolutely the principles which follow can be applied.

1. Specificity Constraint	The groupings of data or content that comprise an "information asset" will vary from one organization or use case to the next.
2. Recognition Constraint	Information cannot be represented in auditable financial statements, nor be capitalized as other assets (per current accounting standards).[17]
3. Jurisdiction Constraint	The provenance, lineage, ownership, and sovereignty of an information asset may be difficult to determine or legally establish.

4. Valuation Constraint	Valuation and other measurements of an information asset will be inexact but useful, just as are valuations of other kinds of assets.
5. Resource Constraint	Tradeoffs among information asset quality, availability, and accessibility are inevitable.

Principles

Principles are generally agreed-upon axioms that dictate how information assets should be managed, and lead to more detailed guidelines, policies, procedures, and standards specific to the organization.

1. Relevance Principle	Information assets should be managed with at least the same discipline as other recognized assets.
2. Inventory Principle	Information assets should be cataloged, described, classified, related, and tracked.
3. Ownership Principle	By default, information assets belong to the organization, not any application, department, or individual.[18]
4. Authorization Principle	The quality requirements, access, use, protection, and other rights and responsibilities for any information asset, even within the organization, should be contractually established by or with a sanctioned and empowered trustee.[19]
5. Assessment Principle	The quality characteristics, cost, value, and risks of any information asset should be knowable at any point in time, and used for prioritizing and budgeting information-related initiatives.
6. Possession Principle	An information asset should be acquired or retained only if its actual or planned value is greater than its cumulative cost, or as required by laws or other regulations.
7. Replicability Principle	An information asset should be duplicated or derived only to improve its utility or availability, and only if doing so also increases its net value.
8. Optimization Principle	The business is responsible for optimizing the usage and understanding of information; the information management organization is responsible for optimizing information's availability and utility; and IT is responsible for optimizing information's accessibility and protection.[20]

These assumptions, constraints, and principles can be adopted by and adapted to just about any organization. They can form the basis for an enterprise data strategy, for a new information management organization, for defining the role of a chief data officer, or as a framework for a data governance function.

Beyond Overarching Challenges and High-Level Principles

Bracketed by the common information-related challenges examined at the beginning of the chapter and these proposed Generally Accepted Information Principles, let's now turn our attention to what specifics we can extricate and apply from a variety of other asset management approaches. Comparatively, the discipline of information management is new. Other kinds of assets have been managed with some rigor for centuries or longer. And even some IT-related disciplines have exceptionally detailed standards and methodologies that can be related easily to managing information as an actual asset.

Indeed, throughout your career, no doubt you have heard people (probably consultants or us analysts) casually refer to information supply chains or ecosystems. Well, let's first dispense with this nonchalance, and explore what it would really mean to apply supply chain and ecosystem concepts to information assets—and how we can advance as a profession from doing so.

Also, in the following chapters, as we truly concentrate on information as an asset, note that I will be making a subtle shift from talking about "enterprise information management" to that of "information asset management." EIM remains the overall program framework and set of key capabilities, while IAM is more of a new information-centric approach and mindset.

Notes

1. Actual name of the building redacted so as not to identify the particular military institution.

2. James Price, discussion with author, 10 January 2017.

3. Stijn Christiaens, "The CDO's Platform for Success," presentation, MIT CDO IQ Symposium, 12 July 2016.

4. Tom Hogan, email to author, 15 January 2017.

5. Stewart Buchanan, email to author, 29 December 2016.

6. Andrew White, "Strategic Roadmap for Enterprise Information Management," Gartner, 17 March 2015, www.gartner.com/document/3008417.

7. Douglas Laney, "Gartner's Enterprise Information Management Maturity Model," Gartner, 02 March 2016, www.gartner.com/document/3236418.

8. A self-assessment with similar questions and discussions to those presented in the workshops can be found in "Toolkit: Enterprise Information Management Maturity Self-Assessment," Douglas Laney and Michael Patrick Moran, Gartner, 13 June 2016, www.gartner.com/document/3344417.

9. By "actual" or "formal" asset, I'm referring to assets recognized and reportable on balance sheets.

10. John Hershberger, interview with author, 09 September 2016.

11. Nina Evans, and James Price, "Barriers to the Effective Deployment of Information Assets: An Executive Management Perspective," *Interdisciplinary Journal of Information, Knowledge, and Management*, Volume 7, 2012, www.ijikm.org/Volume7/IJIKMv7p177-199Evans0650.pdf.

12. Some like to blame technology vendor marketing for distracting us from the real issues and management solutions, with their shiny new technologies and silver bullets. But I think it's more abstruse than that, relating more to information not being recognized as a formal asset.

13. In his book, *Making EIM Work for Business (Amsterdam: Morgan Kaufmann)*, John Ladley offers a set of Generally Accepted Information Principles meant to align with actual Financial Accounting Standards Board statements. As such, they provide guidance on dealing with information-related expenses and valuation, more so than the management of information assets.

14. It is (can be) owned and controlled, is exchangeable for cash, and generates probable future economic benefits that flow to its owner.

15. For some public sector organizations, its information assets may be part of the public trust.

16. For some public sector organizations, value may be determined in terms of benefits to the community it serves, rather than the organization itself.

17. Exceptions include purchased (not licensed) and acquired customer lists, and content that may be copyrighted or patented.

18. In some public sector organizations, information assets may be part of the public trust.
19. Or "fiduciary."
20. In many enterprises, an "information management organization" is still part of IT.

CHAPTER 6

Information Supply Chains and Ecosystems

A couple of decades ago, especially in the early days of data warehousing and as intimations of "information as an asset" were starting to take hold, information professionals started putting forward the notion of conceiving and architecting the production, flow, enhancement, and availability of information (even just within an organization) as a type of *supply chain*, an "information supply chain" (ISC). The supply chain is an excellent metaphor to visualize, define, refine, and assess the processes and resources for the information lifecycle—particularly for unidirectional analytics environments. Even though the term "supply chain" sounds like it focuses on the supplier, supply chains actually are designed with the customer in mind. Therefore, the concept can help information management professionals keep top-of-mind the kinds of business outcomes highlighted in the early chapters for deployed information assets.

> A supply chain is a system of activities and resources involved in moving a product or service from the point where it is manufactured to where it is consumed.[1]

Typically, a supply chain begins with the harvesting, collection, or generation of some kind of raw material. Although I personally shy away from the pedantic discussion of differentiating data from information, in a supply chain context it may be somewhat relevant to discern raw material from product. But as we'll see, adding value to data to turn it into information is rarely a single step or obvious transformation. In our supply chain metaphor, data are raw, original transactions, text files, emails, images, or the like. They often have utility only in the context of the process that created or captured them.

Applying the SCOR Model to the Information Supply Chain

While it sounds straightforward enough, even the most simple supply chains involve a host of moving and tightly coordinated moving parts. The Supply Chain Operations Reference (SCOR) model lays out these processes as:

- **Plan**—Processes that balance aggregate demand and supply to develop a course of action which best meets sourcing, production, and delivery requirements.
- **Source**—Processes that procure goods and services to meet planned or actual demand.
- **Make**—Processes that transform product to a finished state to meet planned or actual demand.
- **Deliver**—Processes that provide finished goods and services to meet planned or actual demand, typically including order management, transportation management, and distribution management.
- **Return**—Processes associated with returning or receiving returned products for any reason. These processes extend into post-delivery customer support.
- **Enable**—Processes for establishing and operating the supply chain procedures, resources, and facilities, including relationships with all stakeholders and other involved parties.

Borrowing from supply chain best practices, information supply chain (ISC) *planning* should ensure: that the process/flow is integrated from front to back; the ability to simulate what-if scenarios for information production, delivery, and usage; flexibility for demand volatility; and that all individuals and organizations involved understand their downstream and upstream impact. It also involves planning for costs, fulfillment cycle times, return on assets and working capital, demand planning and management, "pull-based" inventory replenishment, inventory recording practices, and dozens of other procedures and considerations, some of which have relevance in in an ISC context.

Sourcing deals with how materials (data) are acquired, how to manage inventory (database, metadata, master data) and supplier network (data source owners), supplier agreements (terms of service with data owners), how to handle payments and revenues (chargeback and payback), and how materials (data) are transmitted and received (accessed and/or streamed, including security controls), and verified (quality controls, data profiling).

Making includes the activities for turning materials (data) into finished goods (information, reports, application inputs). This step may include production activities (cleansing, integration, enrichment), packaging (aggregation, predefined analytics, or reports), staging (data staging areas), and releasing (database loads or updates).

Delivering is the order management (user data/report requests or their actual queries against the data), warehousing (data warehouse, data mart, logical data warehouse architecture), and transportation (query management, API, or web service calls). It also includes product lifecycles (archival, roll-ups, deletion) and import/export requirements (cloud, remote data centers).

Returning refers to the processing of defective product (information, reports), which in an information context may not be so relevant since data is rarely returned. But this process could also include information user support activities.

A few years ago the Supply-Chain Council announced an update to the SCOR model, adding *Enable* as a sixth process. This process represents the management of business rules (data integration logic, data governance, and security policies and processes), regulatory compliance (data governance) and data management (metadata, master data). Other *Enablement* processes translate directly into ISC performance management, resource management, facilities management, contract management, supply chain network management, and risk management.

Information Supply Chain Scenarios

The SCOR model also provides a few levels of detail for scoping, configuring, and process/performance attributes. These details enable the handling of specific supply chain scenarios such as "make-to-stock" versus "make-to-order" supply chain configurations for general and custom goods and services, respectively. Differentiating these two configurations for the supply of information can be helpful in designing for:

1. Generalized information uses such as a data warehouse or data lake, or
2. Specified information purposes such as an architected data mart or report, input to a new application, or partner data feed request.

Typically, make-to-stock scenarios are executed not based on supposition, but upon a forecast. In an information context, this could refer to the *vision* for information described in the previous chapter. Make-to-order scenarios usually require some additional tasks for specing, producing, testing, staging, and releasing in collaboration with an actual customer. The information productization steps enumerated in chapter 4 are representative of a make-to-order scenario.

As supply chains grow more sophisticated, they appear and behave more as networks—complex flows of goods and services among suppliers, distributors, payment processors, and customers. Accordingly, organizations should characterize, architect and document their information lifecycles in this way as well.

Metrics for the Information Supply Chain

The SCOR model includes some 200 key indicators of supply chain operations performance. Although we'll cover information measurement in part III, these metrics can be useful in understanding and crafting an information supply chain. The high-level metrics framework includes the following attributes, definition, and sample metrics, along with performance measures transposed into sample *information* supply chain metrics:

Performance Attribute	Classic Supply Chain Performance Attribute Definition[2]	Sample Information Supply Chain Performance Metrics
Reliability	The ability to perform tasks as expected. Reliability focuses on the predictability of the outcome of a process. Typical metrics for the reliability attribute include: on-time, the right quantity, the right quality.	• Query/update performance • Data quality (accuracy, completeness, timeliness, integrity, etc.)
Responsiveness	The speed at which tasks are performed. The speed at which a supply chain provides products to the customer. Examples include cycle-time metrics.	• Information accessibility • User request turnaround time • User satisfaction survey
Agility	The ability to respond to external influences, and the ability to respond to marketplace changes to gain or maintain competitive advantage. SCOR agility metrics include flexibility and adaptability.	• Utility of information for a range of purposes • Linked data, metadata, and master data measures • Ease of integrating new types of data or changing dimensions
Costs	The cost of operating the supply chain processes. This includes labor costs, material costs, management, and transportation costs. A typical cost metric is cost of goods sold.	• Data acquisition cost • Data management costs • Data delivery costs (Each include labor and technology related costs)
Asset Management Efficiency (Assets)	The ability to efficiently utilize assets. Asset management strategies in a supply chain include inventory reduction and in-sourcing versus outsourcing. Metrics include: inventory days of supply and capacity utilization.	• Information timeliness • Amount of available history • Actual usage (e.g., percent of data touched by users/apps)

A New Supply Chain Model for Information Assets

Certainly the classic product/service supply chain model is useful at a high level, especially to express information management needs to those more familiar with the physical supply chain concept. However, the detailed processes become increasingly unrelated to the specific processes relevant to the management and flow of information. Moreover, I find the product and service-oriented supply chain concept a bit too focused on process and less so on value creation. If infonomics is a concept for treating information as an economic asset, a model or framework for describing its flow perhaps should center more on how each step increases its economic potential.

To that end, let's consider a range of different kinds of recognized assets, or the *stuff* organizations manage:

- Material assets (e.g., raw goods, consumer goods, plant, equipment),
- Financial assets (e.g., cash, savings, various investment vehicles, prepaid expenses),
- Intellectual property (e.g., patents, trademarks, copyrights),
- Human capital (employees, contractors, partners, departments), and
- Information "assets" (e.g., transactions, lists, reference data, content, metadata, etc.).

We will examine the specific processes and standards for each of these in the next chapter.

Financial and material assets are somewhat obvious. It gets a little murkier when discussing people as assets. Today, most organizations consider employees as "human capital." However, this concept only came about fairly recently. In 1964, University of Chicago economist and Nobel Prize winner Gary Becker published the book *Human Capital*. Upon the popularity of Becker's ideas, the term "human capital" became widely used in business, and human resources (HR) executives emerged. Becker and other prominent economists including Milton Friedman then established the economic concept of human capital. So, with employees now considered organizational assets, why aren't they (*we*, that is) on the balance sheet? Does your employer actually own you? No. Thankfully, due to anti-slavery laws in civilized countries, we are "at will" employees, even if under contract. Since ownership and control are key asset determinants, you and I show up as an expense on the income statement, not as an asset on the balance sheet.

And we've already discussed how information—in most cases—is not a recognized asset according to accounting standards.

For nearly any kind of asset (or *proto-asset*, as in the case of human capital and information), we execute a similar set of activities on them, or do certain things to them. We collect or otherwise obtain assets. For manufacturers in particular, we produce them and inventory them in the counting, or accounting, sense. Once we have assets, we might also do things to enhance their *potential economic benefit*, such as enriching them in some way (i.e., employee training), moving them about, or integrating them. And for precautionary reasons, we typically protect them in some way and keep continuous track of them. Organizations do these things to assets to ensure the assets don't lose value and are able to generate future value.

These lifecycle primitives classify the activities we do *to* assets, and represent the *supply side* of the supply chain:

Collect	Prepare	Combine	Enrich
Produce	Inventory	Locate	Secure
Organize	Distribute	Govern	Monitor

Many of these look familiar juxtaposed against the SCOR framework, but note that they are applicable to any and all classes of asset (or proto-asset). Also note that no sequence of steps is implied. They can be combined and sequenced in any way necessary or applicable. These activities focus on value augmentation alone. They are ways to increase the potential or probable economic value of the asset, but not to realize its value.

Now let's consider the ways these various assets generate realized economic value. True to the definition of an asset, value realization happens only once we *do* something with them. These primitives classify the activities we do *with* assets, and represent the *demand side* of the supply chain:

Sell	Lend or License	Share
Spend	Trade	Apply

(You may have noticed I just used the terms *supply* and *demand*. Yes, this is foreshadowing that we're getting to the thrilling topic of information economics a bit later.)

In the case of financial assets, we typically spend them on other assets (including other kinds of financial assets like securities), or lend them to financial institutions to generate interest income. Actually in doing so, we are giving banks a *license* to use our money. Material assets are typically sold as finished goods or applied as raw materials to create finished goods. Human assets are applied to business processes. Yes, sometimes we employees feel quite spent, too!

Intellectual property is most often applied to business processes, as well. But because it's an actual owned asset, it can also be sold or licensed directly, as in the case of a business selling or licensing a patent to another business.

Interestingly, even as an unrecognized asset class, information is at least as flexible on the demand side as any other kind of asset. We can perform any and all of these activities with it. And with a strong information culture, we *should* be performing all of these activities with it. In the first few chapters you probably started thinking about how much information your organization has that—if packaged and marketed properly—could become a salable (licensable) commodity itself. You may be doing this already, but the opportunities to do so are likely much greater than most people in your organization realize.

This book is not about defining a detailed, 976-page (i.e., SCOR) reference model for an information supply chain. Instead I'll leave you with a useful illustration based on these supply-side and demand-side primitives, with a few others added specific to information assets. Hopefully, the most enthusiastic of you will look to adopt, adapt, and build on this concept.

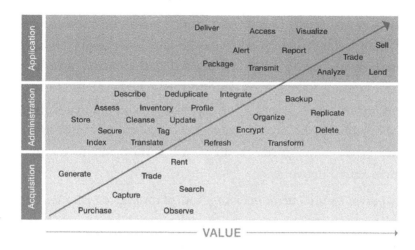

Figure 6.1 *Information Supply Chain Activities*

Figure 6.1 simply shows how information value potential leading to its realization is enhanced along a continuum. Instead of five or six process groupings, it consists of three which I believe represent the main stages of an ISC:

- **Acquisition**—how you obtain raw data or other information.
- **Administration**—how the data is enhanced, or what the machinery the "information factory" might include.
- **Application**—how information is received and used in generating value.

Moreover, as one organization's ISC intersects with another's, as in the case of an information supply *network*, the arrow may loop back on itself. For example: sold, lent, or analyzed information may become the raw data purchased or captured, licensed, or observed by another organization. And so on. This is the nature of our most non-depleting, non-rivalrous, regenerative asset.

Preparing for the Real Information Ecosystem

Speaking of loops, particularly feedback loops, another way to characterize information's relative place in the world is as an *ecosystem*. A supply chain may seem too linear, and even a supply network too static and procedural for today's (and especially tomorrow's) more dynamic business environment. Indeed, supply chains/networks change and increasingly run pseudo-autonomously on business logic, embedded analytics, and always-on communication among stakeholders. But do they really evolve? Do they really sense and respond and adapt to both immediate and gradual shifts in their larger environment the way biological ecosystems do? Only if someone coded them that way. Someday soon we will witness an entire supply chain driven by a neural network.

Perhaps we should be conceiving and planning for that day. Already, certain players in certain supply chains manage and store much of the information flow. Think: Walmart. Or Coca-Cola. As Don Keough, the former president of Coke once said, "Whoever has information fastest and uses it wins."[3] It's probably something Sun Tzu once said, too.[4]

In Japan, keiretsus are the renowned corporate ecosystems formed around trust, sharing, collaboration, and coordination. Today, with companies like Walmart and Coca-Cola and Amazon, we're starting to see the formation of *information keiretsus*. These ecosystems enable trusted partners to readily share and use one another's information. Gartner's Group VP of Data and Analytics, Regina Casonato, has referred to this kind of arrangement as "information without borders." Whatever we want to call it, the behavior of information within and among these entities resembles something flowing or even thriving within an ecosystem.

This flow of information becomes even more important as businesses turn to ecosystems to fuel their digital growth. The Gartner 2017 CIO Agenda[5] survey of 2,598 global CIOs found that top performers create or participate in ecosystems and expect to double their ecosystems in two years. As Andy Rowsell-Jones, vice president and research director at Gartner, said, "Many organizations will need to shift their enterprises from a linear, value chain business trading with well-known partners and adding value in steps, to being part of a faster and more dynamic networked digital ecosystem."

So what we can learn and apply about ecosystems to the discipline of information management? What is an ecosystem exactly?

Ecosystem

[ek-oh-sis-tuh m, ee-koh-]
noun, Ecology.

1. a system, or a group of interconnected elements, formed by the interaction of a community of organisms with their environment.
2. any system or network of interconnecting and interacting parts, as in a business.[6]

Sticking for now with the classical, biological definition, an ecosystem describes a community of organisms along with the inanimate parts of their environment such as air, water, sun, and soil. Ecosystems are defined by how these components are linked via nutrient cycles and energy flows, and how these components interact with one another.

Just as the web can be thought of as globe-spanning information ecosystem, the planet itself is considered by some scientists as a massive ecosystem (or even as a living organism itself!).[7] But most ecologists and biologists prefer to consider ecosystems as more localized.

Which Role Does Information Play in an Information Ecosystem?

We can characterize information within an information ecosystem as a resource, or perhaps as an organism itself. Bear with me.

Consider information as an energy source or resource. Peter Sondergaard, senior vice president of research at Gartner, has referred to Big Data as the oil of the 21st century.[8] Microstrategy's founder Michael Saylor throughout the 2000s repeated his catchphrase, "information like water." These analogies make sense. Information fuels business processes and businesses themselves. It is also a lubricant for commerce. It is fairly abundant (depending on one's climate and topology), can be collected and processed and stored. And it can even be bought and sold as a commodity.

Not to mention, like oil and water, when information leaks, you've got a mess on your hands! But both of these analogies place dubious limitations upon information, disregarding its unique economic and behavioral characteristics.

Perhaps a more compelling, non-obvious, and provocative way to think about information within an ecosystem context is as an *organism* itself. One could argue that information germinates or is born,[9] survives and thrives, replicates, combines and evolves, is affected by climate and topography, and sometimes even decomposes and is recycled. Of course, information does few of these activities on its own. Information doesn't have DNA within it programmed to tell it how to behave, given certain stimuli. Not yet. Information today is programmed from the outside.

But why not flip the information-process model upside-down (or rather, inside-out) to define and prepare for tomorrow's information ecosystem? For decades we've had "stored procedures" embedded within database management systems (DBMS). And more recently we're seeing emerging technologies like those from Pneuron specialize in "moving the processing to the data" rather than the opposite classic approach to information processing. Another fascinating early example of this flip is the inside-out approach from SertintyOne, which embeds security logic within the dataset itself.

Chuck Devries, vice president of enterprise architecture and technology strategy at Vizient, articulated an increasingly common sentiment among thought-leading information executives: "I'm a big believer that you move processing, not data."

On a true ecosystem scale, the New York Stock Exchange and the retail market intelligence company IRI are examples of organizations offering analytic environments for customers to process data in-situ rather than extracting and downloading it. Ash Patel, the CIO of IRI, is also keen on the ecosystem concept. He calls the way they manage data as "liquid" in that "We aggregate nothing. We work on the raw, leaf level of data, and it takes the shape of the container we put it in. Clients come to the fountain to drink, rather than carrying buckets of data around."

Further supporting the metaphor of information as an organism, let's not forget that viruses can infect data, not just systems.

Indeed, most of us in the industry have been using the term "information ecosystem" somewhat casually. This is par for the course throughout much of the IT profession. We use many related terms like "value" and "asset," and even "lifecycle" and "management," without much of a common understanding throughout our organizations or industry. Examining the range of classic, biological ecosystem concepts can yield ways to adapt them for explaining the world of information a bit better.

Adapting Classic Ecosystem Entities Concepts

Classic biological ecosystems involve certain actors or entities, have a range of features and processes, are influenced by various events, and are often managed by humans. An information ecosystem can be classified and described similarly. However, Gartner IT service management expert, Roger Williams, cautions: "The world is littered with the hubris of those that thought they could control the complex. Anyone operating in an information ecosystem must always keep in mind that they cannot direct outcomes, they can only influence them."[10]

Ecosystem Entities

In a biological ecosystem, the main actors are organisms, organic matter, nutrients, and energy. If the biological ecosystem is named for biology, the study of organisms, then it follows that our information ecosystem model would center on information. (Remember, we could adopt the metaphor of information as energy, but then this would suggest applications or business entities are the central actors. "Application ecosystems" or business ecosystems are legitimate models no less, but they are not information ecosystems.)

Other items within the biological ecosystem include organic matter, nutrients and energy, and resources including air, water, and soil. In the information ecosystem, we're concerned with (perhaps) the bits and bytes that comprise information "matter," or the individual units of information that makes up a dataset. And in the information ecosystem we're concerned with resources such as processing, storage and bandwidth, and of course energy just the same. What provides nutrition for information? Let's say transactions or other kinds of events do. We'll get to how these "nutrients" support growth in a moment.

Ecosystem Features

Like their counterpart, information ecosystems involve networks of interactions among information "organisms" and with their environment. It may not be natural to think of information as interacting, but that's just what happens during lookups, searches, integration, query updates, and reporting. These each involve an interaction among disparate datasets such as a sales transaction and a customer or product master data file. It may be more comfortable to call these "intersections" instead since, as I mentioned previously, in these early days of the Information Age information is not yet an autonomous actor.

Both ecosystems also have climates and topographies which determine organisms' access to resources. Information ecosystem topographies are characterized by data and system architectures, and climate relates to periodic or cyclical changes in the availability of resources dictated by *business climate* changes.

Biodiversity is a feature which translates into the variety of information. Ecosystems with high degrees of biodiversity or "infodiversity" are capable of generating a greater amount of goods and services upon which businesses and consumers depend. But these ecosystems may be more complex and fragile. Changes in climate or other influences outlined ahead can adversely affect or unbalance them.

Ecosystem Processes

The types of processes within the biological ecosystem include energy flows, nutrient cycling, and the movement of matter. These sub-processes enable the main functions of decomposition, reproduction, and growth.

The decomposition of organisms is an interesting parallel to the various methods for altering information. Decomposition happens by leaching, fragmentation, and chemical alteration in order to make organic matter more easily absorbed. Similarly, altering information can occur via filtering it, cleansing it, or applying algorithms to it—thereby rendering it more consumable.

The reproduction of information, of course, involves making copies or extracts of it. The movement of organisms is akin to the movement of information. And the growth (volume) of information is due to nutrients (e.g., transactions) and the availability of energy and resources.

Ecosystem Influences

Various occurrences or *disturbances* influence an ecosystem. In the biological world, disturbances may include falling trees or rocks, wildfires, insect invasions, volcanic eruptions, or tsunamis. Using a concept known as "threat modeling" we can imagine and should prepare for similar kinds of disturbances to our information ecosystems such as security breaches, natural disasters, new competitors, or business collapses. Disturbances often lead to *succession*—the term ecologists use to describe a directional change in the structure of an ecosystem due to changes in resource availability. It is the same with information ecosystems. We often see how disturbances bring about or impel structural changes in the way we manage and leverage information.

Even climate change affects both ecosystems. In an information ecosystem, however, the climate is a macroeconomic function. Therefore, it would seem that just as with biological ecosystems, man-made (anthropogenic) global effects upon the business climate may alter or stress information ecosystems.

Ecosystem Management

Many biological ecosystems are managed to ensure the ongoing optimal production of organisms for ultimate consumption (e.g., eating, viewing, playing, commuting, etc.). Correspondingly, information ecosystems are managed to ensure the ongoing optimal production of information consumed by businesses and individuals.

In our biosphere, ecosystem managers alter topologies (tilling, grading), introduce or reduce resources (clear cutting, burning, watering), supplement resources (irrigation, fertilizing), artificially repair organism imbalances (herd thinning, fish stocking), and even help prevent the extinction of species (genetic material banking) in severely distressed ecosystems.

In our *infosphere*, ecosystem managers also perform similar tasks such as reconfiguring hardware and networks; cleansing information; augmenting computing, storage, and bandwidth resources; repairing information imbalances via archiving or enriching data; and even backing up information to help prevent its loss.

Indeed, effective ecosystem planning and management of either kind requires an effective vision, strategy, measurements, governance, and personnel, along with an understanding of the organisms' lifecycles and a set of tools. Sound familiar? Maybe we should look to our forestry and agriculture agencies, water ministries, and national park departments for guidance on how to manage our information ecosystems more effectively. At the very least we should consider borrowing from their model. I look forward to the emergence of information ecologists!

Information ecosystem managers such as CDOs would be well advised to study biological ecosystems to ensure that their organizations' information ecosystems are healthy and sustainable. We have only been managing our biological ecosystems for several millennia. What could those of us in the decades-old information world possibly learn from them? A lot.

One last note on ecosystems: if you think the whole concept of drawing parallels between biological and information ecosystems is a bit whacked, consider that the leading theoretical ecologist, Robert Ulanowicz, has employed modern information theory concepts to describe the complex structure of biological ecosystems themselves.[11]

Lessons from Sustainability

When an ecosystem is healthy, scientists say it is *in balance* or *sustainable*. Since we want our information ecosystems to be sustainable and thrive, let's take a look at how we might incorporate the principles of sustainability or conservation. What was originally known as the "three Rs" of Reduce, Reuse, and Recycle recently have been expanded into "five Rs" which also include Refuse and Repurpose.

Most businesses are compiling information assets so furiously because: 1) they're easily captured or obtained, 2) they're increasingly inexpensive to store, and 3) they have nearly unlimited monetization potential. This makes sense, but as gigabytes become terabytes, and terabytes become petabytes, and petabytes become exabytes, the sustainability of an information ecosystem or architecture or infrastructure can be threatened. Even considering the diminishing marginal cost of storing information, conserving its use and production—and thereby the use of information-related resources—can improve the performance, costs, and risks incurred by your information ecosystem.

Refuse

If you're not going to use it, refuse it.

Refusing an asset is the surest way to prevent any expenses or risks associated with it. Why capture, collect, or generate information you have no intention to leverage? Doing so incurs not only excess storage costs, but also unnecessary costs up and down the information lifecycle such as planning, design, architecture, data integration, backup/recovery, governance, and security. Moreover, bulking up a database with extraneous data can impact operational, analytic, and business performance. Sometimes refusing an asset involves rethinking and reinventing our consumption habits or processes altogether.

Particularly for any kind of private data or information which—if hacked or leaked—could damage your organization, be circumspect about choosing to collect it in the first place.

No doubt, refusing information can be a difficult decision, especially in this age of untold opportunities for monetization and decreasing storage expense. But in many cases, information you don't collect today will be licensable from a partner or data broker when you need it.

Reduce

If you can't refuse it, try to reduce it.

Reducing the use of an asset is about minimizing—rather than eliminating—the expenses associated with it. Information architects and data modelers have struggled with this conundrum daily since the introduction of the relational database: how to balance performance versus storage. If you have never had a debate about how much to normalize or denormalize a data model, then you're not an information professional!

Similarly, customer relationship management (CRM), enterprise resource planning (ERP), and other application architects wrangle with decisions over whether to include or exclude certain fields from the application's data model. *How many different kinds of addresses do we need for a business customer?* Or, *Must we capture the cashier's ID in addition to the point-of-sale terminal number for each sale?* Or other related storage questions such as, *At which level of granularity or detail should electronic media be saved?* Too often business users involved in design will say, "Just capture it all, then we'll decide if or how we're going to use it." Information professionals need to have the ability, authority, and economic models to push back.

However, reducing which information you collect is just one side of the question. The other side is to consider how much information you use. While reducing the amount of data used won't affect the storage and other supply-side expenses, it will affect those on the demand side like processing costs and business performance. Increasingly, information technologies incorporate features like query optimization, but much design work is still manual—e.g., *which fields to present to a user and when*, or *which operational fields to include in a data warehouse or data lake*, or *how much of a large item of content to retrieve and buffer*.

In short, information management professionals should be attuned to reducing the information generated or collected, and reducing the information moved and presented.

Reuse

Especially if you cannot reduce it, reuse it.

Reusing an asset is simply to use it again for the same purpose, whatever that purpose is. Fortunately, such is the nature of information. It is non-depletable. No matter how much you use it, it doesn't get used up. As argued in chapter 1, this is one of the characteristics that makes information highly monetizable. You can't sell or eat the same sandwich or pizza more than once, but you can license and consume the same customer contact data over and over.

True, one can drive the same car again and again, but it depreciates and deteriorates over time. Datasets representing an ongoing business or events don't generally deteriorate, as they are refreshed continuously or periodically. Individual records may lose relevance, accuracy, or timeliness, but not their existence or completeness. As a whole, datasets deteriorate when a business closes (e.g., the customer records of the recently shuttered Radio Shack and Sports Authority stores), unless someone purchases those records and continues refreshing them. Or—to some extent—when a new process replaces an older one.

Therefore, reuse may not be a primary consideration in information ecosystem design, as reusability is a key characteristic of information. However, if you find certain information isn't being reused, such as in the case of "dark data," it may be time to reduce it.

Repurpose

Repurpose on purpose.

Repurposing an asset involves sharing it and enabling it to be used for different reasons. An Uber or Lyft driver's automobile is a prime example: it is used for both taxiing and personal reasons. Repurposing any asset, including an information asset, can lower or spread its net cost of ownership among multiple entities, and it can generate additional benefits that offset its initial expense or ongoing depreciation.

Just as information's non-depletability enables its extreme reuse, information's *non-rivalry characteristic* enables its extreme repurposing. More than just being able to share an asset or resource, non-rivalry, as I mentioned in chapter 1, is the ability of multiple processes or parties to use the same instance of an asset *simultaneously.*

In addition to reference data such as metadata and master data, most repurposing of information tends to be in the form of repurposing operational data for analytics. Or in the case of content it may involve simultaneously sharing on the web, an intranet, broadcast media, or signage. Clever information and enterprise architects recently have been honing their skills at identifying opportunities for repurposing information. Yet, I find most organizations have only scratched the surface, lacking the creativity, the will, or just the awareness that certain information even exists in other parts of the organization, or elsewhere. Issues of "data ownership" we'll discuss in chapter 9 also tend to interfere with information repurposing.

Recycle

No use for it? Recycle it.

Recycling involves breaking down an asset to create a new one. Or in our previous ecosystem terminology: *decomposing* it to provide the building blocks for a new organism.

With transactional or other structured information (portions of a dataset), fields may be parsed and recombined to create new datasets. If the original dataset remains in use, then this is more like reuse than recycling. In any case, architects should look for opportunities to do so rather than discarding the information altogether. Often recycling will involve sharing "decomposed" information with others (even outside the organization) so that they may benefit from creating new information assets from it.

It occurs to me that presently I'm recycling bits and pieces of existing research content from my colleagues and myself, other information sources, and some new ideas to create a new valuable asset: a book.

Remove

Can't reduce, reuse, repurpose, or recycle it? Remove it.

In addition to the "five Rs" of classic sustainability and conservation, there's a sixth "R" specific to non-physical assets such as information: removal. The removal or dumping of physical assets is a last resort, and not much in the realm of sustainability. But with non-physical or *intangible* assets, removing unneeded ones is easy and doesn't harm your or anyone else's information ecosystem. But it can help with lessening personnel, storage, processing costs, and risks. Purging a customer database of old records with dead email addresses (or dead customers!) is one simple example of this.

However, when the actual deletion of information may not be allowable due to regulatory compliance reasons, consider moving the data into an offline archive.

Technically, the simple deletion of information may not always be so simple. Within an information ecosystem, many different kinds of information are linked through other information. Therefore, simply deleting some unused information can cause data integrity problems.

Information as a Second Language

All of these metaphors for information we've devised over the years are not meant to be clever. Rather they're to help information management professionals, IT professionals, business people, and executives communicate about information more effectively using familiar, non-threatening terminology and frameworks. They can make information seem less ephemeral and abstract, and more tangible, helping us convince our business colleagues, executives, and ourselves that information really is an asset to be treated as such.

To consolidate all of these challenges and potential solutions related to "speaking data" within an organization and among business partners, Gartner analyst Valerie Logan recently has introduced the concept of "information as a second language" (ISL). No surprise, ISL parallels the kind of challenges and training afforded to non-native speakers in the U.S. under the moniker "English as a Second Language" (ESL). Logan's ISL idea is a fantastic one and still being developed.

Although rectifying our sloppy or geeky information vernacular can help with communicating throughout the organization, to *manage* information as an actual asset, we still have a lot to learn from other disciplines. In the next chapter we'll investigate other well-honed, well-articulated, and reasonably well-understood forms of asset management to see what we might borrow from these disciplines to improve and extend information asset management (IAM) capabilities.

Notes

1. "What is a supply chain," Canadian Supply Chain Sector Council, http://www.supplychaincanada.org/assets/u/HandoutWhatisaSupplyChain.pdf, accessed 14 May 2017
2. "Supply Chain Operations Reference Model, Revision 11.0," Supply Chain Council, 2012, http://docs.huihoo.com/scm/supply-chain-operations-reference-model-r11.0.pdf.
3. Attributed quote, est. 1988.
4. In fact, he did. In the book *The Art of War* Sun Tzu is quoted as saying: "The general who wins the battle makes many calculations in his temple before the battle is fought. The general who loses makes but few calculations beforehand."
5. Andy Roswell-Jones, Jan-martin Lowendahl, Chris Howard, and Tomas Nielsen, "The 2017 CIO Agenda: Seize the Digital Ecosystem Opportunity," Gartner, 14 October, 2016, www.gartner.com/document/3478517.
6. "Ecosystem", dictionary.com, accessed 14 May 2017
7. The Gaia hypothesis is the idea that the Earth is a single living entity. James Hutton (1726–1797), the father of geology, once described the Earth as a kind of superorganism. Later, in 1979 James Lovelock defined Gaia as "a complex entity involving the Earth's biosphere, atmosphere, oceans, and soil; the totality

constituting a feedback or cybernetic system which seeks an optimal physical and chemical environment for life on this planet." (ref: "The Earth Is a Sentient Living Organism," The Mind Unleashed Website, 15 May 2014, http://themindunleashed.com/2014/05/earth-sentient-living-organism.html).

8. Peter Sondergaard, "Big Data Fades to the Algorithm Economy," *Forbes*, 14 August 2015, www.forbes.com/sites/gartnergroup/2015/08/14/big-data-fades-to-the-algorithm-economy/.

9. With apologies to quantum physicists and information theorists who have proven that information in the purest form can never be created.

10. Roger Williams, email to author, 03 January 2017.

11. Robert E. Ulanowicz, *A Third Window: Natural Life Beyond Newton and Darwin* (Templeton Foundation Press, 2009).

CHAPTER 7

Leveraging Information Asset Management Standards and Approaches

In the mid-1990s, MIT's Media Lab founder Nicholas Negroponte introduced the metaphor of our collective shift from "processing atoms to processing bits" as a means of explaining the transition to a digital economy. However, we shouldn't dismiss everything we learned about processing physical things as we immerse ourselves in all things digital, particularly how to manage them effectively.

We have already examined the barriers to managing information in the enterprise and how to leverage physical supply chains as a model for managing the information supply chain. In this chapter, we will explore the management of other corporate assets to build an approach to information asset management. Yes, we data professionals have really just been improvising for decades.

One of the key issues for chief data officers and those tasked with managing information as an asset is the lack of standards for information. In fact, the only standard related to information management is in the mouthful: "ISO/IEC 27001 Information technology—Security techniques—Information security management systems—Requirements,"[1] Currently, this is the only widely accepted international standard which deals at all with managing information.[2] The standard calls for the inventorying of all kinds of assets, including documenting their classification, owner, usage rules, labeling, control, and handling guidelines.[3]

Sure, the Institute of Electrical and Electronics Engineers (IEEE) has standards for information technology, the North Atlantic Treaty Organization

(NATO) and the United Nations (UN) have standards for information sharing among military organizations and countries, various multinational industry associations such as the World Bank and the International Astronomical Union and have developed regulations for information sharing among member organizations, and various countries alone or together have laws and regulations for information handling. But as for a comprehensive, enterprise approach to managing information, there exists no agreed upon standard.

A Bevy of Non-Standard Information Management Standards

Several associations, collaborative open standards groups, and professional services organizations and industry luminaries have succeeded to various degrees in filling the gap with their own information management-related methodologies or other tools. These include the Capability Maturity Model Integration (CMMI), Data Management Association International (DAMA), Enterprise Data Management (EDM) Council, Experience Matters, Cicero Group, MIKE2.0, Accenture, CapGemini, Deloitte, EY, IBM, KPMG, Wipro, John Ladley, Rob Hillard, and William McKnight. As well, IT research organizations including Gartner publish a large body of research and consultative guidance on information management trends and best practices.[4]

Each of these bodies of knowledge, approaches, resources, and tools has its unique uses and benefits for information management leaders and professionals. Yet, most of them tend to be lacking in adoption, completeness, integration, and/or usability. Usually these challenges are by design. For example: research organizations are not in the "methodology business"; DAMA and CMMI are strictly focused on methodology maturity; and systems integrators generally do not publish their approaches for competitive and compensatory reasons. And as for accreditation, the ICCP and DAMA offer data management professional certifications, although they are neither widely recognized nor often required.

We're well into the Information Age, and we have been managing electronic information for at least fifty years. Most business models and much of the world is flipping to digital, and in the last ten years many of the most successful companies have monetized information more than they have monetized products and services. Still, most organizations have their IT department (or worse, various business units themselves) managing their information as less of an asset than their technology, and without any generally accepted, enforceable standards.

Across the information realm, however, are other close neighbors such as the specialties of IT asset management, IT service management, records management, content management, knowledge management, and even library science. Each of these fields includes standards and procedures worthy of consideration, as we look to better manage information as an actual asset. In the next chapter, we'll weave these best practices into an approach for improving EIM maturity across the seven dimensions described in chapter 5.

An IT Asset Management Eye-Opener

Recently, I attended an IT asset management conference and had a chance to speak with several attendees about their approaches to managing their company's various software and hardware assets. To my surprise, not only are there entire departments in some companies just for tracking who has which corporate laptops and mobile devices, but there's a whole industry around software solutions and best practices for inventorying, tracking, monitoring, and servicing—along with managing the vendors and contracts—for all manner of technology stuff.

First, there's an entire family of International Organization for Standardization (ISO) standards for IT asset management (ITAM):

- ISO 19770–1 is a process defining best practices for software asset management (SAM) in an organization,
- ISO 19770–2 is an XML standard for inventorying and identifying what software is deployed on a given device,

- ISO 19770–3 is a schema describing the entitlements and rights associated with a software license, including how to measure the license and entitlement consumption, and
- ISO 19770–4 is a standard for reporting on resource utilization.

These processes and standards educate end users on compliance, help budget managers make technology redeployment decisions, provide IT service departments with guidance on warranty and other service information, and offer procedures on invoice and IT asset inventory level information for finance departments.[5]

Now, substitute the phrase "information asset" for "technology" or "IT asset." Do information management departments or leaders have a global standard for information best practices? Do they have any kind of inventory standard for information assets? Do they have a standard way to document the contractual rights and privileges for information usage, or to track them (other than for information security or privacy regulations)? Is there a recognized standard for reporting on information utilization? At best, the answer to any of these is: *hardly*.

Now, ask yourself: which is more critical to an organization, the customer information or the hardware upon which it resides? It's no wonder why the ITAM conference attendees I met were dumbfounded when I mentioned no such standards or procedures exist for the management of *information* assets.

I'm not suggesting at all that IT/infrastructure/technology isn't important, only that there's a whole lot that we info-folks can learn and perhaps steal from the impressive discipline around managing it.

IT Service Management—Servicing Information Needs?

A close cousin of ITAM is IT service management (ITSM), a discipline dealing with aligning IT services with the needs of the business. A set of processes, procedures and other tools known as the Information Technology Infrastructure Library (ITIL) is the prevailing standard for IT service management.[67]

ITIL currently specifies twenty-six processes grouped into five high-level areas:

1. **ITIL Service Strategy**: understanding organizational objectives and customer needs.
2. **ITIL Service Design**: turning the service strategy into a plan for delivering the business objectives.
3. **ITIL Service Transition**: developing and improving capabilities for introducing new services into supported environments.
4. **ITIL Service Operation**: managing services in supported environments.
5. **ITIL Continual Service Improvement**: achieving incremental and large-scale services improvements.

Imagine if there were such a library of standards and procedures for information management. Or even in advance of one, what if CDOs borrowed liberally from the ITIL cookbook to establish similar approaches for their own organization: *a discipline dealing with aligning information services with the needs of the business.* Such an "information management library" could include:

- An **Information Service Strategy** process that identifies business demand for information, a catalog of information assets, a set of user profiles, patterns of information creation and usage, budgeting and charging for information access, and an operations approach for fulfilling information needs/requests and resolving information service failures.
- An **Information Services Design** for a catalog of information assets and services, service level agreements (SLAs) among users and providers of information and information services, and the management of information capacity and throughput, continuity, and supplier/provider management.
- An **Information Service Transition** process to ensure information services supports continual and periodic changes to information availability, demand, and needed information service components.

- **Information Service Operations** to ensure information demand and delivery are constantly monitored, and that requests, incidents, and problems related to information assets and their required facilities and technical components are managed effectively.
- An **Information Service Continual Service Improvement** process for monitoring, reviewing, and evaluating ongoing information service needs, and learning from past successes and failures.

It's well beyond the scope of this book, but I'd be really impressed with anyone who took the initiative to adapt and adopt ITIL for an information services organization! But wait, we have several other asset management approaches yet to examine and learn from.

Records Management—From Hard Copies to Hardened Practices

Records information management (RIM) is a mysterious function within many organizations that quietly goes about its business of preserving and safeguarding the organization's institutional memory. Often RIM is part of a broader governance, risk, and compliance (GRC) function under the auspices of the legal department, not IT. Although RIM's heredity is in moving about boxes of files among offices and storage facilities, the discipline has kept up with the times. It now includes the management of electronic records as well.

The current ISO standard for RIM, ISO 15489–1:2016, defines records as "information created, received, and maintained as evidence and information by an organization or person, in pursuance of legal obligations or in the transaction of business."[8] [9] The standard describes concepts and principles relating to:

- Records, metadata for records, and record systems,
- Policies, assigned responsibilities, monitoring, and training in support of effective records management,

- Recurrent analysis of business context and identifying records requirements,
- Records controls, and
- Processing for creating, capturing, and managing records.[10]

Even with a somewhat dated set of vernacular, this standard seems like an excellent framework for a set of data governance policies and procedures. Invariably, however, data governance programs are designed from scratch, based on someone else's data governance program, or leaning on a specific practitioner's book or methodology, enhanced with a smattering of best and emerging practices from magazine articles and analyst organization research reports.

RIM standards also introduce some concepts seldom seen well documented at all in data governance programs, such as that of a *defensible solution*—one which can be supported with clearly documented policies, processes, and procedures. One defensible solution I see only occasionally in information management policies and practices is that of "defensible disposition" or "defensible destruction" of records, which defines explicitly which records to destroy/dispose of, by whom, where, and when. Another well-defined RIM concept that would be useful in architecting and articulating an information lifecycle is classifying records as "active," "inactive," or "semi-current," along with their disposition or other handling requirements.

RIM standards are meticulous about defining a record's lifecycle—from creation, through its storage, modification, conversion, movement, circulation, retrieval, and destruction. RIM discriminates different classes of records with different properties and legal status. RIM professionals themselves can become formally certified via the Institute of Certified Records Managers and other societies, and even can obtain a master's degree in archives and records administration from various universities around the world. Surely this is a sound basis on which to build information asset management practices, standards and accreditation, right?

Contending Approaches for Content Management

Enterprise Content Management (ECM) is a discipline for "the strategies, methods and tools used to capture, manage, store, preserve, and deliver content and documents related to organizational processes."[11] In this way, ECM is more workflow-oriented that RIM. Gartner's definition also incorporates the creation, discovery, and usage analysis of content, and its graphical depiction of ECM includes "return on information" at the center.[12] Often the main discriminator between ECM and EIM is a simple artificial one: unstructured versus structured information. Yet they remain almost entirely distinct disciplines with distinct departments and distinct technologies.

Also, within the family of ECM are intersecting, overlapping, and sometimes conflicting disciplines of: Document Management, Digital Asset Management (DAM), and Web Content Management (WCM). Vendors rather than standards bodies tend to drive most of the accepted or expected capabilities and processes.

Because ECM and EIM are closely related, requiring some of the same basic methodological approaches, there may not be much we can borrow from ECM. However, some unique concepts and focus areas from these disciplines CDOs might consider incorporating into their overall information management approach include:[13]

- Specifications concerning the capture or entry and validation of content,
- Storing content in an optimal format/structure,
- Content classification,
- Content findability, searchability, and discovery,
- Digital rights and digital signatures,
- Content as a service,
- Content versioning and derivatives, and
- Collaboration among users in terms of: 1) document workflows and 2) joint content creation and editing.

Very few CDOs also oversee content management, but in the realm of overall enterprise information management, it makes sense that they should. And I believe they will in the coming years. As the founder and CEO of one content management vendor suggested to me, "Other than the different technologies involved and a few unique workflow considerations, data and content management are more like 'brothers from another mother.'" It might make sense they live under the same roof.

Knowledge Management Know-How

Knowledge is a deadly friend when no-one sets the rules. The fate of all mankind, I see, is in the hands of fools.
Peter John Sinfield, King Crimson

More than two decades after release of the album *In the Court of the Crimson King*, rules around compiling and deploying institutional knowledge began to coalesce. Knowledge Management (KM) became a more formalized discipline in the early 1990s, but still sufferers from an unwieldy number of differing definitions. Most center on the identification, capture, structuring, value, sharing, and deployment of an organization's intellectual assets to enhance its performance and competitiveness. Knowledge assets are segregated into *explicit* and *tacit* knowledge. As such, KM is quite human-centered compared to asset management disciplines and draws upon a number of diverse fields, from cognitive science to anthropology to web and document management technologies:[14] [15]

Information leaders such as CDOs would be well advised to leverage much of what KM offers in the way of:

- Adapting and dealing with new and exceptional situations in establishing a vision for EIM, including scenario planning,
- Developing, communicating, and sharing an EIM vision to transmit an "information culture,"
- Collaborating across other areas of the organization, including IT, business, finance, legal, etc.,

- Identifying, capturing, codifying, and sharing expertise as part of defining the information management organization and associated roles (including other resources spread throughout the enterprise),
- Developing, implementing, and improving repeatable, experience-based information asset management methods, and
- Transferring and incorporating knowledge/information assets into business products and services.

CDOs would also benefit by adopting certain KM technologies such as work-flow management, and groupware for capturing and disseminating knowledge.

What's on the Library Science Shelf?

Closing the book, as it were, on formal approaches to other information-related management disciplines, is that of library science, or library and information science (LIS).

Although a French librarian, Gabriel Naudé, published the earliest known text on library operations in 1627, a Bavarian librarian named Martin Schrettinger coined the discipline in the early 1800s with his work, *Versuch eines vollständigen Lehrbuchs der Bibliothek-Wissenschaft oder Anleitung zur vollkommenen Geschäftsführung eines Bibliothekars.*[16] Oddly, Schrettinger opted to organize his library not by topic, but in alphabetical order.

OK, maybe there's not a lot we can learn from old Schrettinger himself.[17] However, many of Naudé's principles endure, and are instructive to infor-mation professionals even today. In Naudé's first chapter of his book, *Advis pour dresser une bibliothèque*, he poses and answers the question: *Why create a library?* His answer suggests he believed there to be no greater honor than collecting human knowledge and sharing it. Naudé goes on to define a plan which includes inspecting the catalogs of other libraries. He advises that the first books curated ought to be those highly regarded books by highly regarded practitioners in a particular field, and they ought to be collected in their original languages to avoid meanings being lost in translation. He also writes that select interpretations or commentaries should be included, that every book has a reader no matter how obscure the topic, and that multiple copies of popular books should be considered. As for arranging the library, he quoted Cicero: "It is order that gives light to memory," suggesting books should be organized by key subjects and subcategories. Additionally, Naudé offered guidance on bookbinding techniques.[18]

Any information professional will recognize several key principles in Naudé's *Advice* which could be readily adopted as part of a vision and strategy for information asset management, such as:

- There is no greater asset than information (if you think your office furniture, laptops, or other equipment are of greater importance, then you're a 17th century *and* a 21st century laggard),
- Learn what information assets are collected and compiled by competitors and others,
- Focus on the most important information first,
- Collect information from respected (high quality) sources,
- Capture raw, original (not transformed) data when possible,
- Include available commentaries (i.e., metadata) on information,
- Recognize that all information has potential and probable value to someone or some process,
- Ensure the availability for high-demand information assets,
- Organize information assets in ways they are easy to locate, and nearby other information assets of similar topic interest, and
- Ensure the protection and preservation of information assets.

Today, the leading LIS governing body is the International Federation of Library Associations and Institutions (IFLA), whose principles include:

- The promotion of high standards for the provision and delivery of library information services,
- Encouraging widespread understanding of the value of good library and information services, and

- Endorsing the principles of freedom of access to information, and the conviction that the delivery of high-quality LIS helps guarantee that access.

Over the past couple of decades LIS has been transformed by the digital age. The IFLA has developed and published conceptual models and digital formats for bibliographic encoding and sharing, and for resource descriptions. Additionally, it offers dozens of formal guidelines on the handling and storage of various media, content curation and sharing, a growing range of library services, ensuring easy resource accessibility for multiple types of user communities, artifact digitization and preservation, and overall operations.[19] Many of these guidelines, no doubt, would offer CDOs and other information professionals fascinating insights and useful ideas to bring into the information asset management fold.

Balance Sheet Assets and Other Major Proto-Assets

Now let's get away from the world of IT and information to expand our exploration of asset management concepts into other areas.

Physical Asset Management—Living in a Material World

On the spectrum of assets (or things that should qualify as assets), physical assets and information assets, no doubt, are at opposite ends. Physical assets are as tangible as assets get, while information is of course intangible. Still, just as with other IT and information-related standards and practices, we can learn much from accepted physical asset management approaches—the primary one of which is PAS 55 (the basis for ISO 55001).

The Publicly Available Specification (PAS) was first published in 2004 in response to demand for a standard for asset management. It's applicable in any organization in which physical assets are central to the business, especially transportation, mining, and energy companies. Increasingly, PAS has relevance for any organization managing operational technology (OT)—devices and equipment differentiated from but often integrated or communicating with information technologies.

Quoted benefits from these implementations range from "it provided a structured basis for coordinating all our efforts into a common, business-prioritized direction," to very substantial bottom-line performance gains. China Light & Power, for example, report a 90 percent reduction in system outages, while meeting a 20 percent growth in demand and, simultaneously, reducing customer charging tariffs by 40 percent.[20]

PAS 55 is structured around the *Plan-Do-Check-Act* cycle of continual improvement, and it introduces a number of essential "enablers and controls" to ensure alignment, integration, and sustainability of efficient and effective asset management activities.

PAS answers five key questions:

1. What assets do you have?
2. What is your risk of an asset-related disaster?
3. Do you know the current condition of your assets?
4. What are the costs of corrective versus preventative maintenance?
5. Should you repair or replace any given asset?

Shouldn't any CDO or data governance lead have the answers to these at hand regarding the organization's information assets? Are there any who do?

Many of these questions are difficult to answer without a framework—and this is where PAS 55 comes into play.

The adoption and sponsorship at the highest levels of many organizations is the primary reason for the success of PAS 55. Leadership sees it as the means to reduce capital investments and operational costs while improving the uptime of key assets. The executive support it garners also helps those maintaining assets to meet their commitments, even when they may conflict with other imperatives.

An Asset Register

Much like ITAM does for IT assets, PAS requires a reliable and comprehensive physical asset register which includes where assets are located and their condition. So in today's Information Age, why would any organization think about foregoing a register of its information assets? Yet PAS even goes a couple steps further, requiring that asset failure risks are recorded, and an accounting of asset depreciation and replacement. The former is certainly applicable to information assets: *What is the impact if a product Universal Product Code (UPC) or SKU is wrong?* Even the depreciation and replacement of information could also be a consideration: *What is the value of our aging customer database, and should we maintain it ourselves or license updates from a data broker?*

Gartner analyst Alan Duncan writes about the state of data cataloging:

"To monetize internal and external business data, chief data officers must learn lessons from traditional asset management disciplines. By using an information catalog properly, CDOs can develop and expand a data-driven culture and derive new value from their organization's information assets."[21]

Duncan cites several challenges with, and inhibitors to organizations being successful with cataloging information assets:

- Classic attempts at cataloging data have been technically focused and are poorly aligned with business outcomes.
- Exogenous datasets are becoming increasingly important sources of business insight, at the same time as the overall complexity of business data is overwhelming human analysts.

- Organizations are often unclear about the extent of their data holdings, or what that data could be used for. Business opportunity is thereby lost, and data-driven innovation inhibited.
- The semantic meaning of data is poorly understood and poorly communicated. Inconsistency arises, contentions occur, and time is wasted on reconciliation, rather than focusing on new business actions.
- The ability to track causal relationships between business data, analytic outputs, and business outcomes is still immature. Diagnostic root-cause analysis is time-consuming and can be applied inconsistently.[22]

Interestingly, PAS 55 addresses most of these issues in relation to physical assets, but with approaches that could and *should* be adapted to information asset.

Asset Risks

Certain kinds of physical risks as well as information risks are as unacceptable as they are preventable. But when there is a maintenance backlog, as there often is with data quality, how do you know which information assets should be maintained first to mitigate risk and avoid catastrophe? Fortunately, PAS 55 provides an approach to determining this.

With PAS, asset categories are established and each asset category is risk-weighted, ranked, and scored. Doing so with information assets would enable data stewards to assign and schedule priorities, establish budgets, and better align resources for their mitigation.

Asset Condition

Just as with physical asset–intensive industries, the overall performance in information-intensive industries is based on the performance of those assets. When those assets are not performing, your organization is either not driving revenue, or is leaking cash or customers or partners. To account for this, PAS 55 offers a comprehensive approach for evaluating asset condition which consider the history of inspections, repairs, and maintenance. For physical assets, Enterprise Asset Management (EAM) systems will generate recommended actions for inspecting, repairing, maintaining, or replacing assets. There's no good reason today why we don't see similar kinds of functionality available for information assets—other than perhaps that the accounting profession has us believing that information assets are not really assets.

Many ERP systems see assets as a single unit. Similarly, most data governance applications see information assets (e.g., datasets) as a single unit. One of the key differentiators for EAM systems is the use of an asset hierarchy. As the relationships among information assets in an organization are often quite complex or even convoluted, an EAM-like solution would certainly help in documenting, understanding, and leveraging these relationships—at a minimum from a maintenance perspective.

Asset Maintenance and Replacement Costs

In the physical asset world, fixing something broken can be two-to-three times more expensive than the cost of maintaining it.[23] Balancing the costs of preventative versus reactive work on an asset can be difficult. Other costs that PAS accounts for include the cost of replacing a failed part or the cost of an unplanned outage. As with other assets, information assets are especially prone to letting quality problems flow downstream. Information maintenance (quality) costs can be a barrier to ensuring the best long-term maintenance strategy.

Maybe this is just the nature of information we've come to accept: it flows, carrying its detritus along with it for the next department to deal with. A preferable strategy and approach—such as those embodied in PAS—would offer rational, quantitative guidance to CDOs and data governance/quality leads, and ensure overall data quality costs are minimized while the operational and analytical effectiveness of information is maximized.

PAS methods could also be used to make fiscally reasoned decisions about maintaining and repairing certain information assets, versus sourcing them elsewhere. Many organizations today struggle with whether and when to rely upon certain open data sources, license data from data brokers, or enter into partnerships in which information assets are exchanged.

However, since PAS 55 is just a framework, various software vendors offer EAM systems to automate the underlying foundation for this process. Although several data governance software vendors like Collibra, Informatica, SAP, and Global IDs support some PAS framework-like considerations for information assets, both the discipline of data governance and data stewardship would benefit from becoming more PAS-like in process and EAM-like in automation.

As Gartner analyst and operational technology (OT) expert Kristian Steenstrup said: "PAS is sort of like 'religion in a box.' All the parts are there and it's useful if you don't already have a religion."[24] Perhaps it's time for CDOs, other information leaders, and senior executives to get the same kind of religion about managing their information assets.

An Investment in Financial Asset Management Methods

With all the media attention and political hand-wringing about banking and financial industry regulatory compliance, surprisingly few standards exist for the management of financial assets *within* an organization. Certainly there are wealth managers, stock brokers, and financial advisors who are held to various established standards and may require certain training and certification. But these roles do not offer much guidance for managing an organization's own information assets with improved rigor.

As a capital investment executive with a major global financial services company confided,

I look at the engineers we work with on deals. They have all sorts of codified standards, but we don't have the same kind of defined procedures in the investment world. I wish we did. We have developed our own internal procedures, but they're not auditable at all, and make collaboration with other parties involved in a deal quite inefficient. Even worse, they're not even the same across different groups within our own company.[25]

Another investment executive, Bruce Weininger, a principal with Kovitz Investment, acknowledged that even as an investment firm, more than half of his time is spent managing information assets: "The financial assets themselves, without other information assets, don't mean much. I spend more time on issues related to gathering and processing non-financial information about our clients than dealing with their financial assets in a vacuum."

Even lacking formal processes, two key items we *can* consider instructive from the world of finance are those of a *fiduciary*, and the common, if not regulated, financial management roles and responsibilities of the CFO.

Fiduciary Responsibility

A fiduciary is an individual who knowingly accepts the responsibility to act in the best interest and for the benefit of another party whose assets he or she is managing. A fiduciary's duties are both ethical and legal. Moreover, fiduciaries cannot benefit personally from their management of the other party's assets. Fiduciaries come in the form of: corporate board members and shareholders, executors, guardians, lawyers, and investment companies. Some types of fiduciaries are certified, but all have an explicit or implied contract with another party.

Back in information-land we talk about and assign data "owners" and "stewards" and "custodians," but it never seems to include anyone with contractual *legal and ethical* responsibilities for the management of information assets. I have long advised clients that their data stewards also take on the role of *advocates* wherein they assume responsibility for improving the enablement and value generated from information assets. But the idea of a true "information fiduciary" (or "trustee") could help elevate the status of information assets and their caretakers (e.g., CDOs).

The Chief Financial Officer

CFOs need little introduction, but the full scope of their role may not be all that familiar. Moreover, the role introduces a few levels of executive responsibility over the organization's financial assets that CDOs should be assuming for their organization's information assets. These include:

- **Controllership**—CFOs must provide accurate, timely reporting on the financial status of the organization. Similarly, CDOs should be compelled to report to the board on the health of the enterprise's information assets.
- **Treasury Duties**—Just as CFOs decide how to invest the company's money, a CDO should be leading or guiding decisions on how best to leverage the company's information.
- **Economic Strategy**—CFOs must financially model the business, taking advantage of available internal and external information. The CDO should be an active participant in this process, helping to identify, curate, and analyze available information and other leading indicators.

Other integral CFO responsibilities include managing budgets and cash flow, measuring the company's liabilities, managing relationships with the financial community (e.g., investors, financial analysts, shareholders), and raising capital. In parallel, CDOs should be chartered with managing information availability and flow, identifying information-borne risks, managing relationships with other information ecosystem participants, and identifying and assimilating needed exogenous information sources.

Human Capital Management

As I mentioned in the previous chapter, people are not assets because we can no longer be owned. (Score one for humanity at the expense of accounting.) Still, labor is expensed on the income statement, and the discipline of human capital has emerged to manage us as if we were assets. If you think I'm kidding, see the 619-page People Capability Maturity Model (P-CMM). It's longer than any of these other standards (other than SCOR), because well, I guess people and organizations are more difficult to manage than most other things.

The P-CMM, first released in 1995, is advertised as "a tool to help you successfully address the critical people issues in your organization . . . [and] guides organizations in improving their processes for managing and developing their workforce." As one of Software Engineering Institute's many capability maturity models, it is more assessment-oriented than methodological.

Oriented toward the chief resource officer (CRO) or chief human resource officer (CHRO) and their organizations, the P-CMM contains guidance on:

- Developing and implementing human capital strategies and plans,
- Managing and developing workforces,
- Nurturing teams,
- Transforming organizational culture,
- Guiding organizational changes (e.g., downsizing, mergers and acquisitions, changes in ownership, etc.),
- Managing individual development and growth,
- Managing knowledge assets,
- Improving workforce practices,
- Motivating individuals,
- Improving retention, and
- Dealing with changing demographics, labor markets, and other external workforce issues.

Similarly a robust information management process should include strategies and plans, "nurture" information assets, help to transform the organization, enable organizational changes, improve the acquisition and retention of business, and respond to a changing landscape of externally available information sources.

As with the Gartner Information Management Maturity Model, the P-CMM's maturity levels parallel a stepwise improvement in planning, competencies, collaboration, and performance. The P-CMM (Figure 7.1), however, includes ten principles upon which the model is based, which are worth calling out:[26]

1	In mature organizations, workforce capability is directly related to business performance.
2	Workforce capability is a competitive issue and a source of strategic advantage.
3	Workforce capability must be defined in relation to the organization's strategic business objectives.
4	Knowledge-intense work shifts the focus from job elements to workforce competencies.
5	Capability can be measured and improved at multiple levels of the organization, including individuals, workgroups, workforce competencies, and the organization.
6	An organization should invest in improving the capability of those workforce competencies that are critical to its core competency as a business.
7	Operational management is responsible for the capability of the workforce.
8	The improvement of workforce capability can be pursued as a process composed from proven practices and procedures.
9	The organization is responsible for providing improvement opportunities, and individuals are responsible for taking advantage of them.
10	Because technologies and organizational forms evolve rapidly, organizations must continually evolve their workforce practices and develop new workforce competencies.

Figure 7.1 *People Capability Maturity Model*

Not to poke fun at these philosophies, but rather embrace them—if we were to substitute "information" for "workforce" and do a little tweaking, we can construct a similar set of philosophies for information management:

1. In mature organizations, information capability is directly related to business performance.
2. Information capability is a competitive issue and a source of strategic advantage.
3. Information capability must be defined in relation to the organization's strategic objectives.
4. Knowledge-intensive work shifts the focus from job elements to information competencies.
5. Capability can be measured and improved at multiple levels of enterprise information, including at a record level, a dataset level, information competencies, and the entire portfolio of information assets.
6. An organization should invest in improving the information-related capabilities that are critical to its core competency as a business.

7. Information leadership (e.g., the CDO) is responsible for the capability of the information assets.
8. The improvement of information capabilities can be pursued as a process composed from proven practices and procedures.
9. The organization is responsible for providing opportunities to use information, and business people are responsible for taking advantage of them.
10. Because technologies and business models evolve rapidly, organizations must continually evolve their information management practices and competencies.

Other Intangible Assets

Finally, let's examine one last class of asset: intangibles. Increasingly we compete in a marketplace of ideas. These ideas manifest not in tangible things like hardware or equipment, but in things you can't hold in your hand, like knowledge, designs, patents, processes, trademarks, domains, copyrights, trade secrets, and even brand. And yes, information.

However, certain intangibles, intellectual property (IP), are recognized as formal assets and property, while others are not. Those most formal which you might find explicitly or rolled-up on a balance sheet include patents, trademarks, and copyrights. Lawyers have long sought to help their clients in protecting IP, but over the past couple of decades an entire industry has cropped up around valuing, licensing, and advising companies on how to manage their IP.

Paul Adams, CEO of Everedge, a New Zealand-based firm that provides such services, told me, "When we talk about IP, most execs are only thinking about valuing and licensing their patents and trademarks. They struggle to realize their larger portfolio of intellectual assets, including their data, is a massive trove of value." Adams's firm focuses on measuring that value to better position its clients for business transactions or risk mitigation, managing the IP to reduce costs and risks, and helping them identify and develop markets for it.

However, Everedge and other IP specialists like Ocean Tomo and a division of Thomson Reuters (which claims to manage more than 20 million IP assets worldwide),[27] keep their methods and models close to the vest. Yes, these processes are *their* IP. Unfortunately however, in the vast majority of organizations, the responsibility for IP is foisted upon the legal staff who typically are not involved in IP planning. As a result, IP tends to be managed in silos rather than as an enterprise portfolio.[28]

Software exists for tracking and valuing and licensing IP, but a comprehensive, standardized approach does not exist. Harvard Law professors William W. Fisher III and Felix Oberholzer-Gee, however, have detailed five IP management techniques for the strategic management of IP, which include:

- Exercising market power by protecting or not disclosing IP as a means to thwart competition and enable differential pricing of your related products or services,
- Selling the IP to generate immediate income from it,
- Licensing the IP to generate an ongoing revenue stream,
- Collaborating with partners or customers, enabling them to leverage the IP for mutual benefit, and
- Donating the IP, which may seem counterintuitive, but placing IP in the public domain can restrict competitors from protecting related IP they may subsequently develop.

But these sound more like ways to *monetize* IP than manage it, don't they? Such is the state of IP management.

A Unified Approach to Information Asset Management

We've taken a protracted journey through the worlds of supply chains and ecosystems, various IT processes and standards, physical, financial, and intangible asset management approaches, and even library science. But not just for fun. These well-honed industry-standard methodologies, capability models, and standards and checklists offer tremendous new precepts for how to manage information, no longer as a byproduct or resource or some ephemeral, nebulous artifact of business, but rather as an actual asset. In the next chapter, I will extract the juicy bits and pull it all together into a manifesto for information asset management.

Notes

1. Part of a body of 40-plus ISO27k standards related to information technology security techniques.
2. ISO 8000, a body of standards dealing with data quality and master data management, has been under development for almost a decade without significant support or adoption.
3. Ironically, ISO/IEC 27001 calls for the responsibility of ascertaining the value of the information with a view to securing it, without providing any guidance on how to perform such a valuation.
4. Other frameworks such as the Control Objectives for Information and Related Technologies (COBIT), The Open Group Architecture Framework (TOGAF), the Committee of Sponsoring Organizations of the Treadway Commission (COSO), and the Business Information Services Library (BiSL) also include some processes related to information.
5. Gartner software asset management analyst, Victoria Barber, indicates that adoption of these standards is low, particularly by software vendors who are key to the standard's success. (ref: email to author 14 December 2016).
6. G.S. Priyadharshini, "ITIL: Key Concepts and Summary," Simplilearn.com, 10 February 2013, www.simplilearn.com/itil-key-concepts-and-summary-article.
7. Another IT service management standard, ISO/IEC 20000, was developed to reflect best practice guidance from within the ITIL.
8. "ISO 15489–1: 2016, Information and Documentation—Records Management—Part 1: Concepts and Principles," iso.org, accessed 09 February 2017, www.iso.org/iso/home/store/catalogue_ics/catalogue_detail_ics.htm?csnumber=62542.
9. Similarly, ISO 30300:2011 defines terms and definitions applicable to the standards on management systems for records (MSR).

10. "ISO 15489–1: 2016(en), Information and Documentation—Records Management—Part 1: Concepts and Principles," iso.org, accessed 09 February 2017, www.iso.org/obp/ui/#iso:std:iso:15489:-1:ed-2:v1:en.
11. "What Is Enterprise Content Management (ECM)?," aiim.org, accessed 09 February 2017, www.aiim.org/What-is-ECM-Enterprise-Content-Management.
12. "Enterprise Content Management (ECM)," Gartner IT Glossary, accessed 09 February 2017, www.gartner.com/it-glossary/enterprise-content-management-ecm/.
13. AIIM, the ECM3 collaborative, Gartner, and others offer maturity models, best practices publications, and other methodological guidance on ECM.
14. "Introduction to Knowledge Management," *MIT Press*, accessed 09 February 2017, https://mitpress.mit.edu/sites/default/files/titles/content/9780262015080_sch_0001.pdf.
15. Note that Knowledge Centered Support (KCS) is a service delivery methodology that focuses on knowledge as a key asset of the organization. It has gained traction in some service desks. Its dynamic model for how to identifies and codify knowledge assets could prove useful in an information asset context.
16. "Schrettinger, Martin," *Deutsche Biographie*, accessed 09 February 2017, www.deutsche-biographie.de/sfz79181.html.
17. Michael Buckland, "Information Schools: A Monk, Library Science, and the Information Age," *Manuscript for Humboldt University Students' Book Project: Bibliothekswissenschaft—quo vadis? = Library Science—Quo vadis?* ed. by Petra Hauke. Munich: K. G. Saur, 2005, pp. 19–32. Revised 12 June 2005, http://people.ischool.berkeley.edu/~buckland/huminfo.pdf.
18. Gabriel Naudé, *Advice on Establishing a Library* (translation of *Advis pour dresser une bibliothèque*) (Berkeley: University of California Press, Westport, CT: Greenwood Press, 1976 reprint).
19. "Current IFLA Standards," IFLA.org, accessed 09 February 2017, www.ifla.org/node/8750.
20. "PAS 55, Publicly Available Specification for the Optimal Management of Physical Assets," assetmanagementstandards.com, accessed 09 February 2017, www.assetmanagementstandards.com/pas-55/.
21. Alan D. Duncan, Douglas Laney, and Guido De Simony, "How Chief Data Officers Can Use an Information Catalog to Maximize Business Value From Information Assets," Gartner, 06 May 2016, www.gartner.com/document/3310017.
22. Ibid.
23. Kristian Steenstrup, email to author, 21 December 2016.
24. Kristian Steenstrup, email to author, 19 December 2016.

25. Capital Investment Executive (Anonymous), interview with author, 23 December 2016.

26. Bill Curtis, Sally A. Miller, and William E. Hefley, "People Capability Maturity Model (P-CMM) Version 2.0," Software Engineering Institute, Carnegie Mellon University, accessed 09 February 2017, http://resources.sei.cmu.edu/library/asset-view.cfm?assetid=5329.

27. "Thompson IP Manager," thompsonipmanagement.com, accessed 09 February 2017, http://ipscience.thomsonreuters.com/product/thomson-ip-manager.

28. William W. Fisher III, and Felix Oberholzer-Gee, "Strategic Management of Intellectual Property: An Integrated Approach," *California Management Review*, Volume 55, No. 4, 2013, pp. 157–183, www.hbs.edu/faculty/Publication%20Files/CMR5504_10_Fisher_III_7bbf941f-fe1b-4069-a609-9c6cd9a8783b.pdf.

CHAPTER 8

Applied Asset Management for Improved Information Maturity

President Woodrow Wilson once said, "I not only use all the brains that I have, but all that I can borrow."

In the last chapter we examined asset management methodologies, processes, guidelines, and maturity models from other domains. Clearly, other asset domains have well-established practices that date back decades—or even centuries—and include concepts that can be borrowed to help organizations manage information with improved rigor and as an actual asset. In chapter 6 we considered how to expand our thinking about information to that of an actual supply chain (or network), and an extended ecosystem with information acting as an "organism." These ideas can be borrowed to advance not just our thinking, but our approach to improved organizational culture around information.

This chapter describes each of Gartner's EIM dimensions (Figure 8.1), along with the typical levels of maturity, common challenges faced by organizations, and the oft-cited remedies to improving maturity. These are based on our recent interactions with hundreds of clients and a series of information management maturity workshops conducted around the globe. Then for each dimension, we will bring together observations and insights from supply chain, ecosystems, and the other asset management disciplines into a supplemental set of ideas and practices to further elevate the concept of enterprise information management to one of *information asset management*.

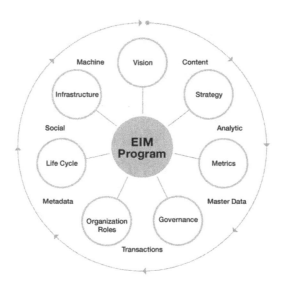

Source: Laney, "Gartner's Enterprise Information Management Maturity Model," Gartner Research
G00289832, March 2, 2016

Figure 8.1 *Gartner Information Management Maturity Model*

Information Vision

A solid information management approach starts with a vision—a vision
for the possibilities of how information can add economic value, or in other
words: be monetized. Vision corresponds to how well business goals that
the EIM initiative must support are defined. EIM should enable people
from across the enterprise to share, manage, and reuse information that
was created in different applications and stored in different databases and
repositories.

But these capabilities do not help the enterprise by themselves. How well
do leaders design their EIM initiative so that sharing and reusing information assets creates business value, and does that value contribute to enterprise
goals? Improving the productivity of individuals, departments, or even a
business unit would not necessarily justify an EIM initiative. An enterprise
goal might be to offer the best service in the market or to become more agile
in adapting to changing business conditions.

The CIO of a major international candy company recently summed up the transformation he's hoping to affect, "I'm trying to get the company, our board and our investors to understand that we're an information company that just happens to make confections." While I wholeheartedly agree, and this is indicative of a solid enterprise vision for information, it's not that easy to enact.

Vision Maturity, Challenges, and Traditional Remedies

The vast majority of information and other leaders place their organizations' information vision as Optimized (Level 2). Rightly or wrongly, they express a variety of reasons why establishing an information vision is so difficult. Most often they cite a lack of experienced resources, competing priorities, and difficulty with untangling legacy systems.

Other reasons mentioned include a lack of cultural acceptance for IM, poor data governance, and leadership throughout the organization being on different pages. It's also difficult to establish an information vision when the organization lacks a well-articulated business vision, or when there's no specific funding for EIM. Finally, some leaders suggest that the abundance of legacy data sources and poor customer and product reference data (i.e., master information) spanning systems also are vision inhibitors.

Typically, the first thing aspiring information leaders do is to establish a steering committee to hash out the objectives for deploying information and goals for information management. The steering committee attempts to align these goals and objectives with organizational priorities in order to help justify the benefits of EIM and secure executive buy-in. Unfortunately, these committees too often lack in business unit representation. Where sufficient leadership is lacking for EIM, often the CIO—but more often lately, the CEO or board—institutes a CDO (or similar) position. This can help to achieve improved cultural acceptance for the importance of EIM, and to help secure sufficient funding. None of these are bad ideas at all, but they may fall short in establishing a true vision of information as an actual enterprise asset. And lacking the means to calculate the value of information itself, even seasoned information executives such as CDOs struggle with quantifying the benefits of information management.

AIG's CDO, Leandro DalleMule, told me that the core of his information vision is an overall philosophy of "data defense and data offense . . . building 'data management in a box' by attacking business cases module by module to create a single source of truth that ultimately pulls data from 3000 systems into one place."[1]

Applied Asset Management for Information Vision

After studying the library science domain, it's clear that information should ascend to a level of importance on par with—or even above—other assets. However, information leaders should promote the principle that information capability is directly related to business process performance and a source of strategic advantage as their colleagues do in human capital management. Information is no longer just a business byproduct or resource. This aligns with the tenet that retained information should have a discernible business context as it does in records management.

The quality of information's value should also be taken into consideration. For example, library science suggests that it's important to note that the potential versus probable value of information must be discriminated and recognized. We can no longer afford to fixate only upon the current value of any information asset. We must be able to visualize its possibilities. Be aware of how others are curating and leveraging information assets. An information asset management (IAM) vision should focus not only upon the organization's own information assets, but also take into consideration how others within and even outside the industry are amassing and deploying them.

Just as with other forms of intellectual property, we must pursue a variety of ways to generate simultaneous value streams from any information asset, not be blinded and limited by a single monetization method. Physical asset management charters are concerned with how to transform assets into business products and services. An information asset vision should include the same dominant principle. Moreover, it should include the ecosystem sustainability tenets of *reusing*, *repurposing*, and *recycling* as approaches for conceiving how to generate more value from information while incurring nominal incremental expense.

For establishing an information culture, existing standards and procedures from knowledge management and human capital can be readily applied. An IAM vision must recognize and support that knowledge-intensive work and business process digitalization shift the focus from the traditional job elements of individuals to information competencies. For example, business professionals of tomorrow who cannot interpret and analyze information beyond high school–level statistics will find themselves of only vocational use, or worse, expendable to their employers. The same with those who cannot creatively curate and deploy information assets.

If we dig deeper into our exploration of likening information environments to living ecosystems, we're awakened to the concepts of climate changes, disturbances, and sustainability, and how to apply them in an information context. Business climates are changing more rapidly than ever. Call it "global business climate change." This affects information ecosystems to the extent that these changes must be anticipated by any information vision. No longer can organizations afford merely to sense and respond to worldwide or industry changes brought about by widespread digitalization, business model disruption, and disintermediation, nor by the resulting orders of magnitude increases in the volume, variety, and velocity of information. In biological ecosystems, the concept of *succession* describes wholesale changes to an ecosystem based on major *disturbances*. To be part of that succession (rather than part of the extinction that often follows), a vision for IAM must either anticipate these disturbances, be flexible enough to handle any disturbances, or recognize your intention to create such disturbances.

Information Strategy

Whereas information vision lays out what you want to accomplish, information strategy deals with the how. It provides the long-term or ongoing plan for realizing this information vision. Information and business leaders cite one or more of three key strategy components their organization lacks: 1) commitment from the enterprise, 2) a roadmap of some sort, and 3) a plan for organizational structures to execute the strategy. Information leadership must lay out an overall approach to managing information in support of current and future planned business initiatives, and in line with anticipated advances in information technology and data growth. *How will information be managed effectively, and by whom?*

Indeed, information strategy covers a lot of territory and it can take a bit of time to cover all the bases. All the more reason to get it right. Recently I reviewed a new information strategy document for a North American airline which read like it was straight out of the late 1980s. Among a host of oversights, it failed to recognize that information is and will be integrated and shared among business partners; overlooked applications and devices as users of information assets; glossed over what kind of metadata would be captured or how; conflated "personal" information with "personally identifiable information"; made no mention of applicable laws or industry regulations; and mentioned nothing about roles, training, certification, monitoring, or enforcement. Worse, the strategy document stated, "After information's original purpose has been served, it must be destroyed." I wonder how anyone is going to get an analytics project authorized!

Strategy Maturity, Challenges, and Traditional Remedies

Like with information vision, more than half of organizations place themselves at a Level 2 (Reactive) maturity. Information and business leaders themselves suggest their top inhibitors to higher levels of information strategy are: 1) siloed thinking about information across lines of business, 2) the lack of a dedicated sponsor, and 3) an immutable corporate culture. They also mention issues with differing business unit opinions about how information should be managed, and being able to define the strategy to secure funding. Less frequently cited, but no less important, are competing IT priorities and the inability to prioritize EIM activities, the fear of IT losing control, and disagreement on approaches by stakeholders.

Unfortunately, many organizations skip vision and jump right to strategy. Trying to determine the how before you've determined the why is never really a good approach. On the other hand, having no objectives ensures you'll never fail to meet them!

As with vision, organizations seek to solicit executive sponsorship and make information strategy a C-suite action item. Doing so can help consolidate various departmental "small s" strategies into an enterprise "big S" strategy, leading to improved prioritization and culture change. But if you're not agile and pragmatic, this can also lead to increased bureaucracy.

Liz Rowe, CDO for the State of New Jersey, told me how she makes the role of business sponsors clear to them: "Whatever I do has to tie with what you guys are doing. My data strategy supports your business strategy. I'm not going to say I have this data strategy without listening to what the business strategy is."[2]

Applied Asset Management for Information Strategy

From the world of knowledge management (KM) we learn how important it is to have repeatable, experience-based methods. The IAM strategy should lay out these methods and indoctrinate the organization on them. However, KM processes also instruct on the importance of being able to adapt to *new and exceptional situations*. As the business climate—and thereby the vision for information—changes, so will the needs of users, applications, partners, suppliers, customers, and (depending upon your industry) regulatory bodies. The ecosystem metaphor reminds us that our IAM strategy must acknowledge the existence of, and plan for the behavior of, information networks formed by the interactions among data sources and other resources such as technologies, applications, individuals, and the business topology. A strategy for the unidirectional, unidimensional flow of information is insufficient.

Moreover, as information sources, technologies, and business models rapidly evolve, organizations must continually evolve their IAM practices and competencies.

Thankfully, library science seems to offer a concise recommendation on where to start with managing information: an IAM strategy should ensure the most important information assets are tended to first. It's too easy and seemingly lazy to treat all enterprise information assets equally. But this too is an inadequate strategy. Under *Metrics* below and in chapter 11, we will begin to surface ideas for how to prioritize information assets. Within an IAM strategy, those methods need to be applied.

Library science also compels us to learn how others are accumulating information assets, while financial management approaches remind us how to identify and assimilate ancillary information sources. The biological ecosystem metaphor explains why. Ecosystems with higher degrees of biodiversity support the production of a greater quantity of goods and services. Similarly, a robust variety of information assets available to the organization breeds improved business production and performance. Still, the study of ecosystems reminds us that there's a balance which IAM strategy must take into consideration: Too much biodiversity (or "infodiversity") can make the system difficult to balance and more susceptible to climate changes. Just as with ecosystem management, information ecosystem management is critical to maintaining an appropriate balance. Three of the "Rs" of sustainability— *Refuse, Reduce,* and *Remove*—suggest strategic approaches to ensure the information ecosystem does not become unnecessarily unruly.

As for delivering information to processes, employees, partners, and customers, IT service management (ITSM) methods and standards express in detail how to define a services approach. Applying this model to an IAM strategy can result in limiting the complexity of the information ecosystem while improving its performance. Rather than designing and developing custom datasets and interfaces for information users, an information services strategy and architecture lays out a defined set of information sources and standards along with ways to access and interact with them. Beyond the scope of this book are the information architecture concepts of data – service

(DAAS), the logical data warehouse (LDW), data lakes, etc. Similarly, services that the information organization provides application developers, IT, and business users can and should be defined along the lines of ITSM and common enterprise content management (ECM) practices and principles. Too often, even in mature information organizations, the services and resources they provide and how to engage them are ill-defined when compared to the discipline of IT service management.

However, the supply chain management (SCM) discipline instructs that it's not possible to pre-plan and predefine all the ways assets are going to be leveraged. Remember, a well-oiled supply chain process has the equal ability to handle *make-to-stock* and *make-to-order* requirements. Even the best data lake or DAAS architecture isn't going to be able to accommodate all information needs. Therefore the IAM strategy must include approaches for creating common information layers *and* handling the intricacies of, and collaboration needed for, bespoke information requirements.

Finally, organizations often have entirely separate, siloed, and disconnected strategies for managing different kinds of data, enterprise content, knowledge, records, and intellectual property—each of which could and should fall under an "information asset" strategy umbrella. James Price, with the information strategy consultancy Experience Matters, recounted for me how one of his Australian clients unwittingly brought several of these domains together:

For the New South Wales Department of Finance and Services, we were engaged to develop a knowledge management framework. We asked them what they were doing for *information* management and they replied that they were building a separate framework. When we showed them what we were doing they decided to have us amalgamate these two initiatives into an "Information and Knowledge Management Framework." We then asked about their unstructured content, and they firmly told us not to touch it. But when we'd completed the framework and started discussing implementation, they were disappointed that the framework hadn't addressed enterprise content too.[3]

Metrics

As we saw with information strategy, many of the challenges lead back to justifying, funding, and prioritizing information management. Rare is the organization which has expressed the benefits and value of information management using measurements and language in business terms rather than just IT terms. Deriving metrics that link the information management goals in alignment with established enterprise goals and metrics is no easy task. *How will EIM, and particularly improvements in IM, manifest in enterprise performance improvements, and when?*

The CFO of an automotive services company confided to me, "Everybody in our business understands we don't manage information assets well. But they don't know what the benefit is by actually managing them a lot better."

And while data usage metrics may be a poor proxy for value, they're certainly a useful indicator. The executive sponsor of a multi-million dollar data warehouse project I led for an Australian insurance company years ago later complained that the data warehouse had not generated any benefits. I asked if people were using the reports that were generating from it. He said he wasn't sure, they had no way to track this. So I suggested putting dummy, ridiculous data into the reports for a couple weeks to see who noticed. No surprise: nobody noticed. Information usage may be a poor proxy for value, but zero usage is an indication of zero realized value.

Metrics Maturity, Challenges, and Traditional Remedies

Most business and information leaders fairly consistently feel their organization's information vision and strategy level of maturity is reactive. Whereas with information-related metrics, we see a fairly balanced split among organizations at the lowest Level 1 of maturity (Aware), Level 2 (Reactive), and Level 3 (Proactive). Interestingly, many of those who have achieved Level 3 seem to have done so without much of a vision or strategy. So one wonders how effective or aligned their metrics actually are.

The top challenges recounted by information and business leaders all relate to or hint at a lack of metrics-related capabilities. They include challenges with: 1) defining effective measurements, 2) developing an understanding of metrics, and 3) lacking quantification know-how. Other challenges frequently mentioned relate to creating metrics at an enterprise level, a lack of clarity on the benefits of EIM, and no organizational focus on measurement at any level. Some leaders also lament not knowing where to start, being mired in short-sighted metrics, being unable to understand the cost of data quality issues, and having difficulty relating information metrics to business processes.

Prior to joining Gartner as an account executive, Brian Ehlers sold enterprise data management solutions. He spoke to me about the lack of interest in metrics about information itself:

There's a vast disconnect between the business and IT sides of the organization. The IT folks are there to protect the data and make sure the data is served up. 99 percent of the time they don't think about the value of the data. More often, they're concerned with the cost of data—but just about the raw cost of owning and managing it, not the value to the business by making it more secure and available, or the cost to the business if it's not. IT execs typically don't look at information with an eye toward business value, just how much it costs per terabyte to store and manage the data.[4]

Defining effective information-related metrics is best achieved by tying actions to metrics. Metrics for information-related programs and activities, and for information itself, require thresholds and triggers, and must be actionable. They should adequately reflect the achievement of strategy milestones and toward the vision. And the data used to generate them should be trusted, complete, and accurate. As we'll consider more in chapter 9, if we're to begin treating information as an asset, there should be metrics defined, captured, and reported about it as well—not just the information management efforts themselves.

One excellent example of this is AIG's analytics environment in which its CDO Leandro DalleMule also spoke with me about how he is incorporating data quality metrics into its data lake so users can determine their own comfort level with information.[5]

Applied Asset Management for Metrics

With EIM, most metrics are for justifying, funding and prioritizing, and gauging the success of initiatives—both those involving the management of information, and business initiatives utilizing information. In addition, metrics typically include those related to data quality.

Traditional supply chain doctrine advises on how to develop a complete financial picture of the information supply chain for any information asset. These factors include: the costs to acquire, administer, and apply an information asset; the fulfillment cycle times; return on assets; and return on working capital. Library science also includes the concepts of measuring an artifact's potential versus probable value. And physical asset management methods suggest measuring the depreciation of inactive information. As well, the entire spectrum of information demand planning and management can be lifted from established supply chain methods.

As we extend the notion of EIM to IAM, many of the measurement concepts from the physical asset domain become relevant. For example, as with the PAS 55 standard, it is not enough to quantify the condition of any asset, but also the costs and benefits of taking corrective action versus performing preventative maintenance, or replacing the asset. While replacing an information asset may be rare indeed, circumstances arise when selecting a new information source becomes a strategy consideration. Human capital management procedures remind us that the quality of any asset can be measured and improved at various levels of granularity.

Unfortunately, most data quality initiatives are undertaken without a financial or business performance analysis of upstream preventative data cleansing versus downstream remediation.

The discussion of supply chain procedures in chapter 8 depicts over a dozen useful information and information management metrics paralleling those from the SCOR model, grouped by: reliability, responsiveness, agility, costs, and efficiency.

Furthermore, physical asset management discipline requires organizations to measure the risk profile of key assets. The security risks alone include hacking, damage, insider theft/disclosure, and accidental disclosure. Assessing these may require a manual audit by security professionals with sufficient expertise. And just as with physical assets, information-borne risks include: the business impact from inaccurate, missing, incomplete, and delayed information; integrity issues between multiple information assets; issues of precision; and information misunderstandings (typically due to a lack of metadata). It may seem cumbersome to assess risk at this level, but with data sampling techniques and data profiling technology, determining most of these metrics on a periodic basis can be straightforward and inexpensive. The trick then is to link these risk metrics to their probable business impact.

Once these probabilities are established they should be applied to the various remediation expenses involved, including:

- Financial data breach penalties,
- Breach notification costs,
- Opportunity cost due to loss of customer revenue,
- Replacement cost of deleted data due to lost customers, malicious or accidental activity,
- Data security remediation tasks,
- Additional data security product purchases,
- Increased cyber insurance premiums, and
- Legal expenses and potential litigation.

and to information risk–related fixed costs such as:

- Dataset acquisition, storage, and processing,
- Audit and compliance processes,

- Data security governance reviews and assessments,
- Data security product purchases, and
- Cyber insurance.

Governance

Decision rights and accountability for acquiring, valuing, creating, storing, using, archiving, and deleting information rarely are specified adequately. Doing so demands a framework of precepts such as the principles, guidelines, policies, processes, standards, roles, and metrics that ensure information will help the enterprise achieve its goals. Moreover, information governance rarely aligns with established enterprise governance components. How will information's management, quality, and use be monitored, measured, and assured to be in line with current and future business needs?

However, no matter how good an organization's policies are, they tend to lack relevance when the business culture from the top down doesn't value information as a business asset, or when that value isn't well articulated. As James Price, managing director of the Australian information strategy firm Experience Matters, told me: "Data governance policies sit and gather dust; that is, until the next time some issue with information leads to something the investment community would consider 'material.'" One data governance expert suggested that some business people would prefer "plausible deniability" over knowing how poor quality the data is they're creating or using.

Sometimes people have challenges with basic information governance concepts. For example, another analytics project for a U.S. financial services company resulted in users complaining that the new reports didn't match the old ones. The project manager then, and now Gartner analyst, Mark Beyer, recounts how, "They insisted we re-introduce the errors from their old application that we'd fixed in the new one! So I had to give them a spontaneous tutorial on the difference between balancing and reconciling."

Then there are situations in which the information governance process is ill-conceived. Too often, including at a major U.S. pharmacy and convenience store chain, over-exuberant new heads of information governance can't wait to start creating policies. There's no better way to turn off business people and struggle at information governance than to skip the collaborative, culture-building part of the process that starts with agreeing on overarching principles and guidelines.

Governance Maturity, Challenges, and Traditional Remedies

Over one-third of organizations self-assess their information governance capabilities at Level 3 (Proactive) or above, with nearly two-thirds still in a reactive or lesser level of maturity. Leaders weighing in on the topic of information governance relate their top three challenges as: 1) moving accountabilities from IT to the business, 2) cultural/organizational buy-in, and 3) an understanding of the role of governance. Other typical hurdles declared include: understanding the role of governance, executive sponsorship or CDO, and the notion that it is seen as extra work that nobody wants to own. Some information leaders suggest that a resistance to standard data definitions are limiting factors. One CDO lamented, "Exceptions are the rule, and legacy data cannot be standardized."

Usual recommendations and efforts surrounding information governance also include the formation of a council, with defined information trustees, stewards, and custodians who develop and rally around a set of draconian policies—policies that are difficult to monitor or enforce. Some organizations have dispensed with the notion of an information owner (for reasons I'll cover in chapter 10), indicating a clear delineation of information responsibilities and privileges. Sometimes incentives are introduced when policy adherence can be measured. And more frequently we see effective prioritization methods, such as Andrew White's "three rings" approach,[6] or those proffered by John Ladley, Robert Seiner, David Plotkin, and others. These enable the organization to focus better on the most important information assets rather than being overwhelmed by trying to govern them all equally (i.e., poorly).

Applied Asset Management for
Improved Governance

Information governance (or "data governance," as it's more commonly called) deals with establishing and enforcing the principles, guidelines, policies, procedures, and standards for information within an organization.

No two organizations have a complementary set of information governance precepts, let alone a consistent process. Still, other than *having* a well-defined process, many of the lessons from other asset management domains are reflected in common approaches to (or at least attempts at) information governance.

Particularly with physical asset management, the prevailing standards detail a serious discipline around maintaining a register for recording the location and condition of key assets. Software for information catalogs, data dictionaries, and metadata management have been maturing for decades. But in my estimation they have not advanced in step with increased business needs and importance. Similarly, the procedures for maintaining them are scant in most organizations—typically a function of small budgets reflecting the low priority given to inventorying information assets. Even leading data governance software companies have yet to introduce detailed procedures and standards, or work to collaboratively develop industry accepted ones.

Physical asset management standards also impart the importance of, and steps for, documenting asset classifications, hierarchies, and relationships, and for tracking their utilization, failures, and maintenance histories.

One such company that has is Dell EMC. Barb Latulippe, its chief data governance officer, shared with me how she is able to tie data quality issues to various short- and long-term economic business impacts: "I can show people 'a day in the life of data,' including where data quality issues manifest and how they affect cash flow."[7]

From library science, information governance should adopt the idea of including commentaries in information asset metadata. Detailed descriptions and explanations of information assets would be invaluable to most users—that is, if they were also accessible whenever and wherever a user needed them.

Finally, the world of financial management offers the concept of a true asset *fiduciary*—an individual with official, legal authority to manage and authorize the use of a particular asset or portfolio of assets. Typical information governance practices involve the assignment of data owners and stewards, but as I argued, the notion of "ownership" carries baggage, and often lacks the formalized, contractual significance of a fiduciary or trustee. Such a role would enable an organization to establish a system of rights and privileges for interacting with any information asset or class of information asset, and to document the economic benefits of these asset interactions.

People

The ability to establish specific roles and organizational constructs is critical to getting anything done in an institutionalized, accountable way, as is needed for information management. Otherwise the IT organization is forced to tackle information management, often as an off-budget, project-by-project initiative lacking business backing or involvement. A solid cross-section of dedicated skills and experience will keep the EIM initiative focused on attaining enterprise goals. *Who will be responsible for and involved in key EIM activities, and how will they be organized and managed?*

"It's not my job," stated the head of business analytics for a major health care provider in reference to data preparation. "I'm in charge of getting data out, not getting data in. And I really don't know who that is, or even if I have a counterpart over there at all." This is a sure sign of an anemic organizational structure and ill-defined information responsibilities. Not only does this individual not know who's responsible for data sources or the data warehouse, but "over there" implies a sorry and inefficient us-versus-them organizational culture.

People-Related Maturity, Challenges, and Traditional Remedies

More information and business leaders believe their organization structure and personnel installment has achieved Level 4 (Managed) maturity than any other of the seven dimensions. Yet over two-thirds still believe that they are reactive or less mature in this regard.

Most often they lament that the larger organization: 1) lacks an understanding of the importance of information management, 2) does not see information-related roles as a worthy investment, and 3) is fearful that growing an information management organization will just lead to personnel layoffs. Often there's a perception that the CIO does not agree with the concept of a CDO for turf reasons, which may coincide with 65 percent of CDOs being requested by the CEO or board of directors, and only 29 percent of CDOs considering the CIO a "trusted ally."[8] This sentiment interferes with information leaders from moving data accountability outside of IT. Other leaders claim they have challenges with determining whether information-related roles should be centralized or whether they should be distributed regionally or divisionally. And funding difficulties are a common undercurrent throughout all of these challenges.

Most organizations seek to boost their maturity in this area by attempting to educate the organization on the importance of information. Unfortunately this may be putting the cart before the horse. Who is making this case effectively if not someone in an executive information role, like a CDO? It usually falls upon the CIO's shoulders. Yet when we see large jumps in organizational maturity, it often involves bifurcating the IT organization, or at least designating a formal information management group within IT. Other advances in organizational maturity involve creating and budgeting new roles for curating and harvesting information, information architecture, data science, content management, metadata management, master data management, full-time information governance, and other newer roles.

Applied Asset Management for People-Related Improvements

The EIM dimension dealing with organization and roles is meant to ensure there are personnel resources and organizational structures for delivering the various capabilities of information enablement.

As we look to the personnel needs for IAM, the knowledge management discipline offers procedures and standards for aligning responsibilities with required capabilities, and for providing the training and certification for key roles. Moreover, it provides guidance on how to capture, codify, and share experience, including the creation of an "expert roster" to help identify and connect with designated resources and accomplished amateurs in various information competencies. KM is also strong in how to collaborate across the organization, providing information leaders and specialists with guidance on engaging others. Although documented KM standards seem to stop short at the four walls of the organization, they're certainly applicable across an extended information ecosystem.

Supply chain management principles emphasize the importance of identifying each of the individuals and organizations up and down the supply chain. Who is affected downstream by changes to the way information is managed, and how is upstream IAM affected by changes in the way information is created, captured, accessed, and used? From the worlds of physical and financial asset management, the well-honed procedures and practices for supplier and partner relationship management should be applied to managing relationships with participants throughout the information ecosystem. Too often these relationships with data brokers, business partners, and information management vendors are handled indelicately or haphazardly.

As we learned in chapter 6, the language of information is important, and a recently emphasized concern yet lagging competency. With the data and analytics discipline now spanning well over twenty-five years, the diversity among professionals who lead, architect, design, and use information-related solutions has never been greater. Diversity related to business-IT heritage, veterans-versus-rookies, data-versus-analytics backgrounds, along with industry vertical diversity, creates an environment of professionals who do not share a common language, thereby creating a deficiency in information literacy.

Whether describing how the array of advanced analytics techniques can be applied to mine vast internal and external datasets, or explaining to data scientists the underlying data infrastructure complexity, or helping translate to the board how information manifests in company use cases, the information discipline is becoming the new language of the digital economy. The "speaking data" as a language is rarely recognized, but it is starting to be embraced as the new language of digital business. The rise of storytelling, customer journey maps, infographics, and visualization techniques signals the demand for an enhanced communications medium to convey the business impact of applying information to the business moments that matter most. The ability to speak this new language is a new organizational readiness factor: information literacy. Borrowing from language learning methods can help an organization on its "information as a second language" (ISL) journey.

Last but certainly not least is the concept of leadership. The human capital management (HCM) discipline emphasizes the importance of, and defines the characteristics of, strong leadership over key assets or resources. Until recently there's been a void in the land of information management. Only lately have we seen the rapid ascent of the chief data officer (CDO) role, and the bifurcation of IT departments into autonomous "I" and "T" groups at companies like PNC Bank in the U.S., Coles Supermarkets in Australia, and the State of New Jersey, among others.

Later in this chapter we'll cover the role of the CDO in some detail. HCM best practices support this notion, suggesting that one executive should be responsible for taking advantage of an asset, and another executive should be responsible for making it available.

Process

This may be the most difficult to define—and therefore most difficult to implement—of the seven EIM dimensions. The lifecycle processes of a unit or set or group of information within a well-defined set of information architecture and flows (conceptual, logical, and physical) supports information governance precepts, information value optimization, and business objectives. Lifecycle processes document and enable the proper flow of information from its creation or capture through to when it is ultimately archived or deleted. It answers the question: how will data movements, availability, and retention/disposal be architected in line with current and future business, application, and user and governance needs?

The challenges of prioritizing information lifecycle processes are summed up by a managing partner at a legal firm, "We're not running an oil rig where someone's going to get killed if we don't follow the manual," and by a government agency's chief knowledge officer, who declared that "It's not going to save someone's life."[9] Yet the effective management of information assets can mean life or death for a company. Or many companies: In 2005–2006, I consulted to one of the major financial rating firms later implicated in the banking crisis. I assessed its financial derivatives surveillance (rating) process for acquiring, integrating, transforming, calculating, and sharing rating-related data. The 100-page report advised on how the defective process should be repaired. As evidenced by the mortgage crisis and subsequent recession, apparently it never was.

Process Maturity, Challenges, and Traditional Remedies

Likely due to varied conceptions about what information processes or lifecycle means, enterprises' maturity self-assessments for this dimension also vary. More people feel they're reactive (Level 2) than at any other level of lifecycle maturity.

Among the most often cited information process concerns are: 1) a "keep data forever because we might need it" mentality, 2) a lack of understanding of the concept of an information lifecycle, and 3) once information is out of sight, it's out of mind. Other challenges include: complications from differing country regulations, information architects lack influence, and that tending to lifecycle issues will impede time to market. Sometimes we hear about a lack of lifecycle ownership, information hoarding, a lack of rules, and the lifecycle procedures being time-consuming as additional roadblocks.

Information processes center on the lifecycle—procedures developed to execute the flow of information based on your information strategy, metrics, and governance. So the primary way to improve lifecycle maturity is to ensure that when developing your strategy, metrics, and governance you also are defining procedures associated with them. Too often, attention to lifecycle is deemed optional and the failure to plan becomes a plan to fail.

The question of risk also comes into play. *What is the risk of copying or storing or deleting certain information assets? Who makes this determination? How are we quantifying this?* With these questions answered, determine how you will operationalize those answers. Ratcheting information process maturity also can commence with simply knowing what information you have, where it is, and how it's used today. And it ends with automating as many lifecycle processes as possible.

Applied Asset Management for Improved Information Processes

As we recall, information management processes perhaps are the most difficult of the EIM dimensions for information leaders to wrap their heads around. In short it's the activities involved with defining an information architecture and the movement of information in support of the EIM strategy, within the constraints of information governance.

Elevating the concept to IAM really requires the introduction of a supply chain management (SCM) approach while acknowledging that information actually flows in manifold and increasingly unpredictable ways throughout an information ecosystem. The main objective of SCM is to specify and enable the activities and resources for moving a product from the point of manufacturing to the point of consumption. In this regard, the SCM metaphor and associated processes are particularly applicable to external information monetization such as creating information products.

Barb Latulippe at Dell EMC mentioned to me how she draws heavily upon her manufacturing background to encourage the management of data as an asset, including maturing it throughout its lifecycle up until its release to users.[10]

Established SCM standards for specifying the creation or capture of information assets, along with their storage, modification, conversion, movement, circulation, retrieval, and destruction, provide one handy framework for laying out an information asset's lifecycle. A common simplified version which may work for some organizations is the set of *source—make—deliver—return* supply chain phases. This may even be an excellent way to organize and manage IAM resources, and support architecting the feedback loops endemic to an ecosystem. Also, to adapt this model better for IAM, consider replacing "return" with "service."

Alternatively, as discussed in chapter 7, one could apply the straight-forward *Acquire—Administer—Apply* framework I offered, including the eighteen information supply chain primitives (i.e., basic actions) for what is done *to* and *with* an information asset. This model may offer more specific information lifecycle steps, but can still draw upon SCM procedures and standards for managing the information lifecycle.

Other novel ideas from the supply chain domain for improved IAM lifecycle enablement include: the ability to simulate what-if scenarios for production, delivery and usage, demand-based inventory replenishment, and ensuring demand volatility can be handled via process flexibility and the ability to render resources dynamically.

Additionally, a couple key concepts from library science provide further information lifecycle guidance:

- Collect information from the most respected sources in the original format whenever possible, and
- Organize information in ways that make it easy to locate and near other related information assets.

Infrastructure

Information infrastructure refers to a range of information-related technologies used throughout the organization. Effective connection and coordination among disparate technologies, including the logical and physical integration of information, are paramount. IT and information management are expected to coordinate on selecting, implementing, and maintaining an integrated set of infrastructure components for enabling EIM. These components must support current and planned information architecture and application needs. *How will information structures and infrastructure technologies be determined and administered, and what are the strategies and procedures for upgrading and replacing them, as and when appropriate?*

As with organizational deficiencies, certain language used may indicate technology deficiencies. "We don't know where data is or how to get it," "I don't know how much I can trust the data," and "My department creates its own extracts because the data warehouse queries take too long," are each the kinds of statements that speak to problems with one's infrastructure.

Infrastructure Maturity, Challenges, and Traditional Remedies

Most information and business leaders, however, contend their level of information infrastructure maturity is at a Level 3 (Proactive), with less than one-third admitting to being in more of a reactive mode or worse.

The top three concerns from organizations about their information infrastructure are: 1) business units demanding their own tools and engaging vendors on their own, 2) IT's poor response time, and 3) an undefined information architecture. They also lament that migrating from legacy systems, having a clear strategy and direction, and tying investments to benefits are significant inhibitors. And to a lesser extent, the other issues include: how to use cloud with legacy systems, supporting both business units and the enterprise, keeping current with technologies, and finding knowledgeable resources.

Traditional approaches to improving information infrastructure maturity often start with better collaboration between IT (or the EIM organization) and business units. As we have seen a growth in "shadow IT" over the past decade, information leaders typically attempt to set in motion a plan to support it or rein it in and consolidate it. Working with business units and IT also to create a reference architecture for information management can also lead to improved maturity. Other parallel approaches may involve growing IT-related skills and/or moving to cloud and software-as-a-service (SaaS) solutions.

But reference architectures and static plans can only help so much. As Brendan Smith, director of business development at GasBuddy, conceded to me, "With the way we are grabbing, aggregating, and consuming more and more data, it has required us to continually change the tools we're using and bring in a lot of folks to handle the technical infrastructure."[11]

Applied Asset Management Principles for Improved Infrastructure

The information infrastructure includes the technologies used throughout the organization to capture, collect, or generate information; to integrate and transform information; and to move or enable the access to information.

Many of the practices, procedures, and standards from other asset management disciplines suggest the need for, or potential benefits of, additional or enhanced technologies. The broad capabilities of enterprise asset management (EAM) software for automating the tracking physical assets, or software asset management (SAM) for software assets, if reconfigured for information assets, would be a boon for IAM.

Other asset management principles merely support and emphasize the objectives of information technology, such as:

- Library science and financial management tenets assert the need for the primary availability of high-demand assets,
- Library science includes copious procedures for ensuring the protection and preservation of artifacts, and
- Enterprise content management standards require storing content in optimal structure, enabling its discoverability, and laying out workflows to enable content creation and editing collaboration.

Fresh Hot Roles for the *Infosavvy* Organization

While reading this chapter, you might have thought, "*Wow, great (or merely good, interesting, or crazy) concepts for managing information as an actual asset, but who is going to incorporate them and lead these efforts?*" Perhaps you already have an inkling that this chapter was crafted as a set of enhanced management concepts for a senior information executive such as a chief data officer (CDO).

As discussed throughout this book, becoming an *infosavvy* organization means you are beginning to manage and deploy information with the same kind of discipline as your traditional assets. Of course this doesn't happen without strong focused leadership or a variety of more tactical roles. Primary among these are the chief data officer (CDO). However, other key roles are have been in place for a while, including those related to data integration, data quality, information architecture, and business intelligence or analytics. And others are starting to become more mainstream involving data science, metadata, and master data management, along with information governance and stewardship, and information strategy.

We're also starting to see the introduction of novel roles which acknowledge information's emergence as a key economic asset, including those for the curation, harvesting, or "wrangling" of data sources, for specialized information technologies, for productizing or otherwise directly monetizing information, and for engineering information into digital business solutions. In addition, there have been sightings out there in the wild of "data journalists," "algorithm librarians," "information attorneys," "digital ethicists," and even "digital prophets," "hackers in residence," and rumors of an ominously titled "lord of dark data" somewhere out there.

The Chief Data Officer: Foresight, Not Fad

The chief data officer role is foresight, not fad. To demonstrate, let's start with looking at the path to the emergence of the chief data officer role itself.

I often speak to individuals including other executives who scoff at the notion of needing another chief somethingorother. Advances in business and management science have always required new kinds of specialist leaders. In the 1940s and 1950s, companies rarely had an executive head of human resources. In the 1960s and 1970s, companies rarely had a chief marketing officer. And in the 1980s and 1990s, few had an executive risk management leader. However, these roles now are common, reflecting the mission-critical importance of these functions and the assets they oversee. Today, a new kind of leader is starting to arise, to take charge of the management and exploitation of the information assets of the firm. However, this is an early stage for the role, and as one might expect, the new role is very roughly formed—giving rise to confusion and false starts.

However, their existence is an important signal that should be heeded. A plethora of new senior titles have emerged that have something to do with managing some aspect of data, and the CDO role is the most logical place for them to converge. They are pioneers of a key future discipline in infonomics.

Today's CIOs may carry the badge "information officer," but they are seldom—if ever—the chief of information in the firm. However, they do exercise authority over the IT systems that are the containers of that information. So they can see—better than almost anyone else—the nature of the information challenges and opportunities.

Indeed, the growing information "asset base" of the firm is also seen by more farsighted CEOs as a great opportunity to be harnessed. Today, nearly two-thirds of instantiated CDO positions are requested by the CEO, CFO, or board of directors, with over half of CDOs given enterprise-wide responsibilities. Yet, over one-quarter of the time, the anointing of a CDO is due to a particular data-related crisis.

Individuals with the CDO title report at various levels of the organization. 38 percent report to the CEO. Most others are still a rung further down the organization chart: 18 percent report to the COO, 11 percent to the CIO, and 6 percent to the CFO. Less often they report to another officer or senior vice president. Those with less positional authority are more often focused on defensive work, such as regulatory compliance or legal support. They also tend to be focused on narrower organizational scope—such as the needs of only one or two departments.[12]

CDOs involved with progressive business strategy and adding new business value tended to be reporting outside of IT and to a higher level. Their span of thinking about the kinds of information to be commanded tends to be wider, and their notion of information as a valuable corporate asset tends to be more complete.

This leads us to the concept of information value and economics. In parts I and II of this book, we covered monetizing and managing information as an asset. Now next in part III let's examine how and why to measure information—its foundational properties like quality, along with its financial value—and ideas about how to fully capitalize on its unique economic properties.

Notes

1.　Leandro DalleMule, interview with author, 09 September 2016.
2.　Liz Rowe, interview with author, 09 September 2016.

3. James Price, email to author, 14 January 2017.
4. Brian Ehlers, interview with author, 10 June 2014.
5. Leandro DalleMule, interview with author, 09 September 2016.
6. Andrew White, and Debra Logan, "Use Gartner's Three Rings of Information Governance to Prioritize and Classify Records," Gartner, 10 January 2017.
7. Barb Latulippe, interview with author, 09 September 2016.
8. Jamie Popkin, Valerie A. Logan, Debra Logan, and Mario Faria, "Survey Analysis: Second Gartner CDO Survey—the State of the Office of the CDO," 13 October 2016.
9. Evans and Price, "Barriers."
10. Barb Latulippe, interview with author, 09 September 2016.
11. Brendan Smith, interview with author 15 May 2015.
12. Popkin et al., "CDO Survey," www.gartner.com/document/3471546.

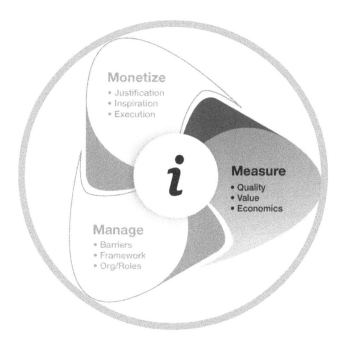

Part III: Measuring Information as an Asset

CHAPTER 9

Is Information an Asset?

At 10 a.m. on Wednesday, July 19, 2000, five distinguished gentlemen filed into the chambers of the U.S. Senate committee on banking, and proceeded to obliterate the tenets of our antiquated accounting system. They included the chairman of the American Institute of Certified Public Accountants (AICPA), a major accounting firm senior partner, a professor of accounting from New York University, and others.[1] Even the name of the hearing didn't soft-pedal what this was all about: the *Hearing on Adapting a 1930's Financial Reporting Model to the 21st Century*.[2] One after another, the experts lambasted the accounting profession for its abject failure to keep up with changes in the global economy. These changes, they argued, had rendered classic accounting practices all but ineffectual at gauging what has become the largest source of value in businesses today: intangible assets.

Steve M. Samek, of Arthur Andersen, lamented that balance sheets and income statements "form the backbone of today's accounting system" but fail to "capture significant sources of value in our economy." He wondered aloud about the actual value of several household-name businesses after pointing out outrageous accounting metrics about them, then questioning, "How much is each of these companies worth? The plain truth is that we cannot readily answer that question because our current measurement and reporting systems . . . do not capture emerging sources of value. The measurements we use don't reflect all the ways that companies create or destroy value in the New Economy."[3]

Samek went on to enumerate the issues this lack of transparency causes, including an inability for business leaders to make informed decisions about the use of resources, an inability of government to track and report on meaningful economic indices, and an inability of the investment community to apply anything more than "guesstimates" (his word) to value companies.

Next, Robert K. Elliott, chairman of the AICPA, stated:

Unfortunately the current accounting model is somewhat out of date. It is very much based on the assumption that profitability depends on physical assets, like plant and machinery; on raw materials, like coal, iron ore, sheet metal, electrical wire, and plastic; in other words, on the tangible inputs needed to produce tangible products. This is the accounting model of the industrial age. But we are no longer in the industrial age.[4]

Elliot suggested that in order for the U.S. to maintain its advantage, it must move to the "next plateau of transparency," as he called it.

Over a decade and a half since this hearing, what has been done to improve transparency or to formally account for information and other intangible assets while the economy has become ever more digital? Not much, according to Tom Linsmeier, retiring board member of Financial Accounting Standards Board (FASB), who said: "[T]he current accounting model fails to provide much information on most internally developed intangible assets, resulting in an often-increasing market to book ratio for these organizations and leaving users with little financial reporting information to make their valuation assessments."[5] Irrespective of what accountants say or do, Linsmeier told me, "Accounting standards boards should be asking for an increased disclosure of internally-generated assets."[6]

Here we are in the midst of the Information Economy, and the eponymous major source of value in that economy is considered valueless by the custodians of what constitutes value!

Throughout the next few chapters, we will explore what constitutes an asset from the perspectives of the accounting profession and the law, and uncloak the increasingly sticky matter of whether information is something that can be owned. Afterward, I will share various methods to help organizations better quantify the value of their information assets, and shed light on how key economic principles break down or need tweaking if they are to be applied to information assets. Finally, I will wrap up with a look at various IT, business, and information-related trends affecting your ability to monetize, manage, and measure information as a true asset.

Awakening to the Information Asset Realization

In interviews with dozens of business executives I conducted at industry events, nearly 80 percent believe that their company's information asset value is represented under goodwill or elsewhere on the balance sheet.[7] Despite meeting all the criteria of an intangible asset, information is absent as an asset class on the balance sheet. Even among enterprises whose core business is the buying and selling of information (e.g., TransUnion, Onvia, HG Data, IMS Health, A.C. Nielsen, and IRI), information assets are nowhere to be found on their balance sheets.

Public companies are required to inventory, quantify, or assess the value of other assets, but not their information assets. Yet, these assets are either their primary source of revenue generation, or increasingly and tangibly contribute to their top line. Even intangible assets, such as copyrights, patents, and trademarks, are recognized and reported. Therefore, the growing disparity between corporate book values and market values is in large part due to the undisclosed value of information assets.

While some executives may claim that information is not possible to quantifiably value, valuation models for other similarly non-depleting balance sheet intangibles are straightforward enough to apply. In chapter 12, we'll show just how to do so.

Information, other than the various ways we represent it, is devoid of physical substance, yet is something we can clearly identify, and a resource owned and controlled by an entity. Recent legal rulings against insurers' denied claims related to data loss or destruction have often confirmed electronic data as a physical property. Information is acquired by recording business transactions or other events, such as communications or processes. As illustrated throughout Part I, information increasingly is wielded as a resource to generate probable future economic benefits, primarily via improved decision making and process performance.

However, people often are tripped up by the common misconception that information only has value when applied—i.e., data has no value when sitting idly in a database. This simply is not so. Just as inventory sitting on a shelf in a warehouse has discernible value, so do idle information assets. This is the difference between realized value and the true definition of an asset, which takes into consideration its probable future economic benefit. All information has a probable future economic benefit. CDOs need to keep this in mind when considering strategies and options for acquiring, administering, and applying information.

Why Does Information's Value Matter?

Throughout our lives and careers, we have been conditioned to talk about the concept of information in either purely technical or strictly contextual terms. Information is something to be created, captured, updated, stored, moved, arranged, integrated, and ultimately accessed, used (or ignored), and retired. The physical nature of information is varied and evolving, first from human gestures millennia ago, then to the spoken and written word in stone and on parchment, and today to magnetic fluxes, radio signals, optical bits, and data streams from billions of IoT devices.

Beyond its technical manifestation and more importantly, information means something. It has context, particularly when applied. Information is a message, an event, or a unit of knowledge. Yet it isn't actually any of those things. Rather, information is merely symbolic of them—a proxy. While the meaning of information ultimately drives business processes and decisions, it is the increasingly efficient, neat, and compact way with which we can technically represent information that allows its nearly unfettered flow and accumulation. Therefore, it is information's meaning, representation, and context that combine to improve business process performance and decision making.

Organizations whose business, information, and IT leaders all recognize this cycle and the growing importance of information, no doubt, are better positioned to take advantage of it. Information should no longer be seen merely as an operations byproduct to be managed, or even as just a business resource to be leveraged, but rather as an enterprise asset to be valued. As seen in the first few chapters, organizations in nearly every industry—including retail, financial services, manufacturing, life sciences, and telecommunications—recognize and realize information's economic benefits, sometimes even above some traditional assets, in its ability to be monetized.

We also discussed that business leaders increasingly recognize that there are things in the business world that financial assets can't buy, physical assets can't perform, and humans can't process. In supply chain and customer relationship domains, for example, most businesses don't want cash from business partners; instead, they desire a cache of information. Businesses that do a better job of compiling, managing, and making available the information assets are more valued as business partners—and more valued by Wall Street.

Until legislation, regulations, and accounting practices catch up, information-based transactions have become a means to avoid taxation and to conceal certain business activity from public disclosure or the prying eyes of competitors. Once the corner store clerk knew his customers' buying habits, families, financial situations, and personal interests. Today, this familiarity must be approximated on a grander scale in a global online information-based marketplace. Information assets and analytics have become the necessary, albeit impersonal, substitute for this personal touch.

Only by considering information as a true enterprise asset are organizations better positioned to manage it and monetize it with the same discipline as traditional assets—leading to vast improvements in the realized value of information.

Real World Evidence of Information's Economic Value

From Pacioli to Digerati

In barely five hundred years, civilization has advanced from Luca Pacioli's elementary form of double-entry accounting still used today to a class of business exclusively capitalizing on information's unique accounting principles. The so-called "digerati" include companies for which information is their primary input and their primary output, or which rely primarily on information as a disruptor to provide new or traditional products or services better, faster, and cheaper than incumbents. For these kinds of companies, information is their currency, their capital, their lifeblood. And because information assets may not be capitalized on balance sheets according to current accounting standards, these companies have a particular advantage over those whose business models rely heavily on traditional assets.

Although it may be commonplace to think of these kinds of companies as unique, unusual, or different, in reality they are merely at one end of a spectrum of information utilization. At the other end of the spectrum are companies just dabbling in analytics—mostly periodic hindsight-oriented reporting—or implementing ERP or CRM systems, or merely running their small businesses on spreadsheets. Further along the spectrum are those that have begun to capitalize on their own information—using data collected from transactions and production to forecast and plan, or even to operate more efficiently in real time. Then there are organizations that incorporate exogenous data from public data sources, data brokers, and/or business partners to better sense and respond to market forces, enhance existing offerings, or develop new ones. But when executives and business leaders start to recognize their organization's information as a direct form of value generation, well, that is when they can really start putting it to work in novel ways and start nipping at the heels of the digerati.

The goal for most businesses when it comes to leveraging information assets shouldn't be to "become" a Google or an Amazon or a Bloomberg, but rather to better monetize the distinct fiscal advantages, flexibility, and performance that information assets offer—a secret that some of these companies' leaders have known for decades or longer.

Investors Prize Infosavvy Companies

"Tobin's q" is a simple ratio posited by Nobel laureate and American economist James Tobin in the 1960s to understand the relationship between a company's market value and the replacement value of its tangible assets. Analysis shows that this quotient has been growing since financial statements were standardized following the Great Depression. "Tobin's q" has more than doubled from 0.4 in 1945 and now regularly eclipses 1.0 in any given year. In fact, this ratio seems to have tripped in favor of market value over tangible assets about the same time data warehousing and business intelligence rose to mainstream popularity in the mid-1990s.

Moreover, a Gartner study found that companies demonstrating *infosavvy* behavior such as hiring CDOs and data scientists and launching enterprise data governance programs, have a q-value nearly 2 times greater than the market average. And little surprise, as they do more with fewer tangible assets, information-based business like those above enjoy a q-value 3 times greater than the market average. In short, investors see something special in *infosavvy* and infoproduct companies.[8]

We can also look at pure-play information companies to get a sense of how financial markets value information assets. When Facebook announced its initial public offering (IPO) in 2012, its S-1 filing with the U.S. Securities and Exchange Commission (SEC) indicated reportable assets of $6.6 billion and predicted a conservative post-IPO market cap of $75 billion. Since the only other non-reportable assets Facebook had, for the most part, were information assets, Facebook had close to $68 billion in information assets.

Or more precisely, its investors expected Facebook to be able to monetize its information assets to the tune of $68 billion. At the time, that meant the information from each user account was worth about $81.[9] Today this figure is well over $200.[10]

No, most organizations do not benefit from a global pool of unpaid content-churning staff and a pure information-based business model. But to remain competitive, they no less must continue to become more information-centric. As emphasized throughout this book, this starts with business leaders and CDOs considering what sources of information are available both internally and externally, envisioning how this information can be monetized in transformative ways, and valuing and managing information as an actual corporate asset.

Indeed, Facebook and the other digerati are extreme cases with extreme numbers to go along with them. Still, these companies are evidence that every leader in every organization must consider the vast amount of data available to their organization, and how if sanitized, packaged, and marketed effectively could introduce an entire new revenue stream—perhaps even self-funding ongoing enterprise data warehouse or nascent Big Data initiatives, as some organizations have done. This is the crux of infonomics.

We know that due to 75-year-old accounting standards, certain intangibles cannot be valued and reported. These unreportable intangibles frequently cited include human capital and intellectual capital. Yet, could these alone have doubled over seven decades? Do corporations of similar revenue have twice the number of employees they once did? Quite the opposite, as we've become more efficient and reliant on technology. Do humans have twice the knowledge capacity than we did back in the day? Even my teenager would fervently disagree with that!

Then what is it that companies have so much more of, that has been accumulating for over half a decade, and that is hidden from balance sheets? Information.

As data formats have evolved from stone to paper to punchcards to tape to disk to and now to flash memory, organizations have amassed evermore information assets (leading up to this era of Big Data) and finding ways to leverage them. Yet the value of information isn't quantified or reported in any way. Even today's infocentric companies whose business models revolve around collecting, buying, and selling data (e.g., Facebook, Google, Experian, Vizient, etc.) have balance sheets devoid of their most valuable asset.

Furthermore, a study by intellectual capital research firm Ocean Tomo shows that the portion of corporate market value attributable to intangibles has grown from 17 percent in 1975 to a whopping 80 percent in 2005, and another seven-point shift to 87 percent in 2015.[11] Information accumulation has not only increased dramatically in businesses, but the importance of information itself has supplanted traditional assets in generating revenue, and therefore in contributing to market value as well.

What are CEOs to do knowing that information comprises a significant and growing chunk of their corporate value? First, forget what the accountants say, and listen to what the market is saying. Stop just talking about information as such an important asset and start treating it like one. Organizations with a chief data officer in place are well on their way to doing so.

What about measuring information's value? It's certainly a best practice we observed in other asset management domains. But many information leaders are hesitant to involve their CFO in measuring the value of their organization's information assets. They think that since information isn't a balance sheet asset, CFOs will dismiss the idea. Remember, the CFO's role includes demonstrating overall corporate wealth and health to the board and investors, and strategic planning based on how to effectively leverage the organization's available capital.

Organizations that treat idle information as anything less than having potential benefit do themselves a disservice. All information has a probable future economic benefit. IT and business leaders need to keep this in mind when considering strategies and options for acquiring, administering, and applying information. This probability varies based on a number of factors, including, but not limited to, its completeness, accuracy, consistency, timeliness, and business process relevance. Like any asset, its *realized* value depends upon the organization's capacity to deploy the information.

Accounting for Information

What is an Asset, Anyway?

When we consider information as the newest class of enterprise asset, we must determine how it stands up to the formal definition of an asset. The common understanding of an asset is that it is merely "something of value." There's more to it than that. While there are differing formal definitions of an asset, we see some key commonalities.

- The Merriam-Webster dictionary defines an asset as: "the entire property of a person, association, corporation, or estate applicable or subject to the payment of debts" or "an item of value owned" among other ancillary definitions related to the military and spy craft.[12]
- Investopedia defines an asset as: "a resource with economic value that an individual, corporation or country owns or controls with the expectation that it will provide future benefit," or "a balance sheet item representing what a firm owns."[13]
- According to FASB, assets are "probable future economic benefits obtained or controlled by a particular entity as a result of past transactions or events."[14]
- Similarly, per the International Accounting Standards Board (IASB) International Financial Reporting Standards (IFRS) framework, an asset is "a resource controlled by the entity as a result of past events and from which future economic benefits are expected to flow to the entity."[15]

However, the lack of mainstream appreciation for the concepts of "future economic benefit" and "control and ownership" has manifested in organizations neglecting to quantify information's future potential.

Moreover, it seems clear that information meets the formal criteria of an intangible asset as defined by accounting standards. The International Accounting Standards (IAS)[16] defines the critical attributes of an intangible asset as:

- Lacking physical substance (and non-monetary),
- Identifiability (capable of being separated and sold, transferred, licensed, rented, or exchanged),
- Control (rights and power to use the asset), and
- Having probable future economic benefit (such as revenue or reduced future costs).

Information clearly meets these criteria, and similar IFRS criteria.[17] [18] [19] Information certainly is salable and generates future economic benefits. There is however the question as to whether information "development expenses" may be determined reliably. We'll deal with that in chapter 11, but suffice it to say that we can do so just as reliably as other kinds of reported intangibles.

Should You Be Reporting the Value of Your Information Assets on Your Balance Sheet?

If information clearly meets the criteria of an accounting asset, why aren't we accounting for it? It's a vexing question that really has not been adequately addressed officially by the accounting profession—other than in one small sweeping statement which appears almost as an afterthought in International Accounting Standard 38 (IAS 38), which after suggesting the criteria for reportable assets (specifically those internally generated) states:

> Internally generated brands, mastheads, publishing titles, customer lists and items similar in substance shall not be recognised as intangible assets.[20]

In this single short sentence, the accounting aristocracy basically says, "Although these valuable things may meet the criteria of an asset, we are not going to allow you to recognize them."[21]

There is one small exception. IFRS Standard 3 requires that customer lists acquired as part of a merger or acquisition, under certain circumstances, are separately recognized rather than lumped into goodwill.[22] Therefore, it would seem there exists some precedence for recognizing information assets after all.

Is Information a Liability?

Occasionally, I come across someone who suggests that information is both an asset and liability. It's clear in these circumstances that they are using those terms casually, not in a true accounting sense. In a casual sense, a liability equates to a risk or something that has negative impacts. There's no doubt information can have dire consequences. Just ask any of the executives at companies whose data has been hacked, especially those in which the data stolen (or more precisely, copied) has been used against them either reputationally or to inhibit business performance outright.

But in a formal accounting and economic sense, a liability is *an asset owed to another entity*. In this case, information fails the definition of a liability. Although information is increasingly liquid, it rarely if ever is something owed to someone else.

One lesson in all of this discussion of assets and liabilities is that we need to be more careful and considerate of how we use these terms. They have different meanings in different contexts, and all too often people using them casually merely confound matters. Language matters. Business people and information professionals alike must learn to be more mindful of the words and phrases they use to discuss information-related concepts, as argued in chapter 6.

When Will the Accountants Catch Up?

In a response to The Great Depression, a committee chartered by the nascent Securities and Exchange Commission (SEC) was tasked with standardizing financial statements. Until that time, both public and private companies could disclose what they wanted, however they wanted. This lack of consistency was blamed in-part for investor confusion leading to the market crash. Part of these new standards included homogenizing the set of recognized asset classes to be reported.

Information was not one of these asset classes. It wasn't until some fifteen years later that the inklings of the Information Age emerged when the accounting firm, Arthur Andersen, computerized the payroll system for a General Electric plant. Only then was the idea hatched that information could be an item separable from its physical manifestation—the paper (e.g., book, magazine, ledger) it was printed upon.

Now, five or six decades since the beginning of the Information Age, the namesake of this age, and the major asset driving today's economy, is still not considered an accounting asset. Somewhat ironically, while information is at the crux of accounting and has been for millennia, even in today's information economy it is not something accounted for itself.

However, there is some movement on the issue. Both FASB and IAS recently have issued discussion papers for open comment, and have met on the topic of how to recognize, value, and report internally generated intangibles. Presumably these include information assets as well.[23] [24] But even after laborious discussions, over 15 years after the accounting gentry were called before the U.S. Senate, don't expect any new significant regulatory changes any time soon. As a stepping stone to GAAP recognition, it seems organizations will be encouraged to include non-GAAP footnotes regarding the valuation of certain intangibles.

One of the key items of contention regards proving the ownership and/or control of certain intangible assets. This is not just an accounting issue—it's one of serious legal and operational concern to many organizations. Who owns the information you generate or collect? And do you actually control it? These are essential questions we'll deal with in the next chapter.

Notes

1. "U.S. Senate Committee on Banking, Housing, and Urban Affairs, Sub-committee on Securities, Hearing on Adapting a 1930's Financial Reporting Model to the 21st Century, Wednesday," Witness List and Prepared Testimony, 19 July 2000, www.banking.senate.gov/00_07hrg/071900/witness.htm.
2. Ironically, it costs $350 to purchase the full transcript of this hearing on the websites of two icons of today's digitalized economy, Google and Amazon, while the Senate.gov site only has limited details.

3. "U.S. Senate Committee on Banking, Housing, and Urban Affairs, Sub-committee on Securities, Hearing on Adapting a 1930's Financial Reporting Model to the 21st Century, Wednesday," Prepared Testimony of Mr. Steve M. Samek, Partner, Arthur Andersen, 19 July 2000, http://banking.senate.gov/00_07hrg/071900/samek.htm.

4. "U.S. Senate Committee on Banking, Housing, and Urban Affairs, Subcommittee on Securities, Hearing on Adapting a 1930's Financial Reporting Model to the 21st Century, Wednesday," Prepared Testimony of Mr. Robert K. Elliott, Chairman, American Institute of Certified Public Accountants, July 19, 2000, www.banking.senate.gov/00_07hrg/071900/elliott.htm.

5. Tom Linsmeier, "FASB, Financial Accounting Standards Board: Tom Linsmeier Looks to the Future as He Leaves the Board," FASB, Q2 2016, www.fasb.org/jsp/FASB/Page/SectionPage&cid=1176168083404.

6. Tom Linsmeier, interview with author, 13 December 2016.

7. Throughout 2011 and 2012.

8. "Maverick* Research: The Birth of Infonomics, the New Economics of Information," Douglas Laney, 03 October 2012, www.gartner.com/doc/2186116. (Analysis updated May 2017.)

9. Doug Laney, "To Facebook You're Worth $80.95," *The Wall Street Journal*, 03 May 2012, accessed 09 February 2017, http://blogs.wsj.com/cio/2012/05/03/to-facebook-youre-worth-80-95/.

10. As of Q3 2016, Facebook's net assets less goodwill was $314 billion. With 1.49 billion active monthly users, the value of each active account is about $211.

11. "Ocean Tomo Releases 2015 Annual Study of Intangible Asset Market Value," Ocean Tomo Insights Blog, 05 March 2015, www.oceantomo.com/blog/2015/03-05-ocean-tomo-2015-intangible-asset-market-value/.

12. "Asset," Merriam-Webster, accessed 09 February 2017, www.merriam-webster.com/ C:\Users\dlaney\Google Drive\InfonomicsBook\Manuscript\Merriam-Webster. http:\www.merriam-webster.com\dictionary\asset.

13. Investopedia Staff, "Asset," Investopedia, 01 April 2016, www.investopedia.com/terms/a/asset.asp.

14. "Statement of Financial Accounting, Concepts No. 6, Elements of Financial Statements, a Replacement of FASB Concepts Statement No. 3 (Incorporating an Amendment of FASB Concepts Statement No. 2)," Financial Accounting Standards Board, December 1985, www.fasb.org/resources/ccurl/792/293/CON6.pdf.

15. "The Conceptual Framework for Financial Reporting," IFRS Foundational Staff, 01 January 2014, www.ifrs.org/IFRSs/Documents/Technical-summaries-2014/Conceptual%20Framework.pdf.

16. "IAS 38—Intangible Assets," IASPlus, Deloitte, www.iasplus.com/en/standards/ias/ias38.
17. Additionally, information meets each of the IFRS criteria for intangible assets.
18. "Technical Summary, IAS 38 Intangible Assets," IFRS, 01 January 2014, www.ifrs.org/IFRSs/Documents/Technical-summaries-2014/IAS%2038.pdf.
19. IFRS criteria for intangible assets include: a) an intention to complete and use or sell it, b) an ability to use or sell it, c) it will generate probable future economic benefits and/or there is a market for it, d) an ability to measure reliably the expenditure attributable to it during its development.
20. "Technical Summary, IAS 38 Intangible Assets," IFRS, 01 January 2014, www.ifrs.org/IFRSs/Documents/Technical-summaries-2014/IAS%2038.pdf.
21. It is generally understood that "similar items in substance" includes information assets.
22. "International Financial Reporting Standard 3, Business Combinations," IFRS, 18 February 2011, http://ec.europa.eu/internal_market/accounting/docs/consolidated/ifrs3_en.pdf.
23. "Discussion Paper, Initial Accounting for Internally Generated Intangible Assets," The Office of the Australian Accounting Standards Board, 2008, www.saica.co.za/Portals/0/Trainees/documents/DPInitialAccountingInternallyGeneratedIntangibleAssets.pdf.
24. "FASB Invitation to Comment, Agenda Consultation: Financial Accounting Standards Board," FASB, 04 August 2016, www.fasb.org/cs/ContentServer?c=FASBContent_C&pagename=FASB%2FFASBContent_C%2FNewsPage&cid=1176168356245.

CHAPTER 10

Who Owns the Information?

In March 2010, U.K. publisher Datateam Business Media (DBM) contracted a third party, Your Response (YR), to manage its database of subscribers. As part of this agreement, YR was given access to the database to perform its management duties. After a year or so, DBM became dissatisfied with YR's services and sought to terminate their contract. A dispute arose when DBM refused to pay the fees it owed YR until YR returned the database which had been moved to its servers. In response to non-payment of fees, YR discontinued providing services prior to the contract termination date yet refused to give DBM access to the database in its control.

This case ultimately found its way to the England and Wales Court of Appeal in 2014. YR had argued that the database should be considered a "physical object" because it "exists in a physical form," and therefore could be held as a lien. YR also argued that it maintained physical control over the database just as if it were a "document," therefore they should be able to claim ownership of it.

The court, however, rejected these arguments, ruling that, "Whilst the physical medium and the rights are treated as property, the information itself has never been," and that rendering a database as physical property would upend property rights law, resulting in "unanticipated consequences in other contexts."

Not every justice agreed. Lord Justice Davis wrote in dissent:

[T]he courts should not leave the common law possessory lien stuck in its eighteenth and nineteenth century origins and development;

rather the courts should go on to give it a twenty-first century application, appropriate to modern times and modern commercial activities. That appeal to modernism has its attractions.[1]

Even as the court ruled information should not be considered property, it also acknowledged such a ruling was based on ignorant notions of information and antiquated property laws, whereas we now live in an electronic world in which information holds legitimate commercial value.

Where does this leave an organization whose executives, business leaders, information leaders, and even legal counsel believe and speak about information ownership, and behave as if it legally owns (not just possesses) information?

This chapter explores the notion of information ownership from several angles:

- What legal precedent exists for claiming ownership of information?
- Do present accounting principles help in answering questions of information ownership?
- What about the casual use of the term "information owners" used within organizations?
- Do we even own personal information about ourselves?
- If we can't own information per se, is there something related to it we can own?

How the Law Weighs In on Ownership

Information ownership is a topic lawmakers have skirted since the invention of the database. Perhaps it could be a simple issue. But when we remember that information can be integrated, moved, stored remotely (even across borders), copied, modified, updated, and deleted without a trace, the issue becomes wildly complex.

The Australian Computer Society's Data Taskforce working paper clearly and concisely articulated the challenge and the solution:

The ability to use, replicate and share data means it cannot be considered in the same way as a physical asset with an "owner." Rather, it is important to think of rights, roles, responsibilities and limitations for those who access data in the various process from collection, use, sharing and storage.[2]

A Brief History of Ownership

The process and mechanisms of ownership, even for tangible assets, are somewhat complex. One can gain, transfer, and lose ownership of property in any number of ways. Laws differ by system (e.g., civil versus common law), differ by property type (e.g., moveable versus immovable, and tangible versus intangible), and differ in the way they interpret and ascribe possession, rights, and responsibilities, and shared ownership, and transfer.

Think about your own home. You may own it. And you may also own the land it sits on. Or do you? In some countries, such as Mozambique, Nigeria, and Cambodia, land ownership is actually a 99-year or less lease—though sometimes only imposed on foreigners.[3] [4] And in countries like the U.S., it is continually contingent upon the future claims of others. This is why landowners in the U.S. purchase title insurance—to financially protect against such claims. And let's not forget that if you have a mortgage, a bank actually shares ownership of "your" home.

The notion of property ownership dates back to biblical times, with the first government statutes appearing in Napoleonic laws to replace a patchwork of feudal laws.[5] And while property law has evolved into big business, such laws have not kept up with the needs and opportunities of the Information Age.

Information Location Matters

Case in point is the case against Microsoft with regard to the jurisdiction of information based on its location. Like most of today's digerati, Microsoft often receives court orders initiated by the U.S. Justice Department for information on its servers. Usually these orders relate to fraud, other federal crimes, or homeland security situations. But one such order gave Microsoft pause. The U.S. court order demanded Microsoft relinquish information in one of its data centers located in Ireland. Naturally, Microsoft believed the data it maintained on foreign soil was ensconced against prying U.S. government eyes, especially U.S. search and seizure laws. This holds true for physical property abroad. At question was the Electronic Communications Privacy Act of 1986, which allows law enforcement agents to obtain information from internet service providers (ISPs) through subpoenas, court orders, or warrants. But in 2014, U.S. District Judge Loretta Preska and U.S. Magistrate Judge James C. Francis IV ruled against Microsoft. According to Justice Preska:

Congress intended in this statute for ISPs to produce information under their control, albeit stored abroad, to law enforcement in the United States. As Judge Francis found, it is a question of control, not a question of the location of that information.[6]

Microsoft's attorney, E. Joshua Rosenkranz, argued that the government was seeking to "conscript Microsoft here in the United States to search files abroad." He suggested that if other countries required Microsoft to provide them with emails of customers located in the U.S., "we would consider that an astounding infringement of our sovereignty." Ironically, that happened the same week as Rosenkranz's argument when officials in China had demanded a password for a Chinese citizen to retrieve emails for a resident stored on servers in the U.S.[7] [8]

This ruling may serve to spook the cloud storage businesses and unnerve the IT and executive leadership of any multinational businesses. Whereas previously we may have believed that the physical location of the servers upon which information sits is a key ingredient in questions of jurisdiction and propriety, apparently neither the U.S. government nor the U.S. justice system concur. Therefore, IT and business leaders are well advised to limit their assumptions with regard to the locality of information.

As for executives becoming unnerved by this issue, Microsoft ultimately took the bold step of having local companies own the hardware and data centers upon which Microsoft data sits. In Germany, for example, the telecom giant Deutsche Telekom now hosts Microsoft's data. This not only keeps the U.S. government's prying eyes away from the data, but also helps Microsoft maintain compliance with strict German data privacy laws.[9]

But what happens when the hardware upon which the information sits is seized? In early 2012, the servers of the then-popular file sharing service, Megaupload, were seized by the U.S. government. Although much of the files are known to be pirated music, films, software, and other content, various businesses used the service for legitimate purposes. Still, the U.S. authorities neglected to sort out how information would be returned or made available to its rightful owners. This presupposes that authorities believe the information is owned or that anyone has any rights to it.[10] [11]

Certainly cloud data storage has its advantages, but the Megaupload situation is a cautionary tale for information and business leaders or CIOs who may be considering storing their information anywhere outside the four walls of their organization.

Infothievery

Sometimes the courts do come through on the behalf of plaintiffs in matters of information propriety.

In 2011, a U.K. court ruled on a case in which Beechwood House Publishing licensed part of its database to Bespoke Data Organisation. The database included a curated set of forty-three thousand doctors and nurses. Bespoke was contractually allowed to use the records once then delete them. However, Bespoke copied the records to its own database. Then two other companies, Guardian Products and Precision Direct Marketing, licensed Bespoke's database and loaded it into their own systems. At this point, over eight thousand of the records were identical or updates to those the Beechwood had originally licensed to Bespoke.

A year later, these second two companies sent mailings to some of the customers in this database. Unbeknownst to them, Beechwood had included "seeds" in its original database. Seeds are contacts in the list with dummy or misspelled names, or other indicators such as fictitious suite numbers. These people, usually employees or employees' spouses of the list-owner's business, keep an eye out for mailings they receive from unauthorized list users. Some of these seeds had received such mailings and reported them to Beechwood.

The court agreed on the unauthorized database use, but then had to rule on the question of whether there was an infringement of rights based on the extraction or reuse of a "substantial part" of that database, per the *U.K.'s Copyright and Rights in Databases Regulations 1997 SI 1997/3032*.[12] Moreover, a judgment against the defendant in such cases also requires that the database in question involved significant human investment to create. In the court's estimation, an unauthorized use of 6,000 intact records and 4,783 modified records comprising 14 percent and 11 percent, respectively, of the total database size did in fact constitute a substantial unauthorized use. And the court further calculated that the database required over £100,000 per year to create.[13] [14]

This case illustrates the peculiar limitations on information rights with respect to the amount of information misused and the cost of the information in question. Even if someone uses part of your data without authorization, it may not warrant legal repercussions.

A Habeas Corpus of Rulings on Information Ownership

To date, there have been several judicial opinions both for and against property rights of information. Juxtaposed, they paint a bleak picture of information-related property law, and serve as a warning to any organization that thinks or behaves as if its information is really an asset on legal par with any of their other true assets.

Some courts have ruled that the loss of computer data was "physical damage" or "capable of sustaining a physical loss" due to "the change in the alignment of the magnetic particles on the hard disk," while other courts have ruled that the loss of a database was a "direct physical loss," that the loss of information was a "commercial loss [of] inadequate value," and that loss of data alone was not "physical damage to tangible property." In one case, a court dismissed a case likening electronic data to other forms of recognized intangible property, and was overruled by an appellate court that merely acknowledged "a document stored on a computer drive has the same value as a paper document kept in a file cabinet."

See appendix B for a list of landmark legal rulings related to the question of information property rights.

The lesson, at least until sufficient and consistent laws are formulated, is to assume that information is *not* legal property and you cannot confidently own it. Therefore, your focus should be squarely on the rights of those to whom you entrust and avail information within your control.

How Accountants Account for Information

Since laws are lacking and courts around the world are confounded by the concept of information as *property*, perhaps we should attempt to determine whether information is, could be, or should be considered a formal *asset*. The accounting definition seems to provide more guidance around the potentiality of information as something which could be considered owned, because it is more precise than an array of random rulings by men and women in robes.

Dictionary definitions range from an asset being a positive characteristic or benefit or advantage, to something of value or piece of property. And "asset" is a synonym for a variety of other words. But as discussed earlier, the accounting definition of an asset is more precise, comprising three conditions or characteristics to designate an asset:

1. Something owned and controlled by an entity,
2. Something exchangeable for cash, and
3. Something that generates probable future economic benefits which flow to that entity.

The Control of Information

Previously we covered questions about information ownership, which according to courts around the world may yet be resolved. However, the asset definition specifies that an asset must be controlled by some entity. Accountants assert that control is easier to establish than is ownership, particularly for intangible assets—so when control alone can be ascertained for something, it is most often afforded asset status.

Control must be asserted or demonstrable via past events such as the asset's purchase or self-creation. Again, there's no arguing that all information is either collected via past events or generated by entities themselves. I would further argue that since information can be copied and shared easily, rendering it indistinguishable from the original, control must be asserted also by maintaining its proprietary nature within and among the entity, its agents, or its licensees. Conversely, if you are publicly and freely sharing your data outside your organization with no contractual protection or means of enforcement, then you have lost control of it. You may retain rights to it, but its external use is beyond your control. Therefore, you cannot legitimately claim ownership of it any longer. As well, information that only you retain may not be within your control if others have rights to it—as is the case with some PII.

To further establish the control aspect of an asset, accounting standards require the condition that it is *identifiable*. This applies specifically to intangible assets wherein there is some question of *separability*—meaning that they are not inexorably bound to another asset or unable to be quantified.

International Accounting Standard 38 (IAS 38) details the requirements for identifying and capitalizing intangible assets. It defines intangible assets as "non-monetary assets which are without physical substance." The standard further specifies that recognizable intangibles must be "identifiable (either being separable or arising from contractual or other legal rights)." This opens up another can of questions. Is information separable? And does (or can) information have contractual or legal rights?

As for separability, many IT people feel or behave as if information is bound to technology (e.g., "the DB2 point-of-sale data"). And similarly, business people often speak about information being bound to an application or system (e.g., "the Salesforce.com customer data"). This only is due to years and decades of information being tightly and unfortunately coupled with technical or process components as a result of: 1) a lack of architectural foresight, 2) the need for expediency, and 3) a propensity for developing systems on the cheap.

Today, information generated by one function is leveraged regularly in a multitude of ways. In effect it is becoming unbound. It may take another generation of IT and business people to see and talk more comfortably about information as its own separate entity.

From a data management standpoint, most types of information are easily separable, even if they are co-located in the same database or content store. For instance, you can separate customer data from transaction data and your vendor contract documents from your employee performance assessments.

Cashing In on Information

The second key condition of an asset is that it is exchangeable for cash. There's no doubt that information is exchangeable for cash (or other goods and services). The hundreds or thousands of data brokers like Bloomberg, Dun & Bradstreet, Acxiom, Equifax, J.D. Power, and others are testament to this obvious fact. And more than 20 percent of organizations claim they're bartering with, trading, or licensing information with partners.

Although information is rarely *sold* outright, including an actual transfer of ownership, there are few restrictions against doing so. Most often the transfer of information asset ownership happens as part of corporate transactions such as divestitures, mergers, or acquisitions.

Probable Economic Value

The asset criterion of generating *probable future economic value* is an interesting one. For those who studied accounting before the late 1980s, the word "probable" wasn't a consideration. Accounting practices changed to allow for capitalizing dormant assets for which one has an intention of and capability for generating economic value. Again, there's no arguing against the fact that information can and does generate actual (and probable) economic value for the entity that controls it. Just as an automobile sitting on the lot of a dealership, or a can of soup on a store shelf, or a patent for which a new product is under planning or development has probable future economic value for the organization that currently owns and/or controls it. So can dormant information assets.

Owning the Usage of Information

This question of information "ownership" proves to be a bit unsettled. There's a catch-22: If information isn't considered property according to a lack of legal consensus, how can it be owned? And if you can't own information according to accounting standards, how can it be considered an asset? Chicken, meet egg.

As we have seen, for the most part information cannot be protected like other forms of intellectual property, but *how* information is created or used can be considered property in the eyes of the law.[15] Specific use contracts among two parties, such as social media site user agreements, can offer some protection, but a particular collection of data rarely can receive the kind of blanket protection copyrights or patents afford. While most information assets cannot be protected as intellectual property, the way you *use* information can be legally protected.

The business method patent offers a vehicle for defining and securing the ownership rights to almost any unique and useful process you develop. This includes algorithms. Algorithms are used to create information and make use of information. But are organizations actually taking advantage of this kind of legal safeguard? Absolutely!

Patent applications for algorithms have grown 30x over the past fifteen years. Nearly 17,000 patents applied for in 2015 mention "algorithm" in the title or description, versus 570 in 2000. They jumped from 2,400 applications in 2011 to 8,000 in 2012, and to 12,000 in 2013. Including those mentioning "algorithm" anywhere in the document, there were over 100,000 applications in 2015 versus 28,000 five years ago.[16] [17] At this post-recession pace, plus considering the increasing interest in protecting algorithmic intellectual property (IP), by 2020 there could be nearly half a billion patent applications mentioning "algorithm" and over 25,000 patent applications specifically for algorithms.[18]

Perhaps consternation over being able to legally protect and formally account for information should be redirected into efforts to obtain patents for the algorithms you develop that rely on your proprietary information assets.

It's not that simple, cautions Nolan Miller, professor of finance at the University of Illinois. He suggested that patenting algorithms may not provide the level of real-world protection one assumes they might:

> The more you use them, the harder it may be for them to be a source of competitive advantage. If your information helps you target customers in a better way, you can bet your competitors will be watching who you are targeting. They don't necessarily need your data or your algorithms. Although the algorithm takes raw data and turns into something valuable for business, once people see you acting on information, maybe they don't need the algorithm, they just need to imitate you.[19]

Miller also suggests there is a set of interesting questions around the option value of using an algorithm, not using it, or using it sparingly when you know or suspect competitors are watching. Similarly, Andrew Ng, a Stanford professor, co-founder of Coursera and now chief scientist at Baidu, reportedly has said: "No one can replicate your data. It's the defensible barrier, [but] not algorithms."[20]

Personal Ownership of Your Personal Information

Personally, most of us are concerned about owning or at least controlling information about ourselves—particularly our financial information, and also our emails, telephone records, and anything that could be used to steal our identity. It's important to note that like information, one's identity cannot be "stolen," per se. Rather it can be electronically copied and used to steal other things. The distinction is subtle but important no less. It manifests in a fixation and improper focus in stymying access to our information, instead of us being mindful and disciplined about establishing rights and responsibilities for others who we want or need to have access to our personal information. Either way—clamping down on our personal information or taking the time and effort to define in all the apps we use who gets which of our data, how much and when—tends to lead to security and privacy fatigue.

In most cases the fine print in software, website, and online business user agreements obtusely specifies that you retain "ownership" of whatever you post, but the company behind the agreement (or notice) retains unlimited, perpetual, and transferable rights to it. And in some cases, as with Uber, its U.S. user agreement indicates it can even *modify* your information before doing whatever they want with it.[21] This is the main reason behind Facebook's $19 billion acquisition of WhatsApp: unfettered access and ability to monetize the content of thirty billion messages and seven hundred million images *each day.* Not necessarily to gain customers. Customers don't meet the criteria of a monetizable asset; information does. Remember, customers, like employees, cannot be owned or completely controlled.

Information ownership can be a legally moot concept. As part of these agreements, such language is merely an attempt at pacifying prose. Given the aforementioned lack of consensus and maturity in information property law, I'd rather have unlimited, perpetual, survivable, and transferable rights to some information than to "own" it. Still, we're usually happy to agree to these terms in return for being able to use the app, participate in some community, or shop online. It's the price we pay. We're exchanging information about ourselves in return for some free or discounted online service.

This confounding matter of ownership applies to genetic matter as well. We like to think that it's "our" health care record, but it actually belongs to those who collect and maintain the data. For example, in the U.K., a court ruled in favor of the National Health Service, allowing it to use data it collects from individuals during medical exams for alternative purposes. Similarly a U.S. district court ruled that individuals did not own the biological samples (and therefore the genetic information within them) that they had willingly provided to a researcher.[22]

Then there's the matter of one's metadata. Recently, an Australian federal court refused to hear a case in which Telstra claimed account usage data was not data *about* a customer, and therefore believed it was not required to relinquish it to the customer. Telstra claimed such information was "not information about an individual whose identity can reasonably be ascertained from the information in isolation," even if the owner is inextricably linked to the account. Therefore, the Australian Privacy Commissioner's ruling requiring Telstra to release the information stands, for now.[23]

In short, organizations seem cavalier about claiming legal ownership (or at least control) of information they collect from others, whereas the rights of individuals to control information about themselves is still in limbo where industry regulations fail to plug legal lapses.[24]

Internal Ownership of Information by Departments or Individuals

We have already explored the notion of information ownership across organizational borders, but now let's look inwardly. In almost any book or paper on information management or data governance, you will read about defining "data owners" as a key component of any information strategy. Generally these are business people who are responsible and accountable for the definition and policies for one or more types of information, e.g., customer records, transaction data, manufacturing process documentation, maintenance data, etc. However, as indicated throughout part II, the idea of internal data ownership manifests in a variety problems, including:

- Information politics—Information ownership creates a culture of contentiousness and propriety with regard to creating, defining, and using information. It puts some on the inside and others on the outside.

- Lack of shared responsibility—Information ownership implies that one individual or group is solely in charge of, accountable, or liable for the information.
- Reduced data quality and governance—Information ownership discourages others from participating in governing information or helping to enhance its quality and value.
- Lack of information sharing—Information ownership tends to reduce how readily information is shared with others throughout the organization.
- Lack of information availability—Information ownership results in architectures that restrict the flow of information throughout the organization.
- Increased expense—Information ownership often forces departments to source the same information another department does, duplicating the time, effort, and costs to do so.
- Limited information value generation—All of the above consequences of information ownership limit how readily information is put to work for the organization.

Barb Latulippe, the chief data officer at Dell EMC, agrees. When I spoke with her recently, she said:

Ownership? I don't like the term. We're trying to not use it anymore. It just encourages politics and information silos. Our policy states that data is a shared asset and the property of the company, not individual business units or people. It's a policy signed by C-level executives.

Latulippe said she prefers the term "data trustee." It may not have the authoritative connotation "data owner" does, but in the context of a fiduciary, as discussed in chapter 8, it carries both legal and ethical weight.[25]

Similarly, in his book, *Data Driven Leaders Always Win*, Jay Zaidi asserts that "The question of data ownership is critical to governing data since it deals directly with accountability."[26] But Zaidi follows up this point by acknowledging reality. He writes that asking the question "Who owns data?" throughout your firm elicits many interesting answers, including: data producers, data consumers, business units, the owner of the system on which the data resides, the first system that receives the data and processes, the owner of the data warehouse, and so forth. Zaidi makes the poignant observation that, "None of these answers is correct on an individual basis. Data is neither owned by a single business area nor an individual system owner, but is an enterprise asset that is owned by the corporation."[27]

Ultimately, the idea of an "information owner" is difficult or impossible to ascribe, and more important, sets the wrong tone about information as something other than an *enterprise* asset. Even renowned data quality consultant and author Tom Redman, avoids the term "data owner" throughout his several instructive books on data quality. He exclaimed to me recently, "It's one of the scourges of the Earth. It implies I have something that I don't have to give you. And if I do decide to give it to you, you have to pay for it. Inside any organization, that is unconscionable."[28]

That said, the idea of a "data trustee," as Latulippe, Zaidi, and others suggest, establishes information as a shared resource with shared responsibility. Moreover, it acknowledges that the same information can exist in multiple places at the same time (or is *non-rivalrous* in economic-speak). Along the lines of our earlier foray into supply chains and physical asset management procedures, Redman prefers guiding his clients to think more about information consumers and information producers within the organization, and how they can better communicate and collaborate with one another.

Sometimes, it's not that simple. Take McDonald's, for instance. Gokula Mishra, McDonald's senior director of global data & analytics and supply chain, shared with me how McDonald's pan-geographic franchise model can make it difficult to get access to some data. He referred to this as a data sovereignty challenge in which getting corporate access to customer, supplier and employee information in various parts of the world requires an approval process and adherence to various data protection regulations. For example, he said: "From some of our markets in Europe, data regulations dictate how a subject's personal information can be collected, used, shared, and transferred across borders. As such, certain steps need to be taken for a European market's data to be transferred to McDonald's Corporation in the U.S."[29]

Information sovereignty conundrums exist within tighter organizations, as well. Many U.S. states have legislated open data mandates, requiring agencies and departments to make data available among one another, and externally for citizens and businesses.

According to Liz Rowe, the State of New Jersey's CDO, even following the law can be confounding: "The mindset among agencies is that 'This is my data and I don't have to share with you.'" Relating a meeting she was in with two different agencies, she said conflicting regulations don't help at all:

> One agency quotes a federal regulation that 'I must get this data from you.' The other agency quotes another federal regulation stating, 'I cannot share this with you.' So we have these dueling regulations that are confusing and inconsistent with each other.

Rowe shared that it sometimes takes many months and many lawyers to sort out if and how to share information among agencies, and how this hampers the state's efficiency and abilities. One of her goals is to help everyone understand and start behaving as if they and their information are all part of the same organization.[30]

The challenges of sharing information across internal and external borders within an organization also puts an interesting twist on ownership for one automaker whose head of information innovation admitted to me, "Due to regulatory restrictions and the challenges of requesting data from another part of the organization, it's sometimes easier and cheaper for me to buy from a data broker or elsewhere, even if we already have it."

Loaded semantics aside, the definition of an information owner as someone who is responsible and accountable for the definition and policies related to a particular information asset makes sense—just as the earlier Generally

Accepted Information Principles in chapter 5 state. It is the "owner" moniker itself which causes problems.

You and Your Information Are on Your "Own"

Ultimately, attempts to define and execute on the concept of information ownership, either outside the organization or inside the organization, simply may be fruitless. Even worse, they may be a meaningless impediment to what is really important.

Inside the organization, information should be considered an enterprise asset. Information generates more value and reduces costs for the organization when there's a culture of sharing and internal information availability is maximized. Therefore, instead of a fixation on ownership, focus on information stewardship, responsibilities, accountability, governance, definitions, and advocacy.

Outside the organization there is little precedent, exist few laws, and there is questionable support from the courts, accounting standards bodies, or insurance companies on recognizing information as legitimate property or a formal asset. So instead of blindly assuming you or someone in your organization owns your information, focus on specifying the contractual rights and responsibilities for anyone from whom you collect information or with whom you expose information: *Who has the ability to create, read, modify, copy, share, or delete which data, how, and when? What are the penalties for a breach of contract? Is the contract transferable or assumable? How is it to be enforced?*

Perhaps the idea of information ownership should be supplanted with an unusual idea from New Zealand, and in line with the metaphor in chapter 6 of information as an "organism." The Kiwi government has taken an outlandish approach to land ownership. A statute passed in 2014 transformed the Te Urewera National Park into a unique entity which nobody owns, but with "all the rights, powers, duties, and liabilities of a legal person." Now, more than 200,000 hectares of remote wilderness on New Zealand's North

Island is able to go to court. With help from any concerned citizen, particularly designated *trustees* from the land's traditional settlers, the Tūhoe tribe, Te Urewera can defend itself from misuse by corporations or individuals.[31] What if information itself could be imbued with certain rights, and the means to be legally protected? Perhaps someday.

For the time being, let's turn our attention to ascribing a measurable value to information. All assets are measured. As illustrated in chapter 7, most physical assets are tracked at points along their supply chain. The flow of money is meticulously recorded. And even non-assets like employees are assessed. So why not information? Whether it's an acknowledged asset or not, it makes perfect sense that information's quality should be measured to ensure its functional utility, and that its financial value should be measured to ensure its economic benefits. In the next chapter, we will review recently developed methods for generating these metrics, and examples of how they are already being implemented by organizations today.

Notes

1. "Your Response Limited v. Datateam Business Media Ltd," England and Wales Court of Appeal (Civil Division) Decisions, 13 February 2014, www.bailii.org/ew/cases/EWCA/Civ/2014/281.html.
2. "Data Taskforce—Working Document—DRAFT v2," Australian Computer Society Inc. (ACT), Data Taskforce, Working Document, Version 2.1, 06 December 2016.
3. "Foreigners Buying and Leasing Property in Southeast Asia: Thailand, Cambodia, Vietnam, Laos," Runckel & Associates, Inc., www.business-in-asia.com/news/land_in_southeast_asia.html.
4. www.trans-africa-invest.com/eng/index.php?fldr=media&link=realestate-7.
5. Robert B. Holtman, *The Napoleonic Revolution* (Baton Rouge: Louisiana State University Press, 1981).
6. Gareth Halfacree, "Microsoft Loses Overseas Data Privacy Case," Bit-tech, 01 August 2014, www.bit-tech.net/news/bits/2014/08/01/microsoft-privacy-lost/1.
7. "Microsoft Fails to Block U.S. Warrant for Ireland E-Mail," Bloomberg.com, 31 July 2014, www.bloomberg.com/news/articles/2014-07-31/microsoft-fails-to-block-u-s-warrant-for-ireland-e-mail.

8. If you still think information ownership is a straightforward matter, start by trying to unpack the 20-page U.S. Court of Appeals ruling in this case, In the Matter of a Warrant to Search a Certain E-Mail Account Controlled and Maintained by Microsoft Corporation.

9. "Microsoft to Store Data in Germany to Keep It from Third Parties," CNN Money, 11 November 2015, http://money.cnn.com/2015/11/11/technology/microsoft-germany-data-center-privacy/index.html.

10. "U.S. Govt: Megaupload Users Should Sue Megaupload," TorrentFreak, 11 June 2012, https://torrentfreak.com/u-s-govt-megaupload-users-should-sue-megaupload-120611/.

11. "Fumbling Feds Lose Control of Seized MegaUpload Domains—to Saucy Vid Slingers," The Register, 29 May 2015, www.theregister.co.uk/2015/05/29/megaupload_malware/.

12. "Beechwood House v. Guardian Products Ltd. and Precision Direct Marketing Ltd," England and Wales Patents County Court, 20 June 2011, www.bailii.org/ew/cases/EWPCC/2011/22.html.

13. "Patents County Court Rules on Infringement in Database Right Case," Practical Law, 20 June 2011, http://uk.practicallaw.com/1-507-1888?q=&qp=&qo=&qe=.

14. "Landmark Ruling for Database Owners in Relation to 'Seeding' and 'Substantial Part'," DLA Piper, 16 August 2011, www.remarksblog.com/2011/08/landmark-ruling-for-database-owners-in-relation-to-seeding-and-substantial-part/.

15. As Graham Mullier, head of data science services with Syngenta, pointed out to me at a recent Gartner event: data schemas or models can be legally protected as well.

16. "Data from AULIVE, an Aggregator of Worldwide Patent Application Information," November 2016, www.aulive.com.

17. Thirty-three of the top 40 organizations patenting algorithms the past five years are Chinese companies and universities. Only one western company even cracks the top 10: IBM, in tenth.

18. For a more complete analysis of this data on patent algorithms, see: "Algorithm Patents Increased 30x The Past Fifteen Years," Doug Laney, Gartner Blog Network, 24 October 2016, http://blogs.gartner.com/doug-laney/patents-for-algorithms-have-increased-30x-the-past-fifteen-years/.

19. Nolan Miller, interview with author, 09 September 2016.

20. Roberto V. Zicari, "Trends and Information on Big Data, New Data Management Technologies, Data Science and Innovation," ODBMS Industry Watch, 26 January 2017, www.odbms.org/blog/.

21. "Uber U.S. Terms of Use, Effective: November 21, 2016," Uber, www.uber.com/legal/terms/us/.

22. Stephen W. Bernstein et al., "Ownership of Biological Samples and Clinical Data II: U.S. Supreme Court Denies Certiorari in the Catalona Decision," McDermott Will & Emery, 21 February 2008, www.mwe.com/en/thought-leadership/publications/2008/02/ownership-of-biological-samples-and-clinical-dat__.

23. Campbell Simpson, "Your Metadata Isn't Private Personal Information, Federal Court Decides," Gizmodo, 19 January 2017, www.gizmodo.com.au/2017/01/your-metadata-isnt-private-personal-information-federal-court-decides/.

24. The General Data Protection Regulations (GDPR), implemented 2018, will require organizations doing business in the European Union (EU) to provide individuals access to their data, the ability to rectify issues with it, the right to be "forgotten," and the rights to notification, data portability, and limitations on its usage. As a result, placing the control of personal data back into the hands of individuals may cause it to fail one of the prerequisites for valuing it as a corporate asset.

25. Barb Latullipe, interview with author, 18 July 2016.

26. Jay Zaidi, *Data-Driven Leaders Always Win*, p. 131.

27. Ibid., p. 146.

28. Tom Redman, interview with author, 24 October 2016.

29. Gokula Mishna, interview with author, 15 August 2016.

30. Liz Rowe, interview with author, 19 July 2016.

31. https://newmatilda.com/2016/09/08/new-zealand-land-can-person-meanwhile-australia/.

CHAPTER 11

Quantifying and Accounting
for Information Assets

In addition to the tragic loss of life and property on 9/11, there was another type of loss: the loss of corporate information assets.

The terrorist attacks of 2001 happened before off-site backups or cloud-based data storage had become mainstream. In the weeks and months following 9/11, we heard from clients with businesses in the Twin Towers who had lost their data and were struggling to recreate it and somehow remain solvent.[1] Also, just as any organization suffering a loss of property, some of these companies had filed claims with their insurers for the value of the information assets they lost. Although commercial general liability (CGL) policies at the time were not explicit, insurers roundly denied these claims, arguing that information was not considered property (just as some courts discussed in the previous chapter have ruled).

The insurance industry realized it was exposed to claims for the loss or damage of information, and potential legal action after such claims were denied. Adding insult to injury, the U.S. insurance industry updated its CGL policy template to explicitly *exclude* information assets from property coverage, inserting the language: "electronic data is not tangible property." When did the insurance industry do this? October of 2001, *barely a month after 9/11*.[2]

Not to be outdone, the accounting profession followed suit a few years later with an update to a key financial standard (IAS 38) stating explicitly that certain intangibles including customer lists and the like (generally interpreted by accountants as "any electronic data") cannot be capitalized. In short, the value of information assets cannot be included on auditable financial statements.

So while we revere the 9/11 first responders, there's reason to consider that there were some *worst responders* as well.

Regardless, in this chapter we'll ignore insurance industry and accounting profession dictums, in favor of an understanding of why it is prudent for organizations to measure quality and value of their information assets, and how to do so.

Why Measure Information Assets?

Imagine if some of these companies had detailed, accurate inventories of their information assets. Or if they had formal, audited valuations placed on them. In the absence of a CGL policy exclusion clause for "electronic data," their claims would have had to be taken more seriously, and likely would have been upheld by the courts. There are plenty of other reasons why organizations should quantify the value or other measurable aspects of their information assets, including both information-related and business-related benefits.

Mark Milone, senior legal counsel to Information and Analytics at Boeing had the answer to this question, but not the answer as to how to do it:

> It's important to know how much your data is worth. What's the financial risk to the company if data is lost or corrupted? And what are the ways it can add benefits to the business? But the firms we spoke with that specialize in venture capital and IP valuation had no answer how to value information. It made me wonder how are they able to price M&A deals in today's information economy?

Boeing now is one of several companies relying on the information valuation models I will detail later in this chapter, and benefiting from them in several of the following ways.

Information-Related Measurement Benefits

Improved Information Management and Culture

Outside Chicago from 1905–1983, a large Western Electric factory complex called the Hawthorne Works employed forty-five thousand workers at its peak. In the 1920s, industrial researcher and organizational theorist Elton Mayo ran a series of famous experiments at the plant resulting in the coining of the *Hawthorne Effect*,[3] which he describes as a positive emotional effect due to the perception of an interested or sympathetic observer.[4]

Just as with other assets, the mere act of measuring and reporting on information's quantity, quality characteristics, usage patterns, and the various ways it is used sheds a spotlight on it that alone can change the way people capture, produce, manage, and use it.

The Hawthorne Effect may have inspired the quote often misattributed both to the father of quality management, Edward Deming, and the father of modern management, Peter Drucker: "You can't manage what you don't measure." Regardless, this quote holds perpetual sway among management professionals in all disciplines. But since it elicits disdain from others, I might suggest that "*It's easier to manage what you measure*" or "*It's best to measure what you intend to manage*," are more reasonable takes on this famous aphorism.

Prioritizing Information-Related Initiatives

As GE Power's CDO, Christina Clark, told me, "I haven't yet come up with the right analogy for how big the challenge is. If the CDO did everything the CDO could to help manage the enterprise's data better, it would require an army or a complete reorganization. Prioritizing is the key to survival and sanity."

Understanding which information assets are used by the most processes, are the most critical to business outcomes, have the biggest quality challenges, or present the greatest compliance, security, or privacy risks makes a start to prioritizing information asset management (IAM) activities and initiatives.

Creating a Common Language About Information

As highlighted in chapter 6, my colleague Valerie Logan has identified that overcoming issues related to the vernacular surrounding information is one of the keys to improving its management. The ability to describe data quality, security, availability, or value generation needs and challenges in numerical values offers a way for IT, business people, CFOs, information professionals, and even regulators and business partners to communicate more effectively about information.

Justifying and Proving the Benefits of Information-Related Initiatives

Various leading and trailing indicators, forecasting methods, and value determinations of IAM activities can and should be supported by a range of metrics. Whether it's determining ROI or simply connecting the dots between information characteristics and business outcomes, quantifying information's quality and valuation are critical.

Improving Information Security

Several years ago, I spoke with Carsten Casper, Gartner's managing vice president of digital workplace security, about how organizations budget for data security if they don't know the value of what they're securing. He suggested that most employ one of two methods, either: 1) the "Keep up with the Joneses" method of spending what other organizations like their own do, or 2) waiting until some kind of catastrophic event like a breach, then spending enough to make sure that this or something like it doesn't happen again. I refer to this latter method as "blunderfunding."[5]

As covered in chapter 9, knowing the value of what you're securing—along with the risks and expenses of various kinds of data security events—seems to be the only reasonable method for data security budgeting.

Business-Related Measurement Benefits

Improving Information Monetization

Few of the information monetization stories highlighted in the earlier chapters would have gone beyond prototype or pilot stage without the ability to measure their benefits—not just the outcomes, but how those outcomes were linked to particular information assets. These stories beget other stories. In other words, the publicized success of one information monetization initiative can lead to a dozen others within the organization. Moreover, they illustrate to business people throughout the organization the latent value in dormant or underutilized information assets.

Sometimes just the mere act of putting a cost or market value on an information asset leads to the realization that it can and should be monetized in a variety of ways, such as those shown in chapter 4. If acquiring and administering an information asset has a measurable expense, shouldn't you be recouping it, at least? And if an information asset has an identifiable market value, shouldn't you be realizing that value somehow? Performing these kinds of calculations can induce information monetization efforts.

Understanding Corporate Value

Senior executives, boards of directors, and investors have an incomplete picture of a company's value today, with only a summation of the company's reportable assets and its speculative market value (if the company is public). Regardless of what GAAP and IFRS regulations dictate, why shouldn't company execs also have a more complete valuation of *all* assets? How else can a CFO align corporate strategy and budgets without knowing the contribution of information assets to business performance? Perhaps this is why some CDOs even report to their company's CFO.

Growing Market Valuations

As highlighted in chapter 11, investors seem to reward companies with *info-savvy* behaviors by a factor of 2:1. Also, a recent study indicated that nearly half of equity analysts consider a company's information along with its analytics capabilities in valuing the business as a whole.[6] If those who are valuing your business are paying attention to the value of information, why isn't your CFO? And as we saw again and again in part I, organizations that identify and plan alternative ways to leverage existing information assets are inherently growing their own market value.

Making an Impression on Investors

Moreover, what about potential merger and acquisition (M&A) situations? There's evidence from IP advisory firms to suggest that companies internally valuing their information assets, even though they are non-auditable per accounting regulations, are rewarded by potential suitors.[7] Conversely, a failure to internally account for the value of one's information assets can prove detrimental, as in the case of Caesar's Entertainment that has been sued by investors for surreptitiously shifting customer loyalty information among its corporate entities.[8]

Measuring the Value of Information

As we start to express various approaches for measuring information's quality, impact, relevance, cost, and value, it's important to keep in mind the sage words of the celebrated statistician Dr. George Box: "*All models are wrong; some models are useful.*"[9] Models are meant to approximate reality using available inputs and accessible formulae; they are not a substitute for reality itself. The models presented here have been proven useful by a number of organizations in driving data governance and data quality initiatives, prioritizing other information asset management initiatives, justifying analytics initiatives, and spurring information-led innovation.

Assessing Data Quality

As information becomes a more critical asset to organizations in driving both performance and transformation, its quality characteristics must become a paramount concern to business and IT leaders. Poor data quality can have grave consequences, from strategic decisions that can lead to the death of a business to operational decisions that can lead to the death of individuals. Typically, poor data quality characteristics have a detrimental effect on business performance, innovation, and competitiveness.

A business with annual revenue of around $5 billion loses $2.1 million per year as a result of poor decisions made on the back of bad quality data, and 40 percent of all failed business initiatives are a result of poor data quality.[10]

Data quality consultant Martin Spratt assessed that 23 percent of the workforce at a major Australian bank cannot perform their primary job adequately because of bad data, and that 13 percent of the workforce at an energy retailer and 24 percent at a health insurance provider suffer the same problem. Some *business people* are taking up to 30 hours per week to deal with data quality issues, in some cases leading to hundreds of millions of dollars of previously unmeasured "commercial damage," Spratt said. The larger concern is that "IT people don't want to hear it because it makes them look bad, and besides, they're not compensated on good data the way others around the company are compensated on the quality of the assets they produce or manage." Spratt demonstrated he can even predict employee attrition based on a company's level of data quality, and believes that impaired information assets should be a CFO write-down.[11] Particularly in the realm of Big Data and orders of magnitude increases in volume, velocity, and variety of information, these issues and their economic impact are greatly amplified.

Organizations that take seriously the notion of information as a corporate asset should engage in the same quality assessment discipline as with their traditional physical and financial assets. Just as other assets are periodically inventoried or audited, information assets should be appraised periodically for improvements or degradation. To gauge and improve any measure of information's value, various characteristics should be assessed periodically as part of data governance programs and by data stewards.

Gartner data quality expert Ted Friedman has identified a dozen data quality (DQ) indicators, including both objective and subjective dimensions. Subsequently, Friedman and I devised the following basic means to quantitatively evaluate each dimension. Note that some measures require a degree of manual checking while others may be automated or even extended using a data profiling tool or custom queries. In general, we also recommend statistical sampling for expedience and performance for quantification purposes.

Additionally, while these dimensions apply as equally to unstructured data as they do to structured data, DQ measurements against unstructured data tend to require greater subjectivity, advanced profiling techniques, and/or alternative metrics.[12]

Objective Data Quality Metrics

Validity: how well non-missing data accurately represents reality, irrespective of precision or format. For most structured data, use a binary (0,1) value, but for unstructured or more subjective content, consider degrees of partial accuracy.

Completeness: the percentage of instances of data you have recorded versus the total available (that is, within your business ecosystem or market), and/or the percentage of missing fields in a record.

Integrity: the existence and correctness of linkages to and from a record, and often the legitimacy of relationships among attribute values within a record.

Consistency: the number of different forms, formats, and/or structures data takes when stored in multiple datasets or records.

Uniqueness: the percentage of alternate or duplicative forms of the data instance that exist. Identifying alternates forms of a field requires subject-matter expertise to proactively search for them (for example, "CompanyName" versus "CompanyName Inc." versus "CompanyName Incorporated" versus "CNI").

Precision: the degree of exactitude of a value (or the level of detail for unstructured data). While the value may be completely accurate, its applicability for some business processes may be suboptimal because of its lack of precision.

Timeliness: the probability that a local data record reflects its original source at any given time. Often online transaction processing data is perfectly fresh, whereas data warehouse data is updated periodically (that is, it has "periodicity"). While the tendency may be to gauge timeliness solely in "clock time," it is more important from a business perspective to gauge the confidence that the existing local data is in sync with its original source.

Accessibility: the estimated number of business processes or personnel that can benefit from the data and that are able to retrieve it.

Subjective Data Quality Metrics

Existence: the degree to which business events, objects, and ideas of importance to the business are represented in corporate information assets.

Scarcity: the probability that other organizations (particularly competitors and partners) also have the same data. Scarcer data is likely to have greater relative business benefit than data that is commonplace among business partners and competitors. Like relevancy, scarcity is not a direct quality dimension, but is representative of intrinsic data value.

Relevancy: the number of business processes that use, or could benefit from, this type of data. Higher relevancy is a handy indicator of relative business usefulness. Relevancy isn't necessarily a quality factor per se, but is included because it is reflective of the data's cost-to-benefit ratio.

Usability: the degree to which data is helpful in performing a business function and can only be measured via user surveys.*

Interpretability: the degree to which data has a unique meaning and is easy to understand, which can only be measured via user surveys.*

Believability: the degree to which the data is trusted, and can only be measured via user surveys.*

Objectivity: the degree to which the source of the data is believed to be impartial, which can only be measured via user surveys.[13]

Information Asset Valuation Models

To assist organizations in putting infonomics principles into practice, my collaboration with valuation experts, accountants, economists, and clients over the years has resulted in a variety of methods to compute the value of an information asset. These include both *fundamental* and *financial* valuation approaches.

The fundamental models consider the quality-related aspect of information or its impact on alternate performance indicators. The financial models measure value in monetary terms by adapting accepted methods for valuing traditional assets. When adopting financial models, it is wise to solicit the support and involvement of your CFO.

Some of these methods adapt acknowledged approaches for asset valuation, although none has been accepted or endorsed as yet by any accounting standards body. For now, the models are exclusively for the internal use of organizations in gauging and comparing the value of their information assets.

While the discrete, point-in-time valuations generated are certainly useful, they may not be as meaningful as:

- Understanding the gaps between the realized, probable, and potential value of an information asset,
- Tracking the improvement or impairment of the value of an information asset over time, or
- Juxtaposing or combining metrics for more meaningful or implementable insights.

All asset valuation-related methods such as internal rate of return (IRR) or economic value added (EVA), along with all accounting methods for any kind of asset, are based on a set of assumptions. It is important that assumptions are properly described and consistently applied.

The models generally work best when treating a class of information (for example, customer data, product data, maintenance data, call center data, or employee data) as a portfolio of information. While it may be easier to apply these models to specific datasets, you will likely find more benefit in applying them to logical groupings (portfolios) of related information assets.

Finally, we offer multiple models for various needs and circumstances (Figure 11.1). Selecting which to use and when to use them depends on your objectives. Some are leading indicators, while others are trailing

Figure 11.1 *Gartner Information Asset Valuation Models*

indicators and some can be used as either. The fundamental models are oriented toward improving IAM, while the financial models are more for assessing an information asset's business benefits. You may find that it makes sense to apply several models for the benefit of different IT, information, financial, and business leaders—or for different kinds of information assets. Later, I'll share how some organizations are using them in combination.

Fundamental Valuation Models

The following fundamental valuation models are for organizations or departments that are not yet ready or have no pressing need to ascribe a monetary value to their information assets. These models are useful for assessing an information asset's quality and potential-versus-actual utility to help in improving IAM efforts. They may also be useful as leading indicators of an information asset's potential economic benefit.[14]

Intrinsic Value of Information (IVI)

OVERVIEW

The intrinsic value of information is its presumptive benefit that enables broad comparisons across information classes regardless of how the information may currently be being used. This method gauges how correct and complete the information asset is and how likely other organizations are to have it. The suggestion is that higher quality and available information that is more proprietary or exclusive has greater intrinsic value potential. This method can be useful to prioritize information-related investments among differing information sources or initiatives. For example, the intrinsic value of information (IVI) is particularly useful to guide data quality or security-related efforts and investments.

FORMULA

The IVI is a function of:

- **Validity**. Percentage of records deemed to be correct.
- **Completeness**. Percentage of total records versus the universe of potential or supposed records.
- **Scarcity**. Percentage of your market or competitors that also likely have this same data.
- **Lifecycle**. The reasonable usable length of utility for any given unit (record) of the information asset (e.g., in months).

$$IVI = Validity * Completeness * (1 - Scarcity) * Lifecycle$$

IMPLEMENTATION

This model is ideally suited for use by data stewards to compare the potential utility of multiple types of information, or for tracking the improved (or degraded) potential of particular information assets over time. The optimal IVI is a 1.0 (specifically, perfect data accuracy and completeness with no copies or versions of any part of this data available outside the organization). For information with a high IVI, you may want to increase or ensure its broad availability and use. For information with a low IVI, you may want to redouble information governance and quality efforts (see above for ways to measure these and other data quality attributes).

BENEFITS AND CHALLENGES

The IVI is the simplest of the information valuation models to use. The data quality factors can be determined via automatic profiling and a basic market understanding. It can help quickly compare the potential of different information assets, identify data quality, data privacy, or information governance issues, or identify data that perhaps shouldn't be retained. However, the IVI does not consider relevancy of data (actual or potential) for any particular business purpose.

Business Value of Information (BVI)

OVERVIEW

This method considers the utility of an information asset to actual business usage (unlike the previous IVI method). It addresses how good the information is, how applicable it is to the business, and how up-to-date the information is. This method is handy to get a quick take on information's potential real-world benefit. For example, when there are competing business priorities, this model can be used to align information-related priorities with them.

FORMULA

The BVI is a function of:

- **Relevance**. How useful the information could be (or is) to one or more business processes (0 to 1).
- **Validity**. Percentage of records deemed to be correct.
- **Completeness**. Percentage of total records versus the universe of potential or supposed records.
- **Timeliness**. How quickly new or updated instances of the data are captured and available to be accessed.

$$BVI = \sum_{p=1}^{n} (Relevance_p) * Validity * Completeness * Timeliness$$

Where p = the number of business processes or functions.

IMPLEMENTATION

To implement this method, it is handy to have a general breakdown of business functions throughout the organization. This can be as high level or detailed as you consider practicable. Measuring the gap between information's actual value versus its potential value (specifically, using actual versus potential relevance estimates) can quickly identify opportunities for better utilizing your dark data.

The BVI relates data to actual business value. It is relatively simple to implement and can consider actual versus potential scenarios. This model is useful to identify "dark data" and make "defensible disposal" decisions. However, *business relevance* can be highly subjective and may demand a time-consuming functional analysis to determine.

Performance Value of Information (PVI)

OVERVIEW

This approach looks at the realized (or estimated) impact of an information asset on a business objective that is represented as key performance indicators (KPIs). This answers the question: How much does having this information improve business performance? In short, it requires running a controlled experiment (or conjecturing one), but this method results in a definitive, empirical value measure.

As a trailing indicator of information value, this method may be less useful than the IVI or BVI models for prioritizing information-related initiatives or determining potential information value. However, it is a preferred approach for measuring realized business benefits against established business metrics and as a leading indicator of information asset's financial value.

FORMULA

The PVI is a simple ratio that calculates KPI improvement by incorporating a given information asset, extrapolated over the usable life span of any given instance of data:

$$PVI = \left[\left(\frac{KPI_i}{KPI_c} \right) - 1 \right] * T\!\!\Big/_{t}$$

(Or for multiple KPIs, the overall PVI can be expressed as the mean of their individual PVIs.)

Where:

- KPI_i = Business process instances using the information asset (informed group).
- KPI_c = Business process instances not using the information (control group).
- T   = The average usable life span of any data instance.
- t   = The duration over which the KPI was measured.

IMPLEMENTATION

Using the PVI model ideally requires running a controlled experiment in which certain instances of a business process incorporate a certain information asset that other instances do not. It is a classic A-B test. A positive PVI demonstrates that the data is valuable for this process; a negative PVI indicates that the additional data somehow impedes the process. In determining the PVI, it is important to keep all other aspects of the revenue process constant during the trial.

BENEFITS AND CHALLENGES

The PVI yields hard, empirical measurements that are an excellent predictor or proxy for financial measures. It introduces a real-world scenario without the need for business-function level analysis. However, the PVI requires running one or more experiments, potentially involving system or process changes. The way in which data is integrated into the process affects the outcome, and this model does not take into consideration the expense of incorporating the data into a process.

Financial Valuation Models

A financial information valuation model is useful to organizations that need to determine how information assets perform compared to other assets; what to invest in their collection, management, security, and deployment; and how to express their value when used in business transactions (for example, merger and acquisitions, data syndication, information bartering). These economic models are variants on established asset valuation models that are used by valuation experts and accountants to value traditional assets. However, these models have been adapted to accommodate one of the nuances of information's unique characteristics including that they are non-depletable, non-rivalrous, and more licensable than salable.

Cost Value of Information (CVI)

This method simply assesses an information asset as the financial expense required to generate, capture, or collect it. An optional term that considers the impact to the business if this information asset were rendered unavailable (for example, damaged, lost) or stolen (specifically, copied) is also included. This method is preferred when there is no active market for the information asset and its contribution to revenue cannot be determined adequately. Additionally, this model can be used to assess the potential financial risk of an information asset's damage, loss, or theft.

FORMULA

$$CVI = \frac{ProcExp * Attrib * T}{t} \{ + \sum_{p=0}^{n} \text{Lost Revenue}_p \}$$

Where:

- ProcExp = The annualized cost of the process(es) involved in capturing the data.
- Attrib = The portion (percent) of *process expense* attributable to capturing the data.
- T = Average life span of any given instance of data.
- t = Time period over which the *process expense* is measured.
- n = The number of periods of time until the information is re-acquired, or until business continuity is no longer affected by the lost or damaged information.

IMPLEMENTATION

The process expense and portion attributable to information capture can be tricky to ascertain, given that it may be collected in the course of business operations, in which case it is normally expensed. If the portion of the process allocated to the acquisition of that information asset were determinate, this amount ostensibly could be claimed as an asset value instead of being expensed (current accounting regulations notwithstanding). The cost of reputational or competitive risks should also be considered, should this information be exposed publicly or stolen by competitors.

BENEFITS AND CHALLENGES

The CVI is the best means of estimating information replacement cost and negative business impact if lost, stolen, or damaged. Accountants prefer this method as a more conservative and less volatile approach for initially valuing most intangible assets. However, some factors require estimation and subjectivity. Remember that these costs most likely are expensed already, so the CVI merely expresses the value of information in terms of shifting it from an expense to an asset.

Market Value of Information (MVI)

OVERVIEW

This method looks at the potential or actual financial value of an information asset in an open marketplace. Typically, data monetization is transacted among trading partners in return for cash, goods, or services, or other considerations such as preferential contract terms and conditions. Yet, increasingly, companies are selling their data outright via hosted data marketplaces (for example, ProgrammableWeb, Quandl, Qlik Data Marketplace, Data Republic) or industry-specific information brokers.

This market value method, generally, is not applicable for most types of information unless they are licensed or bartered. However, as organizations become more sophisticated and aggressive at leveraging their information externally, they should consider this approach.

FORMULA

Our modification of this traditional method recognizes that most information is not actually sold (specifically, ownership transferred); rather, it is licensed.

Therefore, we have included a factor for the diminished marketability of information as it becomes more ubiquitous to the marketplace. This is represented as a variable discount factor (represented as an inverse premium) applied to a hypothetical ownership transference (exclusive price) of the information asset:

$$MVI = \frac{\text{Exclusive Price} * \text{Number of Licensees}}{\text{Premium}}$$

IMPLEMENTATION

Use the MVI when considering monetizing information via sale or barter. Ideally, use the CVI or EVI model to determine the exclusive price—specifically, how much you might demand to transfer complete ownership of (or exclusive rights to) the information asset to another entity (licensee). Then determine or estimate how many probable parties will license this data over the average life span of any given record. Traditional market analyses methods for determining market sizes can also be used to determine the number of likely information licensors. Additional surveys of potential licensors can determine the premium factor, by asking: "What premium (multiple) over any given licensing fee would you pay for exclusive access to or outright ownership of this data?"

BENEFITS AND CHALLENGES

The MVI is most useful for determining the value of a saleable or barterable information asset. It can also be useful for determining the price point for an information product, or it can also be adapted for ensuring acceptable licensing fees for another's information product. However, this model is not particularly applicable or useful for nonmarketable information assets. It includes highly subjective factors that may require extensive market analysis, such as determining or estimating the exclusive price for an information asset.

Economic Value of Information (EVI)

OVERVIEW

This method generates the net financial value of an information asset by applying the traditional income approach for asset valuation, then subtracting the information's associated lifecycle expenses. Like the PVI, this method empirically calculates the information asset's actual value. As such, it is more of a trailing indicator than a leading indicator of information value—unless the first revenue term can be estimated adequately.

FORMULA

The EVI considers the realized change in revenue when a particular information asset is incorporated into one or more revenue generating processes. Then, the cost to acquire, administer, and apply the data is netted out:

$$EVI = [Revenue_i - Revenue_c - (AcqExp + AdmExp + AppExp)] * T/_t$$

Where:
- $Revenue_i$ = The revenue generated using the information asset (informed group).
- $Revenue_c$ = The revenue generated without the information asset (control group).
- T = The average expected life span of any given information instance or record.
- t = The period of time during which the EVI experiment or trial was executed.

IMPLEMENTATION

As a financial variant of the PVI method above, the EVI requires running a trial over a period of time. However, in this method, revenue is the only KPI, the value is monetary rather than a ratio, and the life span of the information asset is factored in. First, measure the difference between how much income is generated with versus without using the information. Then subtract the lifecycle costs of the information. (Refer to the previous CVI model for guidance on computing lifecycle expenses.) Finally, multiply this sum by the ratio of the information assets life span (T) to the duration of the trial (t). In determining the EVI, it is important to keep all other aspects of the revenue process constant during the trial.

BENEFITS AND CHALLENGES

The EVI is an empirical analysis of the contribution of information to the top and bottom line. There is no need for a functional analysis, other than in establishing information-related expenses when data is duplicated and/or applied in multiple ways. The EVI, however, requires a live experiment and the ability to estimate information supply chain costs. Many traditional business leaders are still uncomfortable with the contemporary concept of experimenting with revenue-producing processes. Also, the EVI is a trailing indicator, although results can be used to prioritize IT and business initiatives.

Other Information Valuation Approaches

These models are by no means the only methods for valuing information that have been posited. Others worthy of consideration as well include:

- Douglas Hubbard's "applied information economics" methodology strictly for measuring the decision value of information.[15]
- Bill Schmarzo's "data economic valuation" approach also strictly for measuring information's contribution to decision making.[16]
- Paul Strassman's macroeconomic method of comparing the competitive gains of organizations with similar tangible assets, after accounting for all other valuation premium factors.[17]
- Dilip Krishna's methods for attributing business outcomes to specific information initiatives (Business Impact Model); an adapted discount cash flow model (a Monte Carlo simulation method); and a comparative analysis approach similar to Strassman's but using a pure-play information company for comparison.[18]
- Tonie Leatherberry's and Rena Mears's "net business value" method that considers information's present and discounted future value to each department, various risks, and total cost of ownership.[19]
- Robert Schmidt's and Jennifer Fisher's promising but loosely defined and abandoned patent application for an amalgam of information cost, accuracy, and other quality factors, along with information usage/access.[20]

- Mark Albala's conceptual valuation model, similar to that of Schmidt and Fischer, in which information value is based on information requests, usage (royalties), and outcomes.[21]
- Dave McCrory's concept and formula for what he calls "data gravity" that defines the proximal relationship among data sources and applications.[22]

As well, software and services companies such as Schedule1, Pimsoft, Everedge, ThreatModeler, Alex Solutions, Datum, Alation, and Real Social Dynamics (RSD) [in collaboration with the Geneva School of Business Administration] have developed exclusive approaches for measuring information value and/or risk in economic terms specific to their core offerings.

Of course, countless papers and books have been written on the value of information from an engineering, communications, and theoretical standpoint, dating back to Claude Shannon's seminal work on information theory. Even the term "business intelligence" predates any Gartner or IBM paper, having been first used in the 1865 book, "Cyclopaedia of Commercial and Business Anecdotes" in describing the value of information on military battles.[23]

Understanding and Closing Information Value Gaps

Enterprises repeatedly fall into the trap of getting diminishing returns from buying and applying more complex and leading-edge IT to the same narrow sets of data, rather than doing simpler things with the data that has the highest value gap. It's like a farmer who buys new equipment, hires more workers, and drenches a certain crop with fertilizer and water when other crops have greater growth and profitability potential.

Determining the value of any information asset using the cost approach (CVI) can offer a baseline, nominal, and conservative value of the information, regardless of how it is or could be used. Note that the CVI is consistent with the way that accountants prefer for initially valuing most intangibles. Your goal then should be to determine ways to generate a market value (MVI) or income value (EVI) for the information asset that's greater than its CVI.

Since the late 1980s, accountants have allowed for the value of an asset to be recorded as representing its "probable future economic benefits." This means that a currently unutilized asset may have a formal measurable value. It also means that any asset has three degrees of value:

1. A *realized* value based on the economic benefits it is currently delivering,
2. A *probable* value based on its intended uses, and
3. A *mostly* theoretical potential value if it were to be optimally applied.

The implication for information assets is that even dark data (that is, unutilized or underutilized data) has both probable and potential value. So people who suggest that information (or any asset) has value only when consumed are somewhat mistaken—although their intentions may be good.

These three degrees of value (Figure 11.2) also give us a way to apply the Gartner Information Value Models to identify value gaps: the information performance gap and the information vision gap:

> **Information Performance Gap**—The difference between the realized value of an information asset and its probable value.

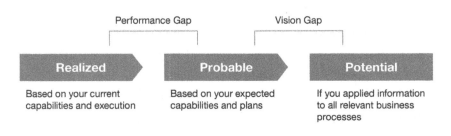

Figure 11.2 *Information Value Gaps*

This gap shows how information will likely deliver benefits. For example, maintenance data may be used currently to identify failing components and reduce their downtime, but systems being developed are not yet in place to predict failures. Both the MVI and EVI models can be used as actual and projected approaches to estimate the performance gap. After measuring this gap, your objective should be to accelerate its closure and increase the probability that the information actually will be applied in intended ways.

Information Vision Gap—The difference between the probable and potential information valuations.

This gap appraises how much (or little) vision the organization has concerning how its data is leveraged. For example, even after predictive maintenance systems are put in place, there are identified opportunities to license this data to component suppliers in return for favorable pricing, plus a range of other potential ways to leverage the data. This gap is usually much larger than the performance gap, but also a bit more speculative. So how can you possibly identify all the ways an information asset could possibly be used? One answer is to identify the actual versus potential business relevance (BVI) of information assets and then conduct information innovation exercises (see the following section) that focus on those with the largest gaps. And with previously unidentified potential uses of an information asset now in mind, you may choose to plan to implement them, thereby increasing the information asset's probable value and, in turn, your own organization's market value.

Applying the Information Valuation Models in Combination

As I mentioned earlier, these information valuation models may have greater utility in combination than as standalone methods. Some organizations already are leveraging the models in creative ways I had not envisioned. Additionally, most organizations (with my encouragement) modify the parameters of one or more models to suit particular needs. Some of these uses include:

Prioritizing IAM Investments

Several companies including an international retailer and a major manufacturer[24] have identified information assets with low data quality metrics but high business relevancy to help them focus their information asset management (IAM) activities and resources. To do this, they used using variations on the intrinsic (IVI) and business (BVI) models (Figure 11.3).

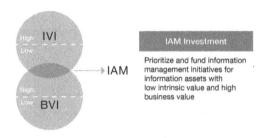

Figure 11.3 *Using Information Valuations to Prioritize Information Asset Management Investments*

Proving the Benefits of Information Governance

Other organizations including a federal agency are gauging the causal relationship between improvements in data quality and business outcomes. This helps them demonstrate, and thereby fund, the benefits of the information governance initiatives behind improved data quality. A global financial services company is using a similar approach to gauge and improve the utilization of its data lake. With IVI-like data quality metrics available to users alongside the information assets themselves, the trust and usage of the data lake can be determined (Figure 11.4).

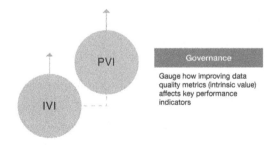

Figure 11.4 *Using Information Valuations to Justify and Prove Information Governance Efforts*

Innovation and Digitalization

One of the most clever ways of leveraging the valuation models has been developed and deployed by the information strategy consultancy, Cicero Group.[25] Consulting to a major security systems company, Cicero helped it identify information assets with high business potential that currently were generating little significant economic value (Figure 11.5)—remember that the BVI model can be used to identify the realized or potential business relevancy of an information asset. Then Cicero helped its client devise over twenty IT and business initiatives to better leverage those underutilized information assets. As a result the client claims it has added $300 million in market value (over a 15 percent increase).[26]

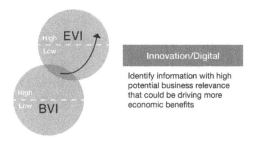

Figure 11.5 *Using Information Valuations to Spur Innovation and Digitalization*

Monetization and Analytics

Working with a few software-as-a-service (SaaS) clients, a prominent online retailer, and other companies looking to determine which information assets are most ripe for external monetization, we have concocted a basic approach to mixing three of the models (Figure 11.6). It involves identifying

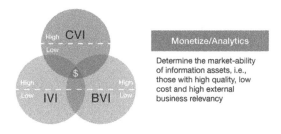

Figure 11.6 *Using Information Valuations to Identify Monetization and Analytics Opportunities*

information assets with a low cost to harvest, generate, or otherwise obtain, along with those that have high data quality and high business relevancy (to potential licensees). A similar approach has been presented to several data brokers as to how they should be thinking about repackaging and introducing new information products and services.

Expanded Revenue

Some companies are just starting to toe the water with monetizing their information assets externally. To help them build a business case for doing so, I have recommended looking at how the external market value of certain information assets of theirs could expand the economic value they're already delivering internally (Figure 11.7)—and how large that unrealized value gap is. This approach helps these companies look at ways to license their data, barter with it for favorable terms and conditions or discounts, attract partners, or any of the various monetization methods we covered earlier in the book. For example, one country's national archives has entered into a partnership to monetize its artifacts by digitizing them. Which ones to digitize and how to price them were based on their expected market value.[27]

Another example of this approach in action is the work the IP consultancy Everedge mentioned earlier did with a business that was looking to get acquired. The client thought its most valuable assets were on the balance sheet. But instead of targeting buyers for the business (for which the client expected a 2x book value valuation), Everedge found buyers for its information assets, yielding a 32x EBITDA (earnings before interest, tax, depreciation, and amortization) deal size.[28]

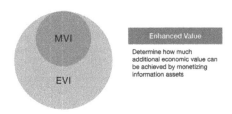

Figure 11.7 *Using Information Valuations to Drive Expanded Economic Benefits and Revenue*

Reduce Information Lifecycle Expense

Remember in chapter 6 the discussion of the five (or six) "Rs" of sustainability? One company, MISO Energy, has put these models to work to *reduce* unnecessary information assets. MISO's Principal Data Architect, Ruchi Rajesekhar, first scoped the analysis to certain information assets with low business relevancy (BVI), then computed the difference between their economic value (actually in this case, the loss to the business without them) and their retention cost (acquisition + human capital + infrastructure). In doing so, MISO was able to defensibly dispose of certain information assets with a negative net value, thereby saving the company $1.1 million annually (Figure 11.8).

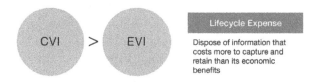

Figure 11.8 *Using Information Valuations to Reduce Infrastructure-Related Expenses*

Architecting for Information Value

Even practicable—if not perfect—models for measuring information's value in various ways cannot convey enough about information's behavior as an asset. Quantifying an information asset's potential or probable or actual value provides us useful indicators to prove or justify ways to improve how we manage and monetize it. But such models fall short of telling us how information behaves or how we can bend its behavior to our benefit. For this we must turn to the field of economics. Although designed for traditional goods and services and human behavior, economic principles and models can be applied to information assets as well—with some tweaking.

In the next chapter, we'll examine how certain economic concepts can provide guidance to CDOs and other information leaders, along with business, enterprise, and application architects, by substituting the concept of information assets into established economic models.

Notes

1. At the time I was an analyst with META Group, subsequently acquired by Gartner.
2. www.irmi.com/articles/expert-commentary/the-2001-iso-cgl-revision.
3. Sometimes called the Observer Effect, not to be confused with the quantum theory effect of the same name which itself is often confused with the Heisenberg Principle.
4. R. McCarney, J. Warner, S. Iliffe, R. van Haselen, M. Griffin, and P. Fisher, "The Hawthorne Effect: A Randomised, Controlled Trial," *BMC Med Res Methodol*, Volume 7, 2007, p. 30. doi:10.1186/1471-2288-7-30.
5. Doug Laney, "Blunderfunding: How Organizations Use Failure as a Basis for Budgeting," Doug Laney, 18 January 2012, http://blogs.gartner.com/doug-laney/ blunderfunding-how-organizations-use-failure-as-a-basis-for-budgeting/.
6. "Data and Analytics: A New Driver of Performance and Valuation," *Institutional Investor Research and KPMG*, June 2015, p. 6.
7. Paul Adams, interview with author, 17 December 2016.
8. Kate O'Keeffe, "Real Prize in Caesars Fight: Data on Players," *The Wall Street Journal*, 19 March 2015, accessed 09 February 2017, www.wsj.com/articles/ in-caesars-fight-data-on-players-is-real-prize-1426800166.
9. George E. P. Box, William Hunter, and Stuart Hunter, *Statistics for Experimenters*, second edition (2005), p. 440.
10. Ted Friedman, and Michael Smith, "Measuring the Business Value of Data Quality," Gartner, 07 October 2015, www.gartner.com/document/ code/218962.
11. Martin Spratt, interview with author, 08 September 2016.
12. The toolkit Ted Friedman and I published includes the actual formulas and examples for calculating each dimension (ref: "Toolkit: Assessing Key Data Quality Dimensions," Douglas Laney and Ted Friedman, Gartner, 21 September 2012, www.gartner.com/document/2171520).
13. For user surveys of subjective factors use a 1–5 Likert scale for responses (for example: 1—Strongly disagree, 2—Disagree, 3—Neither agree nor disagree, 4—Agree, 5—Strongly agree).
14. For further guidance on implementing these models, including variants and examples, refer to "Why and How to Measure the Value of Your Information Assets" or this book's accompanying website.
15. Douglas W. Hubbard, *How to Measure Anything: Finding the Value of "Intangibles" in Business* (Hoboken, NJ: John Wiley & Sons, 2007).

16. Bill Schmarzo, "Determining the Economic Value of Data—InFocus Blog | Dell EMC Services," InFocus Blog | Dell EMC Services, 11 July 2016, https://infocus.emc.com/william_schmarzo/determining-economic-value-data/.

17. Paul Strassman, "The Value Of Computers, Information and Knowledge," 30 January 1996, www.strassmann.com/pubs/cik/cik-value.shtml#RTFToC8.

18. Dilip Krishna, "Inf. Valuation (1)—Valuing an Organizations Information . . .," Course Hero, accessed 09 February 2017, www.coursehero.com/file/8383468/inf-valuation-1/.

19. The Fourth MIT Information Quality Industry Symposium, 14–16 July 2010. *Data as an Asset: Balancing the Data Ecosystem.*

20. Robert Schmidt et al., "Valuation of Data," U.S. Patent Application No. 13/316055, 09 December 2011.

21. Marc Albala, "Recognition of Information Value," SlideShare, 15 November 2016, www.slideshare.net/mcalbala/recognition-of-information-value.

22. "Business Intelligence" coined by Frazar Kirland in 1865, p. 210. Published by D. Appleton and Co, New York, NY.

23. Richard Seroter, "Dave McCrory Unveils Initial Formula for Principle of Data Gravity," InfoQ, 29 June 2012, www.infoq.com/news/2012/06/datagravity-formula.

24. Assisted by Gartner Consulting.

25. Cicero Group is also the first known consultancy to have a formal infonomics practice, although others including Gartner Consulting offer similar services.

26. Client project documentation provided under non-disclosure, 2015.

27. A Gartner Consulting project.

28. Paul Adams, interview with author, 17 December 2016.

CHAPTER 12

Adapting Economic Principles for Information

Although it may be characterized as the "dismal science," the field of economics offers another lens for understanding and applying information assets, and for optimizing information-related investments. Business, information, and technology leaders now must develop and optimize business models, applications, information products, and digital solutions with the economics of information in mind. Unfortunately, classic macro- and microeconomic principles were developed to better understand and improve the consumption and value of traditional goods and services, not information assets.

As we have explored throughout this book, information behaves differently than other assets. Moreover, the type of user increasingly consuming information is not human—rather it is an application, machine, or some kind of device. Technology doesn't feel degrees of satisfaction—a key economic determinant. Nor does technology tire as people do. And information itself doesn't get used up, like metal or wood. The unique qualities of information assets and the way they are produced and consumed compel us to re-examine economic principles and models, and adjust them as necessary for this new age asset.

For decades, and even centuries, classical economic principles have been a critical determinant for making ongoing investments and decisions about expected ROI of products and services. Decisions concerning the production, sizing, packaging, pricing, marketing, and purchasing of goods and services all hinge on an understood canon of economic conventions. However, in the current information-driven society and increasingly digitalized world, sentiments are shifting from the economics of tangible assets to the economics of information—"infonomics"—and other intangible assets.

I have relegated the examination of information economics toward the end of this book, not just because it is the "-nomics" in the "infonomics" portmanteau, but because it is opening a portal to an unexplored universe of ideas. Thought leaders like Barb Wixom and Erik Brynjolfsson at MIT have researched and taught on monetizing information and the information economy, and UCSD's Jim Short is researching data valuation. Others like Gartner's Andrew White, Alan Duncan, Alan Dayley, and Brian Lowans, along with practitioners including John Ladley, James Price, Tony Fisher, Thomas Redman, Kelle O'Neal, Danette McGilvray, Theresa Kushner, Maria Villar, and Rob Hillard, have been pushing the envelope on how to manage information more like an asset. But even as Urs Birchler, Monka Bütler, James Surowiecki, and Hal Varian have offered advanced thinking on information's role in economic phenomena, to my knowledge there's a void in exploring and practicably applying the array of standard economic principles and models to information itself.

University of Illinois professor Nolan Miller cautions about the term "economics of information" or "information economics", noting they are monikers for an established field concerning information's role in human behavior, especially decision making.[1] "Infonomics" on the other hand is about how information behaves *as* an economic asset itself—the topic of this book, and I believe, a greenfield subdiscipline for economists and a future core competency for CDOs, other information professionals, and enterprise architects.

Applying Economic Concepts to Information

While economists are concerned about the economics of information, CDOs, CIOs, and enterprise architects in particular should be concerned with infonomics. It's not part of their profession and, formally, never really has been. Certainly, architects make design decisions based on information availability, volume, velocity, and variety, and may unwittingly weigh various economic factors about the supply and demand, cost, or marginal utility of information. CDOs and CIOs make strategic decisions based on similar factors, but each are largely untrained in principles like diminishing marginal utility, productive efficiency, externalities, elasticity, and excess burden, or behavioral implications of asset availability—certainly not as they apply to information assets. Would knowing these concepts and how to apply them to information assets be beneficial to their employers? Absolutely.

Indeed, many if not most microeconomic and macroeconomic principles can be applied to information assets. Some are obvious and need little treatment, such as the diminishing marginal cost of information (a feature of any storage device or service). Yet others like Ricardian Rent, Nash Equilibrium, and Bekenstein Bounds are out of bounds for a book of this nature. Therefore, we'll explore only those which have the greatest relevance in the context of information assets, and that require some reformulation to guide information producers and consumers such as CDOs, CIOs, and enterprise-, application-, and data architects. They include:

- How the principle of supply and demand operates differently with information than with other assets.
- How to understand and apply the forces of information pricing and elasticity.
- How understanding the marginal utility of information for both human and technology-based consumers of information should drive business and architecture decisions.
- How the opportunity costs of certain information assets must be factored into selecting and publishing them.
- How the information production possibility frontier affects information-related behavior and investments.
- How to use Gartner's information yield curve to conceptually integrate the concepts of information monetization, management, and measurement for improved information-related and business strategies.

The Supply and Demand of Information

Information is an unruly asset. As pointed out earlier, it does not deplete when consumed, it can be used simultaneously, it is representative of some other entity or activity, it costs comparatively little to store or transmit, and it can instantly transform or disappear. At once, its supply can seem both infinite and its demand insatiable. Yet most organizations strive to generate or collect ever more information, even as their ability to consume it struggles to keep up. Regardless, demand for it throughout your organization goes largely unfulfilled. This is an indication of an information supply chain inefficiency, not so much an information ecosystem imbalance.

Supply and demand is the most fundamental of economic principles. Demand refers to the quantity of something someone is willing to obtain for a given price, while supply represents how much of that asset is available.

But wait: If the same unit of information can be sold (licensed) and delivered (transmitted) to multiple buyers (Remember the *non-rivalry* principle?), isn't the supply of available information infinite?[2] How can its price achieve some market equilibrium? Accordingly, why isn't all information freely available? Clearly classic supply and demand breaks down for information assets. Remember the Cost Value of Information (CVI) and Market Value of Information (MVI) models from chapter 12? They can be used not just for valuing information, but also to guide the behavior of suppliers and consumers of information assets. The CVI sets a minimum price for information based on the costs involved in producing/collecting, managing, and delivering it,[3] while the MVI expresses how market saturation of the same information devalues it, thereby reducing its demand.

Executives, business leaders, and architects need to understand how this price equilibrium operates differently with information than with traditional goods and services. It is not based on balancing supply and demand, but rather on a more sophisticated function of information costs, viable uses, and market saturation. Consumers of information should not expect to buy it merely at some nominal cost premium. And suppliers of information must consider how attenuating market saturation will affect the number of buyers at any given price point (and vice versa), and how this in turn affects its attributable revenue stream. Achieving an information price equilibrium, it would seem, involves a bit of game theory well beyond classic supply and demand, and the scope of this book.

Information Pricing and Elasticity

Increasingly, much information is purchased by organizations—not just produced, either directly from data brokers or social media aggregators, or indirectly in the form of trading goods or services. Accordingly, this puts a microscope on the issue of information pricing. As we saw with the market value of information (MVI) model in chapter 11, and the topic of supply and demand in the previous section, pricing information can be more convoluted than pricing traditional goods and services. There are few "open arms-length marketplaces" (as accountants would say) with which to establish viable market valuations for most kinds of information. And most information bartering is off-book because information is not a formal capital asset.

But perhaps as important as—or more important than—fixing a price for a unit of information is how its price changes in response to other factors (i.e., its *elasticity*)—primarily information's supply and demand.

The price elasticity of information supply measures how much a supplier (publisher, producer) of an information asset chooses to supply in response to a change in price. But since information is inherently replicable, why would a supplier like a data broker or book publisher limit the supply even with downward price pressure? Simple: to prevent the price from approaching zero, resulting in negligible or negative profits. In most cases, however, it makes more sense for information suppliers to increase supply up to the point in which market saturation creates significant downward price pressure. This is the theory and mechanics behind the MVI valuation method.

On the other hand, the demand elasticity of information suggests that at some price point, an information consumer will seek an alternative (*substitute*) source. When fewer alternative sources (e.g., retail pricing data, or IT research) are available the information asset is critical, and/or switching costs are prohibitive, then the price premiums can be maintained, and vice versa. Therefore, enterprise efforts to identify and curate information sources can be important not just for improving information's utility, but also for negotiating the price of current licensed or bartered information sources. Moreover, the growing variety and availability of information sources (especially open data published by government organizations and others) compels information suppliers to differentiate either with expanded information sets, improved quality, and/or additional services such as analytics or integration.

The Marginal Utility of Information

The supply, demand, and pricing of information are in part determined by its utility. Economists define utility as a general measure of happiness or pleasure. This is not to be confused with value, in which benefits *and* costs are juxtaposed.

Marginal utility is the additional satisfaction gained from consuming one additional unit of a good or service. Economists and marketers use it to determine how much, or how much more, of an item a consumer will buy or consume. In most situations, each subsequent unit of something consumed has less utility than the prior one; this is the *law of diminishing marginal utility*.

Positive marginal utility occurs when the consumption of an additional unit of a good or service increases the consumer's total utility (for example, when a child receives an additional outfit for her doll). Conversely, *negative marginal utility* is when the consumption of an additional unit decreases the total utility (such as when that extra scoop of ice cream makes you feel unwell).

Below are some highlights of how to consider and incorporate the marginal utility of information into business models and system designs.[4]

Marginal Utility of Information for People

Publishing or directly exposing people to repeated identical information leads to rapidly diminishing marginal utility and very little increase in total utility for each unit of information published. However, marginal utility can increase for the first few units of information assets, and negative marginal utility can be experienced much more quickly than when consuming tangible products or services.

Creators of information (such as journal publishers, advertisers, and data brokers) will find a high level of initial marginal utility among consumers for "original content" or new units of information, but not nearly as much for messages repeated beyond the first few. However, since information is not depleted when consumed and is non-rivalrous, this high level of initial marginal utility can be capitalized on simultaneously across multiple consumers. This is a key principle of information monetization. Information architects therefore should seek to design systems that increase information availability for *multiple* human and/or machine consumers.

Nonetheless, publishing the same information to the same individual repeatedly results in fast-diminishing marginal utility for humans, quickly leading to negative marginal utility and diminishing total utility. Information producers and publishers must therefore strive to achieve a balance between pushing information to individuals in a frequency and periodicity that matches the preferred consumption characteristics of those individuals. Understanding information consumption patterns across increasingly granular segments of individuals can optimize the total utility of the information published. For example, publishing an enterprise performance dashboard of strategic indicators to executives on a daily basis can result in rapidly diminishing marginal information utility, and ultimately disuse—whereas publishing daily changes or a monthly dashboard may retain high levels of marginal information utility.

Marginal Utility of Information for Technologies

For technologies such as systems, applications, and devices, which increasingly are becoming the primary consumers of information assets, the marginal utility principle must be adjusted to accommodate the following two scenarios:

1. Repeated identical units of information received by a component of technology offer zero marginal utility and constant total utility.
2. If we consider the total cost to process or ignore repeated units of identical information, total utility could be perceived to decline with each successive piece of identical information received.

Therefore, information and solution architects should filter out redundant information and instead only collect or stream changes (or deltas). In remote IoT environments, where bandwidth and edge processing is limited, this becomes an important consideration for the transmission of remote sensors' current status (rather than only a state change). For example, thermostats are designed to take periodic readings and only activate HVAC units upon temperature deltas of a prescribed magnitude (such as 2 degrees or more). If, instead, thermostats were designed to activate and deactivate HVAC units based on continuous and often identical temperature readings, these devices would soon suffer damage.

Architecting for Optimized Information Utility

Three basic solutions to architecting systems can avoid the undesirable conditions caused by streams of identical information:

1. Transmit only *distinct data* if and when it is produced and filtered by the publisher. IoT devices, for example, might only send updates when their state changes.
2. Transmit only *differential data*, which includes the delta between subsequent data points. Examples include the aptly named differential backups, and also accelerometer sensors and water leak detectors.

3. Produce and transmit only *derivative data*. Examples include publishing a revision to a previously published book or article, or applying different algorithms to a piece of information in order to craft uniquely differentiated messages for particular customers.

Opportunity Cost of Information Choices

While marginal utility deals with the diminishing benefits of consuming additional units of the same thing, *opportunity cost* refers to foregone benefits from choosing to consume one thing rather than another. In the sphere of infonomics, this constitutes selecting one information source over another, or performing minimal analysis in the interest of expense or expediency. As asserted in chapter 4, enterprise inertia often keeps organizations publishing pretty pie charts when deeper insights from advanced analytics like machine learning are readily available. As mentioned in chapter 3, most organizations are unaware of the variety of alternate information sources available, while they continue to use less accurate, complete, or timely sources "because that's the way we've always done it." The economic principle behind this is called the *endowment effect*, in which people ascribe a greater value to something merely because they possess it. The endowment effect quietly motivates business people to resist information and analytic progress.

It's the job of the CDO to ensure that opportunity costs for information and analytics are understood and employed to drive related strategies. As new information sources and analytic capabilities are continually presenting themselves, information and analytic opportunity cost assessment must be a periodic activity. Moreover, CDOs, business leaders, and enterprise architects must be aware of potential unintended consequences (or *externalities* in economic parlance) when planning to shift to new information sources or analytic methods. In addition, Externalities are a major consideration for any organization publishing information, either publicly or privately. Information can be used in an endless array of contexts, so CDOs especially must anticipate and prepare for how others might use (or misuse) information the organization shares.

The Production Possibilities of Information

Sometimes the inhibitor to improving the production or quality of information, or to implementing more advanced analytic capabilities, is due to its internal information *production possibility frontier*. That is, the organization would have to shift available budget and resources away from one activity, say developing ERP application functionality, to support such information-related improvements. This of course assumes the organization is operating at near optimal information *productive efficiency*.

Production possibility frontiers are a common reason particularly for stagnant data governance efforts. People are busy. They don't have the extra time to deal with developing or adhering to additional information principles and policies, without sacrificing other tasks (i.e., producing other things). However, there are several ways to overcome information-related production possibility frontiers:

- Embed information-related activities into other activities to soften their impact on resources.
- Automate information-related activities, or other activities, to free resources.
- Use ROI modeling to justify additional resources, thereby expanding the production possibility frontier outward.
- Or, as Michael Smith, principal contributing analyst at Gartner, and I recently posited: apply the future alternate economic benefits of an information asset to fund additional resources today.[5] (Remember, information is *non-rivalrous*, meaning the same information can be used for multiple purposes. So, plan for new ways to use information, and funnel the expected revenue or savings into additional information-related resources.)

Improving Information Yield

Ultimately, each of these economic factors influence—or should influence—how and when you make information-related investments. As discussed in chapter 5, these investments come in the form of vision and strategy development, devising and incorporating information-specific and information initiative metrics, data governance, skills and processes, and of course technology. But how is an organization, or more specifically its CDO, to gauge the appropriate level of investment? When do—or should—investments in information asset management (IAM) pay off? What happens to IAM maturity when information assets—along with related procedures and technologies—are merely maintained, not improved? Conversely, what if you accelerate information-related investments? And, how mature should you be or need to be, especially related to your competitors?

This leads us to a examination of *information yield* (a concept loosely inspired by the traditional *yield curve*[6]) for expressing the rate of improved value per unit of information-related investment. The *information yield curve* brings together, conceptually, the concepts of information monetization, management, and measurement. As we all know, information asset management (IAM) involves numerous moving parts. And as enumerated in chapter 5, many factors exert upward or downward pressure on information maturity. But what does this maturation curve look like? And where are you on it?

The *information yield curve* which my Gartner colleagues Andrew White, Joe Bugajski, Frank Buytendijk, and I devised a few years ago is intended to answer these questions. Not computationally, but more along the lines of how the popular Gartner Hype Cycle[7] sets maturity expectations for technology users and suppliers, the information yield curve sets expectations for how information-related investments affect IAM maturity—and thereby your information's rate of return.

In short, low-maturity organizations will see accelerating improvements in the rate of return on their information assets from information-related

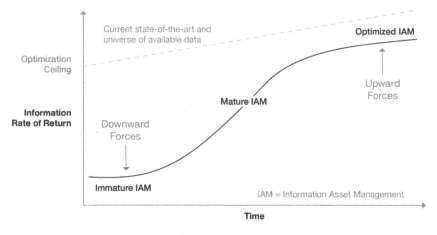

Source: White and Laney, "Increase the Return on Your Information Investments With the Information Yield Curve," Gartner Research G00250593, December 30, 2015.

Figure 12.1 *Information Yield Curve*

investments, while high-maturity organizations will see decelerating rates of return as they approach an optimization ceiling. Similarly, low-maturity organizations that accelerate their information-related investments will experience a maturity bump that begins to level off. For example, moving to a more sophisticated analytics platform will have quicker returns initially until your competitors catch up, market dynamics change, or the platform becomes overwhelmed by the increased volume, velocity, and/or variety of information assets—such as we have observed in recent years with traditional data warehousing approaches.

The forces exerting upward pressure to improve and accelerate maturity should be embraced and cultivated. Many of these can be found in the information management maturity challenges mentioned in chapter 5, such as information quality, accessibility, compliance, analytics, governance, and so forth. The downward forces that limit and tend to decelerate IAM maturity include the volume, velocity, and variety of information, the increasing ubiquity of information assets, the speed of business, regulatory mandates, organizational resistance/inertia, information hoarding and underutilization, and lack of information trust (metadata).

Your organization will find itself, or choose to be, on different relative positions along the curve. These positions can be classified as:

- **Industry Average** (in the middle of the curve): You're tracking along with the industry pack, making similar investments, dealing with downward pressures on par with others, and therefore receiving an average return on your information assets.
- **High Performer** (above on the curve): You didn't get a jump on others in your industry, but your investments are paying off better and/or you're doing a better job of mitigating downward value pressures. Therefore, your information yield is greater than most others.
- **Low Performer** (below on the curve): You are not effectively deploying IAM solutions you've invested in and/or are succumbing to downward pressures more so than other organizations. Therefore, your return on information assets is lower.
- **Leader** (ahead on the curve): You got a head start on your competition and have continued to reap the rewards of greater information maturity, for now.
- **Laggard** (behind on the curve): You're off to a slow start in making information-related investments, and therefore are not generating as much value yet from the information available to you, yet.

Indeed, these positions on the curve are subjective. Nonetheless, a combination of IAM maturity scoring[8] and information asset valuation, along with certain relative industry performance indicators, can give you a sense of where you are on the curve—and therefore an indication of how well your information-related investments are increasing (or will increase) your information's yield. In turn, these indicators, along with the infonomics considerations throughout this chapter, can and should influence business and information vision and strategy.

Vision and strategy are all about the future—defining it, getting there without stumbling or spending too much . . . and hopefully before your competitors. However, vision and strategy are not only influenced by economic principles, but also by trends. So in the final chapter we'll examine various information, business, and technology trends affecting how you will be able to and should monetize, manage, and measure information assets over the next several years.

Notes

1. Nolan Miller, interview with author, 09 September 2016.
2. I'm not talking about generating *new* information here.
3. Supplier costs may include those to market it as well.
4. In our research report, "Applied Infonomics: Designing for Optimal Marginal Utility in a Digital World," Dale Kutnick, Saul Brand, and I detail how the concept of marginal utility and diminishing marginal utility must be adapted for both human and machine-based consumption of information assets. (ref: "Applied Infonomics: Designing for Optimal Marginal Utility in a Digital World," Douglas Laney, Dale Kutnick and Saul Brand, Gartner, 16 December 2016, www.gartner.com/document/3546617).
5. Douglas Laney, and Michael Smith, "How CIOs and CDOs Can Use Infonomics to Identify, Justify and Fund Initiatives," Gartner, 29 March 2016, www.gartner.com/document/3267517.
6. The standard yield curve plots the yields or interest rates for bonds or other debt instruments of differing contract or maturity lengths.
7. "Gartner Hype Cycle: Interpreting the Hype," Gartner, accessed 09 February 2017, www.gartner.com/technology/research/methodologies/hype-cycle.jsp.
8. Douglas Laney, and Michael Patrick Moran, "Toolkit: Enterprise Information Management Maturity Self-Assessment," Gartner, 13 June 2016, www.gartner.com/document/3344417.

CHAPTER 13

Infonomics Trends

There's no doubt that infonomics as a concept and a set of disciplines is in its infancy. Organizations are beginning to generate significant economic benefits from their information assets not just in the original ways intended, but in expanded ways—both internally and externally. As well, few organizations have gone beyond just talking about information as an asset in taking the first steps to apply true asset management approaches. Very rare indeed is the organization that generates much more than occasional and rudimentary data quality measures, to implementing a spectrum and combination of information valuation approaches—as they do with other assets.

Various global business and technology trends are subtly or not so subtly urging business, IT, and information leaders to treat information as a legitimate economic asset. Chief among them are:

- The commoditization of many physical assets, products, services, and even workforces compels business leaders and innovators to look toward information as a new source of margin.
- The cornerstone of digital business is the ability to identify and respond to business moments which almost invariably are represented by an information stream or alert.
- Continued globalization demands that organizations participate efficiently and quickly in expanding and dynamic business ecosystems via improved information sharing and ingestion.

- Smart government services are based almost entirely upon a platform of information.
- Cyber insecurities will require organizations to identify, assess, and minimize information-borne risks more formally.
- Privacy regulations increasingly will mandate the improved handling of personal information.
- The rise of the machines, algorithmic sprawl, and the promise of artificial intelligence (AI) depend upon accurate, complete, timely, granular, and unique information sources.
- The internet of things (IoT) will become the single fastest growing source and most voracious consumer of information.
- Digital twins that precisely represent models of physical things and their state rely on a variety of metadata, along with condition and event information.
- 3D printing is entirely contingent upon information-based representations of objects, and their ability to be monetized and managed effectively.
- The institutionalization of ethics in the face of commercialized and politicized misinformation will require the generation and management of new information sources to emerge with built-in trust indicators.

Key Information-Related Trends

Closer to home for information leaders and professionals are trends related to information itself. These trends will affect the monetization, management, and measurement of information assets. They include:

- Big Data and beyond,
- Organizational inhibitors,
- Information rights conscientiousness,
- Advanced analytics, algorithms, and artificial intelligence,
- Information infrastructure, and
- Information security and privacy.

Most Big Data Projects Will Fail, and That's a Good Thing

Monetizing information is the number one challenge among those planning to invest in Big Data. This is an indication that many organizations are embarking on Big Data projects speculatively and without any strategy or defined business outcomes. Some Big Data projects are driven by IT without buy-in from the business, or have been initiated inside a department without any buy-in from the rest of the organization. In both of these cases, the ability to demonstrate value from Big Data will be at risk. This can lead to the project being abandoned as a pilot because crucial funding and support to get it into production will be missing.

Big Data projects are inherently experimental, and most experiments fail. Some projects will not deliver value and will justifiably be discarded. Others may last short term and be shelved after providing some insight. These outcomes should be expected, but having failure as the common case does not mean Big Data projects should lack a desired business outcome.

Recognizing the Organizational Roadblocks to Information Monetization

While the recent and ongoing diminishment of Big Data hype is a relief, fast followers and late adopters will struggle to achieve the kind of innovative and high-value successes that many early adopters had with Big Data. Even as technologies and techniques for accumulating, managing, and deploying Big Data have matured, most organizational cultures and business models remain garrisoned against information-based innovation.

It's true that Big Data skills—especially real data scientists—are in short supply. This will continue for several years. However, most limiting is the continued inertia toward thinking about and using data merely for generating ever more reports and spreadsheets, rather than evolving to consider information a strategic asset and raw material for transforming businesses, products, and services. Digitalization and a shift toward the data-driven organization, of course, require a sophisticated application of information assets, as opposed to more aesthetic pie charts. Finding ways to make use of orders of magnitude, higher volume, velocity, and variety of data can require drastic business model changes for which many are simply unprepared.

Giving the Gift of Information to Your Competitors

Digital industry change will seldom be initiated by incumbents—instead it's the technology providers and startups that will often take the lead. The master agreements of these technology providers often gives them the right to take ownership of their customers' intellectual property, even (in some cases) that which may have been designated as confidential.

To date, as a result of digitalization, a small number of industries have been deeply disrupted and fundamentally redefined. Examples of these industries include music, books, newspapers, travel agencies, local advertising, and photographic film. However, developments over the last five years show that now every industry must be considered as susceptible to deep disruption.

With digital remastery of an industry or company, the intellectual property and knowledge that differentiates your company is virtual and IT-driven. Perhaps, because of this, we are increasingly seeing that the protagonists responsible for some of these industry changes and digital remastery have not originated from the industry incumbents, but rather have derived from technology-savvy and information-savvy companies outside the industry.

The Great Chief Data Officer Balancing Act

To derive value from information assets, organizations must focus first on data quality and data governance. This is the primary reason to hire a CDO. Once the data management aspects of risk, audit, and compliance are addressed, CDOs should shift focus to maximize the value of information assets consistent with the business's strategies.

As CDOs mature in their role and improve their organization's ability to better manage the risks associated with data (such as data quality, security, and data breaches), their roles will evolve and different priorities will emerge. While still responsible for the strategy and execution of data policies in support of compliance and risk mitigation, CDOs will adjust focus toward maximizing the business value of information assets. Specifically, in the age of Big Data, CDOs will be tasked with raising the analytic competency of their organizations. CDOs will show how information assets and analytics enhance the customer experience, increase market share, and deliver new forms of information innovation to improve brand recognition.

CDOs also will become tasked with identifying barter deals for information assets, participating in information exchanges with partners and suppliers, and driving other sources of competitive differentiation across their ecosystems. In this evolution from risk to value, CDOs will apply advanced analytics and information valuation techniques to measure and communicate the economic value of their data assets. And value-focused CDOs, will deploy information assets to generate supplemental and significant revenue streams.

Advanced Analytics, Data Science, and Artificial Intelligence

Not just a global trend, but also a technology trend, advanced analytics solutions are becoming increasingly popular in driving business innovation and experimentation—and creating competitive advantage by monetizing available information assets inside and outside the organization. Over the foreseeable future, enterprises will be seeking to adopt advanced analytics and adapt their business models, establish specialist data science teams, and rethink their overall strategies to keep pace with the competition.

Machine learning, represented by neural networks are supplanting most forms of advanced analytics due to their dynamic nature that adapts to changing and unknowable inputs. These types of algorithms can help to monetize almost any kind of information, be it granular IoT data or macro-level economic figures. Expect these kinds of algorithms to be a standard component in the vast majority of data scientist toolboxes and increasingly accepted by business leaders, despite their "black box" models. As a result, many data science tasks will become automated, increasing the productivity of data scientists and enabling a class of "citizen data scientists" to emerge. This will put significant pressure on information asset supply chains and information curation efforts, and engender a boom in information monetization ideas from all corners of the organization across all industries.

Increasingly, predictive analytics solutions that make copious use of available information assets within and external to the organization will evolve into artificial intelligence (AI) solutions capable of automating decision making and processes. Around the beginning of the next decade, some industries will attribute up to one-third of their net new revenue growth to information-fueled AI solutions. Still, humans will remain involved. Many machine learning implementations will require dedicated workers to help train, monitor, and guide them. Expect these roles to be mandated by various industry regulations. As well, industry regulations will require AI applications and their underlying information sources to be audited able, thereby presenting a new set of challenges.

Information Infrastructure

Information infrastructure is moving toward a complementary environment that encourages simultaneous deployment on premises and across multiple cloud environments. An increasing pressure to manage data in multiple deployment models, while also optimizing its access and retrieval, is enabling extended information ecosystems, while making an organization distinct information supply chain more obtuse.

Over the coming years, organizations with data virtualization capabilities will spend significantly less time on building and managing data integration processes for connecting distributed data assets. The ability to logically connect data sources, rather than physically integrate them (and do so with nominal performance degradation) will enable expanded information ecosystems, and reduce the security risks associated with information sprawl.

As well, data transformation flows increasingly will make use of machine learning algorithms. I have long anticipated and referred to this as "self-organizing information." Early attempts at this, however, will be plagued with erroneous interpretations of the data, both by the algorithms themselves and unsuspecting recipients (humans and applications).

Blockchain is worth mentioning as well, since it is a hot (if overhyped) topic at present. Into the next decade, expect most blockchain efforts to miss the mark, either due to performance challenges endemic to the technology or the misapplication of the technology by overzealous architects. That said, blockchain may very well prove useful for rationalizing metadata or master data long before being practicable for managing most high volume/velocity/variety information assets themselves.

Information Asset Privacy and Security

Other global trends with specific information-related implications are privacy and security. Information asset risk-related concerns increasingly will demand serious planning and robust execution in the areas of privacy and security. This will involve the vast majority of enterprises continuously monitoring for sensitive data incidents. First, however, this will require organizations to automatically inventory their information assets and scour their systems for instances of sensitive data such as PII. And these efforts will lead to the use of automated information masking or similar pseudonymization techniques, along with monitoring the information's usage itself. To further buffer against missteps, most large organizations that process personal information will perform periodic impact assessments and more formal audits.

For information asset security implementations, many organizations will continue to attempt to implement manual data classification policies. But these will be fraught with limited deployments and insufficient tangible benefits. Formal (and eventually standardized) calculations for information asset liabilities will supplant these efforts to provide a degree of economic risk modeling and security prioritization. Within a few years, a small percentage of penetration tests will begin to be conducted by machine learning–based systems.

The Future of Infonomics

Textron is the parent company of Bell Helicopter, and Beechcraft, Cessna and maker of other specialized technology products. Few traditional manufacturing companies embrace the possibilities and potential of infonomics so well. "We no longer differentiate ourselves primarily via the performance of our products. Rather we gain advantage from our ability to monitor enormous amounts of data from inside and outside our business, find insight in that data and act on it more quickly than our competitors" said Matt Cordner, Textron's director of Global ERP and Analytics. "Our finance people used to chuckle about the idea of information as an asset, the reality is that for most employees, our business is data. 70 percent of our employees don't touch aircraft, but everyone touches data."[1]

So to close, let's also ruminate about what the future of infonomics holds as a concept and a discipline for companies like Textron, or those in any industry. Just as it's difficult to tell what the future holds for a young child, I can only speculate where business leaders, information leaders, chief executives, financial executives, academics, and others will take the nascent notion of infonomics. Hopefully it will be to places I have not yet envisioned!

Information Monetization

In part I we looked at dozens of ways organizations of every size—and in every industry and geography—are generating measurable economic benefits from their own and external information assets. One can only imagine that what we've seen the past few years is information monetization in its infancy. Today, information monetization efforts are targeted, functionally specific, or experimental. Most are limited to just a few kinds of information and are deliberate, customized solutions. Tomorrow, expect a wider variety of information monetization approaches, and the emergence of standardized models, mechanisms, and technologies for doing so.

Moreover, I anticipate robust industry markets for data and content, automatic information trading, and an economic fluidity for information approaching or even surpassing that of cash. Remember, certain unique economic and behavioral characteristics of information render it more useful than other assets in some circumstances. This infonomics boom will lead to organizations finding unimaginably creative ways of harvesting or generating valuable information assets, and of marketing them.

Information Management

In part II we considered how current information management standards fall far short of the discipline with which other kinds of assets are managed. In examining the concepts of the supply chain and ecosystem, and traditional asset management approaches, we can envision how information assets may (or should) be managed with orders of magnitude improved discipline.

The emergence of the chief data officer (CDO) role in many organizations, and across all industries, indicates a growing recognition of information as a strategic business asset. Although today most CDOs are "chiefs" in title only, I expect IT organizations will begin to bifurcate into separate "I" and "T" organizations, thereby elevating the CDO to a level of prominence, influence, responsibility, and budget aligned with other CXOs within the organization. At this point, no longer will information be considered the domain of the IT organization, but a distinct business asset in its own right.

One of the greatest IAM challenges, particularly for CDOs, will be the continually dissolving walls between one organization's information assets and those of another. Information assets increasingly will be shared in the cloud, not transmitted, among business partners and customers, creating true information ecosystems with established protocols, rewards, and penalties for its participants. In addition to pure IAM challenges, these information ecosystems will stress the notions of information rights, control, ownership, and sovereignty. Adopting and institutionalizing precepts such as the Generally Accepted Information Principles suggested in chapter 9 should help to lay a foundation for IAM within and among organizations.

Building on the popularity of cloud storage, combined with an age-old banking business model, I have long anticipated the emergence of "information services organizations." Such companies will provide not just storage and access to information assets, but also a full range of banking-type services including: lending (licensing), interest (enrichment and cleansing), investment (new forms of monetization), credit (using information as a form of payment or collateral), portfolio analysis (measuring and reporting on information health), and advice.

Information Measurement

As we just covered in part III, the impetus to improve the way information is monetized and managed will lead to organizations measuring it in a variety of ways. Information quality, performance, relevance, impact, cost, and value measures deployed independently by organizations will become mainstream competencies, later giving rise to industry standards. At first, industry regulators and investors will require them. Later, insurers—realizing they could be offering new "information insurance" products—will solicit or generate information-related risk and value measurements. Once insurers acknowledge information assets as a form of insurable property, the accounting profession will be compelled to acknowledge information as a capitalizable asset. Although, this could happen in the reverse order—accountants followed by insurers. It's uncertain which profession will blink first.

Eventually, the formalized measurement of information value and risk will lead to multi-billion dollar industry opportunities not only for the insurance industry, but also for accounting firms to offer formal information auditing services. In addition, accounting and valuation firms will start offering enhanced M&A services that rightly consider the value of a firm's information assets.

Finally, I expect CDOs, enterprise architects, business leaders, and economists to begin thoroughly looking into how to apply classic economic models to information—not as some nouveau academic exercise, but as legitimate means for determining how to better understand and harness information's unique characteristics and behavior. This is the promise of infonomics—information's emergence over the past couple of decades from that of a business byproduct and business resource, to a performance fuel and marketable commodity, and ultimately to a true, recognized economic asset.

Note

1. Matt Cordner, interview with author, 23 June 2016.

APPENDIX A

Information Management Maturity Challenges

The following information management maturity challenges are verbatim those articulated by participants in Gartner EIM Maturity workshops throughout 2016. Information leaders should anticipate these kinds of challenges and resistance, and take sufficient measures to avoid or overcome them.

Vision Challenges

- Information is seen as a source of power
- Information is managed in silos
- Data fiefdoms
- People spend time arguing about whose information is correct
- People spend time arguing about who owns data
- Little effort to seek uniform availability of information assets
- A general acknowledgement that information management (or lack thereof) is a serious problem
- Efforts by IT to formalize objectives for information availability are hampered by:
  - Culture
  - Contradictory incentives
  - Organizational barriers
  - Lack of leadership and executive support
- Different types of information are still treated and managed separately
- Poor awareness of exogenous data such as that from public data sources (open data), data brokers, or social media

- Information is seen as disposable
- Information is poorly linked across business areas or applications
- Information is not perceived as a fuel for innovation and transformation
- Information is not perceived as a competitive differentiator
- Information is not a central component of business strategy or enterprise architecture
- A focus only on Mode-2 (transformation) than on Mode-1 (operations)
- Customers and partners are not involved deeply in defining information uses
- The language of information is imprecise, and dialects differ throughout the organization

Strategy Challenges

- IT taking the reins for information management
- A static, annual planning process
- Too much planning, not enough doing
- Information hoarding or begrudged sharing by individuals and departments
- Lack of executive support and executive-level leadership (e.g., no CDO or similar)
- Obliviousness to what information exists
- Vision is lacking upon which to base a strategy
- EIM enablers have both process- and people-oriented gaps
- Being too focused on technology
- Executives are consumed by expense management
- Controls and standards get in the way of information enablement
- Corporate strategy is set without consulting information leadership
- An ill-defined or incomplete information management organization
- Lack of funding
- Information only being defined in terms of the value it brings, not its intrinsic characteristics
- No consideration of the larger info-ecosystem of partners, suppliers, and customers
- Information strategy being a separate work task, poorly linked to business operations

Information Metrics Challenges

- Measures and goals are purely subjective
- The achievement toward goals is rarely tracked, at least in any quantified way
- Information management is not an IT budget item, and certainly not an enterprise budget item
- Simple, often predisposed, cost-benefit models are used to justify independent information management investments, but not collectively
- Cost-benefit and ROI metrics and prioritization merely are part of IT projects
- Priorities and goals are based on:
  - Influence peddling
  - Failure prevention
  - User surveys
  - Expense reduction, or
  - Scaling infrastructure performance or capacity
- A proliferation of mostly incompatible nonfinancial metrics
- Qualitative metrics don't link to business KPIs
- Data quality is not measured or performed only downstream for specific IT or business projects
- Information value, cost, and risk go unmeasured
- Information is not treated as an investment (e.g., an information portfolio)

Governance Challenges

- The culture allows few official (if any) policies to exist for the handling or use of most information, other than those required by law and industry regulations
- A lack of governance culture as evidenced by limited governance in other domains
- Ad hoc data quality efforts are favored or simply budgeted that way
- A lack of data definitions (metadata) result in low data trust and usage, and therefore no imperative for governance

- Emerging policies are mostly for particular information silos.
- Information is too easily copied, resulting in information sprawl
- There is no mandate or precedence for monitoring or enforcing policies, which leads to policies being regularly circumvented
- Information owners (or "trustees") are assumed, not actually designated
- Limited authority for anyone entrusted with information to do anything about its quality or policies
- Lack of sponsorship or organizational structures and budget for information governance
- A "project" mentality in which information is merely an input or output for that process
- A fixation on policies, rather than a well-crafted, integrated hierarchy of precepts
- A fixation on control, rather than governance as an enabler of information
- A lack of defined information principles
- Lack of information inventory—not knowing what needs to be governed
- Data stewards without advocacy as part of their role
- Data stewards (for business information) who are part of the IT organization
- IT running the information governance initiative

People (Organization and Role) Related Challenges

- Information-related responsibilities are resourced on an application-by-application or project-by-project basis
- Business people are resigned to circumvent IT in an attempt to source and manage their own data, or must queue up in the IT backlog
- Lack of change management as part of EIM initiatives
- A lack of pooled or centralized database administrators, data administrators, information architects, data modelers, etc.
- The above resources being part of the IT department
- Information not being perceived as an enterprise resource or asset (hoarding)

- Lack of budget and executive sponsorship for such roles or structures
- A fixation on traditional information-related roles at the expense of emerging and increasingly important roles such as the CDO, data steward, information curator and information product manager, master data manager
- CDOs without budgetary authority or resources beyond a small "office of the CDO" team
- A lack of understanding of the larger information ecosystem beyond the immediate enterprise
- Information management being perceived as a cost center rather than as a revenue generator or business innovation enabler

Process (Information Lifecycle) Challenges

- A lack of understanding of information even having a lifecycle (Most managers and users of see information or part of it at a certain point in time, or they don't see it at all as it's embedded and obscured in systems and applications.)
- Information silos where it languishes
- Information is copied with wild abandon rather than being accessed in place
- A tendency toward local (single application or system) efficiencies
- Information is deleted early due to a lack of infrastructure or policy
- Infrastructure asset budgets are planned independently of information assets—which usually are not even budgeted
- Data integration may be effective in linking disparate sources, but efforts to semantically align them are lacking
- Metadata management is mostly manual (e.g., spreadsheets) and is specific to information assets for specific projects or applications
- A lack of interest or perceived business importance in defining information flows or architecture
- A lack of data architects owning or driving the definition of information asset lifecycles
- Little concern, planning, or innovation regarding older information

- An impression that information lifecycles are IT workflows or tasks rather than business processes
- No means to value information assets or balance this against their assessed risk

Infrastructure (Information Technology) Challenges

- A tendency to push information storage and processing capacities to their limits, rather than allowing for dynamic business needs or growth
- Application-specific technologies leading to technology-sprawl
- Redundancy in tools
- Lack of defined information architecture or reference models
- A preponderance of shelfware
- Unused licenses or superfluous capacity
- IT backlogs which perceptibly inhibit business performance
- Information silos limiting business interoperability, both internally and with business partners
- IT spending "spill over" as business units invest in their own tools
- Shadow IT organizations emerge
- Multiple or personal data extracts used for analytics instead of a common analytic structure (e.g., data warehouse or data lake)
- Applications are integrated but semantics and ontologies are inconsistent among them
- Overpaying for prior generation technologies with order of magnitude lesser capacity or performance
- Reliance on application-specific DBMSs for analytics
- Lack of a data-as-a-service architecture (e.g., logical data warehouse)
- Application- or department-specific master data, metadata, and governance/policy implementations
- Stubbornness and misconceptions about cloud security and privacy
- A focus on tools over solutions
- Non-elastic, non-scalable technologies
- Excess storage and processing capacity not shared among business units (i.e., "capacity hoarding")

APPENDIX B

Sample Legal Rulings Related to Information Property Rights

Rulings affirming information property rights:

- In *American Guarantee & Liability Insurance Co. v. Ingram Micro*, a U.S. federal court ruled that the loss of computer data was "physical damage."[1]
- In *Lambrecht & Associates v. State Farm Lloyds*, an appellate court ruled that "data" stored electronically "dictates that such property is capable of sustaining a 'physical' loss."[2]
- In *Switzerland Insurance Australia v. Dundean Distributors*, an Australian appellate court ruled on the corruption of data as: "The physical alteration was the change in the alignment of the magnetic particles on the hard disk of the computer . . . which had the effect of rendering the system useless in a practical sense until the particles had been realigned."[3]
- In *Southeast Mental Health Center v. Pacific Insurance*, a U.S. court held "that the corruption of the pharmacy computer constitutes 'direct physical loss or damage to property' under the business interruption policy."[4]
- In *Thrifty-Tel v. Bezenek*, a U.S. appellate court ruled that, "It would follow if ordinary electronic data (rather than just the disk) is 'property' capable of being stolen or trespassed, that insurance coverage for 'property' would encompass such ordinary data in the amount of 'the value of the information on the disk, not the de minimus price of the disk.'"[5]

- In *Seagate Technology v. St. Paul Fire and Marine Insurance*, a U.S. federal district court ruling strongly implies that loss of data alone is not "physical damage to tangible property."[6]

Rulings denying information property rights:

- In *Ward General Insurance Services v. Employers Fire Insurance Co.*, a U.S. appellate court ruled that the loss of database alone did not constitute "direct physical loss."[7]
- In *AOL v. St. Paul Mercury Insurance*, the court held that "Computer data, software and systems are not 'tangible' property in the common sense understanding of the word. The plain and ordinary meaning of the term 'tangible' is property that can be touched. Computer data, software, systems are incapable of perception by any of the senses and are therefore intangible."[8]
- In *Rockport Pharmacy v. Digital Simplistics*, a U.S. court of appeals concluded that the loss of data represented nothing more than "commercial loss for inadequate value and consequential loss of profits."[9]
- In *Greco & Traficante v. Fidelity & Guaranty Insurance*, because the plaintiff could not prove that the computer glitch in question was the result of a physical loss, a U.S. appellate court held that there was no coverage under the electronic data processing systems provisions in its policy that covered "risks of direct physical loss."[10]
- In *Seaboard Life Insurance v. Babich*, a Canadian court judge ruled that, "There was no physical injury to any asset of the plaintiff nor was there anything which could be described as direct damage to its property. . . . There may be contexts in which computer data will be held, in law, to constitute property. But for the purposes of distinguishing between pure economic loss and damage to property in the law of damages, I consider that it would simply be productive of confusion to treat the loss of the data as anything other than economic loss. In this case, the loss was purely economic."[11]
- In *Thyroff v. Nationwide Mutual Insurance*, a U.S. appellate court overruled a lower court's dismissal of a case involving the application

of law in likening of electronic data to other forms of recognized intangible property, holding that that the strength of the common law is a response "to the demands of commonsense justice in an evolving society" and that "a document stored on a computer drive has the same value as a paper document kept in a file cabinet."[12]

And a couple decisions in which courts refused to rule on information property rights:

- In *Home Indemnity Co. v. Hyplains Beef*, a U.S. circuit court's ruling ruminated on whether electronic data truly exists in "tangible form" but refused to rule on it.[13]
- In *Privacy Commissioner v Telstra Corporation Limited*, an Australian federal court dismissed a case in which the Australian Privacy Commissioner ruled against Telstra, requiring it to release information about a customer's locations and IP addresses of sites he has visited. However, as of this writing, Telstra has only partially complied. At question is whether this kind of information is *about* the customer or about the services provided to the customer—each with different privacy and ownership implications.[14]

Notes

1. www.propertyinsurancecoveragelaw.com/2011/01/articles/commercial-insurance-claims/the-physical-damage-requirement-an-archaic-concept-in-todays-world-understanding-business-interruption-claims-part-57/.
2. http://caselaw.findlaw.com/tx-court-of-appeals/1110884.html.
3. www.computerlaw.com.au/doku.php?id=swiss.
4. https://casetext.com/case/southeast-mental-health-center-v-pacific-ins-co.
5. https://scholar.google.com/scholar_case?case=13124205958630567455&hl=en&as_sdt=2&as_vis=1&oi=scholarr.
6. http://law.justia.com/cases/federal/district-courts/FSupp2/11/1150/2289357/.
7. http://caselaw.findlaw.com/ca-court-of-appeal/1445761.html.
8. http://caselaw.findlaw.com/us-4th-circuit/1330432.html.

9. http://caselaw.findlaw.com/us-8th-circuit/1104409.html.

10. www.leagle.com/decision/In%20CACO%2020090126060/GRECO%20&%20TRAFICANTE%20v.%20FIDELITY%20&%20GUARANTY%20INSURANCE%20COMPANY.

11. http://caselaw.canada.globe24h.com/0/0/british-columbia/supreme-court-of-british-columbia/1995/08/30/seaboard-life-insurance-company-v-babich-1995–1335-bc-sc.shtml.

12. http://caselaw.findlaw.com/us-2nd-circuit/1470623.html.

13. http://openjurist.org/89/f3d/850/home-indemnity-company-v-hyplains-beef-lc.

14. www.smh.com.au/technology/technology-news/federal-court-rejects-application-for-telstra-to-supply-personal-metadata-20170120-gtvc85.html.

Index

About the Author

Doug Laney is vice president and distinguished analyst in the Chief Data Officer (CDO) research and advisory team at Gartner, Inc. Doug researches and advises clients on information monetization and valuation, open and syndicated data, analytics centers of excellence, data governance, and Big Data-based innovation. He is the author of Gartner's enterprise information management maturity model, has compiled several hundred real-world examples of the "art of the possible" with data and analytics, edited and co-authored an eBook on Big Data for the *Financial Times*, and is a two-time recipient of Gartner's annual thought leadership award.

Around the turn of the millennium, Doug originated the field of Infonomics, developing methods to quantify and harvest information's economic value, and positing how to apply traditional asset management practices to information assets. He lectures at leading business schools and conferences on the topic, and his articles have appeared in *Forbes*, *Wall Street Journal*, and the *Financial Times*. Throughout his career Doug held leadership roles with global systems integrators and early-stage software companies, and has been a Gartner analyst for eleven years.

Doug lives outside Chicago with his wife and son where he bikes, cooks, plays competitive tennis and non-competitive golf, is a volunteer Junior Achievement instructor at a local grammar school, coaches area entrepreneurs, and sits on the University of Illinois Department of Accountancy advisory board.

You can follow Doug on Twitter at @doug_laney and on LinkedIn at linkedin.com/in/douglaney.